Kids Learn From the Inside Out

Kids Learn From the Inside Out

How to Enhance the Human Matrix

Shirley L. Randolph, MA, PT
and
Margot C. Heiniger, MA, OTR
with
Kristin M. Tucker

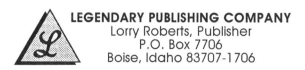

LEGENDARY PUBLISHING COMPANY
Lorry Roberts, Publisher
P.O. Box 7706
Boise, Idaho 83707-1706

Integrated Human Dynamics
Shirley L. Randolph, MA, PT, and
Margot C. Heiniger, MA, OTR
4333 West Plum
Boise, Idaho 83703
(208)342-6463

Library of Congress Catalog Card Number: 98-67048

International Standard Book Number (ISBN): 1-887747-19-2

Printed and bound in the United States of America.

This book is published by:

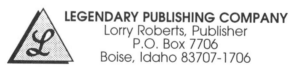

LEGENDARY PUBLISHING COMPANY
Lorry Roberts, Publisher
P.O. Box 7706
Boise, Idaho 83707-1706

Printed by: Gilliland Printing, Inc.
215 N. Summit
Arkansas City, Kansas 67005

Grateful acknowledgement is made to the following for permission to reprint previously published material:

*Garland O'Quinn. Excerpt from *Developmental Gymnastics: Building Physical Skills For Children.* (University of Texas Press, 1978). Permission granted by Garland O'Quinn.

*Ashley Montagu. Excerpt from *Growing Young* (McGraw Hill Paperbacks, 1983). Permission granted by A. Montagu.

*David Elkind. Excerpt from *The Hurried Child* (Addison-Wesley, 1988). Permission granted by Addison-Wesley Publishing Co., Inc., Reading, MA.

*Joseph Chilton Pearce. Excerpt from *Magical Child.* Copyright © 1977 by Joseph Chilton Pearce. Used by permission of Dutton Signet, a division of Penguin Books USA Inc.

*John-Roger and Peter McWilliams. Excerpt from *You Can't Afford the Luxury Of A Negative Thought,* Prelude Press (1990), 8159 Santa Monica Boulevard, Los Angeles, California 90046, 1-800-LIFE-101. Permission granted by Peter McWilliams.

*Pia Mellody, Andrea Wells Miller and J.Keith Miller. Excerpt from *Facing Codependence: What It Is, Where It Comes From, How It Sabotages Our Lives.* Copyright © 1989 by Pia Mellody Enterprises and J. Keith and Andrea Wells Miller. Reprinted by permission of Harper Collins Publishers, Inc.

*John Bradshaw. Excerpts from *Homecoming: Reclaiming And Championing Your Inner Child* (Bantam, 1990). Permission granted by Bantam Books, a division of Bantam, Doubleday, Dell Publishing Group, Inc.

*D.Thomas Verny and Pamela Weintraub. Excerpt from *Nurturing the Unborn Child* (Delacorte, 1991). Permission granted by Dell, A Division of Bantam, Doubleday, Dell Publishing Group, Inc.

*Marshall H. Klaus and John H. Kennell. Excerpt from *Maternal-Infant Bonding* (C.V. Mosby, 1976). Permission granted by Marshall Klaus.

*Barry Brazelton. Excerpt from *On Becoming A Family* (Delta/Seymour Lawrence, 1981). Permission granted by Bantam, Doubleday, Dell Publishing Group, Inc.

*Arthur Janov. Excerpt from *Imprints: The Lifelong Effects Of The Birth Experience* (Coward-McCann, 1983). Permission granted by the Putnam Publishing Group.

*Dr. Frederick B. Levenson. Excerpt from *The Causes and Prevention of Cancer* (Stein and Day, 1984). Permission granted by Scarborough House, Madison Books.

*Nancy Verrier. Excerpt from *The Primal Wound.* Permission granted by Nancy Verrier.

*David Chamberlain. Excerpt from *Babies Remember Birth* (Tarcher, 1988). Permission granted by The Putnam Publishing Group.

*Ken Magid and Carole A. McKelvey. Excerpt from *High Risk: Children Without A Conscience* (Bantam, 1987). Permission granted by Ken Magid.

*Sylvia Ann Hewlett. Excerpt from *When The Bough Breaks.*

To the individuals in the past who have contributed to our understanding and inspiration . . .

To those in the present who have sustained and affirmed our efforts . . .

To those in the future who will continue our concern for the quality of life for all people.

CONTENTS

THE INNATE AUTOMATIC STAGE OF DEVELOPMENT

Chapter 4: The "Fourth Trimester"

THE MOTOR-PERCEPTUAL STAGE OF DEVELOPMENT:
3 - 24 months of age

Chapter 5: The AHA! of Kinesthesia

THE PERCEPTUAL-MOTOR STAGE OF DEVELOPMENT
18 months – 4 years of age

Chapter 8: Systematic Exploration

THE PERCEPTUAL STAGE OF DEVELOPMENT
3 1/2 – 7 years of age

Chapter 9: Ready for Action

APPENDIX

Preface

Kids Learn From the Inside Out: How To Enhance The Human Matrix provides the essential information for raising children according to the genetically encoded timeline for the human species. The time has come for our children to become our top priority. As our most important natural resource, they deserve to be planned for and provided for. It would be a tragedy if children were to appear on the "endangered species" list!

Some readers may feel awkward or uncomfortable with some of the terminology. This book speaks about assisting healing and repatterning, not about providing physical therapy treatments; about physical challenges, not physical handicaps. It is time to actively change negative self-limiting thoughts and language to the positive, easy, fun language and lifestyle humans are designed to experience.

As we wrote this book and put the material on tape, we were repeatedly challenged to state what we really believe. From this challenge came our Nine Fundamental Laws of Integrated Human Dynamics:

1. Humans develop according to a genetically encoded timeline.

2. Departure from the timeline limits human potential.

3. Efficiency diminishes with departure; that is, the further we are from our timeline, the less our efficiency.

4. Problems arise from the point of departure.

5. Physical behavior pinpoints deviations and compensations.

6. Human potential is always available.

7. Activation can begin at any age.

8. Restoration requires need, desire, understanding, and commitment.

9. Divine human potential occurs with full engagement of the natural developmental process.

As you read this book, consider these five outcomes:

1. You will learn to be one with the way you are created.

2. You will understand why you are designed the way you are.

3. You will understand the importance of the natural developmental process and its contribution to creating dynamically integrated human beings.

4. You will learn how to provide the environment that keeps you connected to the natural developmental process.

5. You will be committed with confidence in being the divine creature you are designed to be by applying the Nine Fundamental Laws of Integrated Human Dynamics.

In reading this book, you may find the material brings up old memories: that is OK. You may have some unusual body memories: that is OK. You may have some unusual body sensations, which are really body memories: that is OK. You may also have some very strong wants or desires that surface: that is OK. Be assured when any of these things happen you are at the point, the threshold, of your own healing. Make an agreement with yourself to allow whatever happens to be OK. You may want to keep a tablet nearby that you can immediately write down thoughts, feelings, sensations, and body responses. Allow yourself time to really experience what is happening, and to acknowledge, accept, and validate the *YES* that is *TRUE*. In this way the information will become alive and provide you with a wealth of knowledge and understanding that you will be eager to share with everyone you know.

This simple, vital information is essential to transform childraising practices and enhance the human matrix. We must use positive language (I can! I am! I will! I choose! I have! I love! I enjoy! I create! I empower!). Imagine what the planet will be like ten years from now, when every child is provided the proper environment for the natural developmental process.

Partner with us to spread the word so we can all be the dynamically integrated human beings we are divinely created and designed to be.

Shirley and Margot

Acknowledgements

First, we would like to acknowledge our partner, Kristin M. Tucker. Her wonderful creativity provided the people and stories that make this book come alive. Her ability to take our medical jargon and turn it into everyday usable words is deeply appreciated. The love, support, and trust created during the writing of this book will be cherished all our lives.

We would like to acknowledge Robert and Helena Stevens for their love, support, and living example of the real difference it makes in lives when we *come from* imagining our highest choice for our lives, our wish fulfilled. By living in the promise that there is enough love, joy, peace, enthusiastic abundance, and enlightenment in the moment, creates and allows the miracle of life for which we are created.

Professionally and personally we would like to acknowledge A. Jean Ayres, Newell Kephart, Clara Chaney, Nancy Miles, Margaret Rood, Dr. and Mrs. Karl Bobath, Maggie Knott, Dorothy Voss, Roxie Morris, Frances Ekstam, Kathryn Young, Frances Corley, Edward Snapp, Drs. deQuiros and Schrager, Dr. A.A. Tomatis, Dr. William Emerson, Barbara Findeisen, Judie McReynolds, Helen Adams, and EarthThunder. All of these people in their own personal way have contributed to our professional knowledge and growth and our personal convictions.

A special thanks to those people who previewed the manuscript and provided their support and endorsement.

Thank you to our editor Jean Terra for her timely assistance.

Lastly, a huge thank you to Darice Peltier, our talented and creative computer person, who did what had to be done so this book could happen.

WHAT IT'S ALL ABOUT

CHAPTER ONE:
Learning From the Inside Out

Three-month-old Emily* squirms and wiggles as she lies on her tummy on the kitchen floor. At mealtime, she cuddles against her mother's breast.

For his first birthday, Curtis was given a foam ball. He and his daddy love to play catch together. When Daddy's not around, Curtis chases the ball as it rolls across the floor.

Renae and Wes, both age four, are playing at the park. Some days they swing and slide, or ride the merry-go-round; sometimes they climb the wooden play structure, or roll down the grassy hill. Today, as they run across the meadow,

> "For a young child, physical movement is the source of discovery, the vehicle of expression, and the method of survival."
>
> (O'Quinn. *Developmental Gymnastics.* p. 3)

they are pilots of invisible jet planes, racing towards destinations yet unknown.

---

*Emily, Curtis, and other children and adults described in this book are purely fictional characters, created by the authors to illustrate the concepts of this book. The appendix includes actual case studies from the authors' professional experience.

Children don't worry about the mortgage, the stock market, the meaning of life. Kids just are. That's the work of kids – and the magic of childhood: experiencing life completely with body, mind, and spirit. That's how kids learn – *from the inside out.*

Just three months old, Emily is learning where she is, what she is, who she is. The slick floor makes it easy for her to move her arms and legs (which she has just discovered): up and down, side to side, away from and towards her body. At meal time, Emily is held in her mother's familiar arms where she experiences trust as her most urgent and obvious need, hunger, is met.

With the foam ball, year-old Curtis learns to sequence body movements. Through discovery, practice, and experimentation, he is learning that he can control some body actions, and that he has some control of his world. As he plays with his father, Curtis is developing the foundation for healthy relationships.

At the park, Renae and Wes are learning a more complex sequence of movements, activities, and interactions. Their imaginative play challenges their bodies and minds, as they develop self-awareness and learn social skills.

Through physical activity and relationships with others, Emily, Curtis, Renae, and Wes are discovering who they are, and are finding their place in the world. Each experience helps to build basic skills and confidence. But learning *from the inside out* isn't always so positive.

Tami is a colicky baby. She fusses and frets day and night. Her stomach hurts, so she cries – and her stomach becomes more upset. She gets little sleep, and her parents sleep even less. Stress builds as the days wear on.

Matt is clumsy. His body just doesn't do what he wants it to do. When throwing a ball, skipping, or running, he's not as coordinated as the other kids. And sometimes he gets frustrated when he has to work to do something that others do easily. So Matt doesn't play with other kids much. He watches television and snacks on chips and sodas; gaining weight adds to his clumsiness and his self-esteem slips even further.

What happens in our bodies affects our minds and our spirits. Tami's colic and Matt's poor motor skills initiate chain reactions that affect their self image, perception of the world, social interactions, academic progress. These chain reactions continue with one negative experience leading to another.

With early intervention, such a chain reaction can be broken and the impact minimized. In fact, intervention can be effective at any time if it addresses the problem in the background and not simply the obvious difficulty. But too often, we fail to recognize that our problems (and those of our children) are built on a complex foundation of body memories, behavioral patterns, and stress.

This book will teach parents and caregivers how to see what is in the background, behind the visible problem; to recognize the "core issue" or "missing piece" that is troubling a child; and to implement the most effective intervention strategies. Our strategies have been developed over the past 20 years, and have been implemented with hundreds of children, including children with behavior problems, learning disabilities, chronic illnesses, genetic defects, and spinal injuries. Our goal is to help children's bodies work as they should, to nurture children along their developmental timeline, to help children learn from the inside out.*

Without intervention, we can anticipate what might be in the future for Tami, our colicky baby. If she spends much time in an infant carrier or jump-seat, she will be propped up where she can see what is happening– but at a safe, hands-off distance from real activity. With constant stomach problems, stress, and inactivity, she is likely to be small for her age and she probably will have many food allergies and dislikes. Because of her size and frailty, her parents may be wary of allowing her too much physical activity; consequently, Tami won't spend much time playing with balls, riding tricycles, or running in the park. If her muscle tone doesn't have a chance to develop, she won't do well at sports. Her penmanship may be poor because she won't develop fine motor skills. She may have a short attention span and little personal initiative. And because she won't be able to do what the other kids are doing, she is likely to be a temperamental student.

By high school, Tami may face a myriad of problems. Assigning her to the school "resource room" or providing academic tutoring may provide some remedial help in specific areas. Yet these measures will have limited effect because they don't address the underlying problems.

Effective intervention begins by looking beyond Tami's visible problems, so we can recognize colic as her stomach's response to

---

*Throughout this book, key references are noted CNx.x , indicating that additional information can be found in the chapter notes in the appendix section, where we introduce Heiniger and Randolph's earlier book, *Neurophysiological Concepts in Human Development.* CN1.1

stress. Milk that should have brought comfort to Tami's "innermost inner" brought distress instead. Perhaps a milk allergy began a stress reaction that became self-perpetuating as the pleasure of eating was replaced by the pain of indigestion. Or perhaps indigestion began as a response to Tami's anxiety as a newborn baby. If Tami spent her first hours after birth in the isolation of a neonatal nursery, far from mother's familiar heartbeat and loving embrace, that early anxiety and the fear of abandonment may have festered in the only place it could: Tami's empty tummy.*

Realistically, we may be unable to completely and precisely examine the background of Tami's problems. Yet, reviewing even a few memories can provide insights into the cycle of problems that began in the first months of life. Tami's healing requires breaking through that cycle as early as possible to avoid further traumas. Whether Tami is ten days old or ten years old, now is the time to help her re-learn from the inside out.

This process must begin with a wholistic approach that addresses Tami's emotional needs and enhances her well-being. Her mental development will be stimulated by appropriate activities, non-threatening experiences, social interactions, and opportunities for self-directed play. Specialized treatment may require the expertise of physicians, physical or occupational therapists, hearing specialists, optometrists, and other professionals.

True intervention begins when we accept the complexity of the visible problems – and continues when we are empowered with tools for observing, skills for evaluating, strategies for change, support and encouragement. Change is possible if we are committed to change.

Each Stage of Development is Unique and Important

Human beings develop according to a master timeline in which every learning must be practiced, tested, reinforced, and integrated.

Before birth, human development is sheltered by the safe, secure, consistent environment of the womb. Because physical

---

*A trauma is any significant disruption to development. Any negative experience may be traumatic and has the potential to block, stop, interrupt, or slow development. The trauma may result from a physical experience (such as an injury or disease) or an emotional experience (such as abandonment, fear, or unmet emotional needs). The earlier the trauma occurs, the more disruptive it is likely to be.

needs are automatically met, the growing fetus can tend to its primary agenda of preparing for life outside the womb. Cradled within mother's body, baby has the physical support of the elastic uterine wall, the comforting rhythm of mother's heartbeats, and the stimulation of her constant movement. Development is spiritually nurtured by the life-to-life bond between parent and child. These earliest experiences become "body memories" that

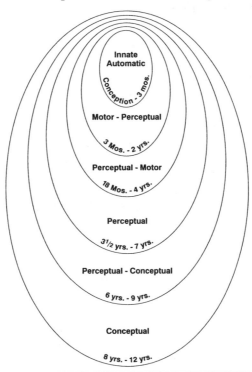

Newell Kephart's Stages of Development

Looking at sensory and motor function, therapist/educator Newell Kephart recognized development as a series of stages: innate automatic (conception through three months after birth); motor-perceptual (three months to two years of age); perceptual-motor (18 months through four years); perceptual (age three-and-a-half through seven); perceptual-conceptual (ages six through nine); and conceptual (ages eight through twelve). Because of individual differences and factors relating to growth and development, the stages overlap slightly. "The order of the stages is more important than when each occurs," Kephart insists. (*Steps to Achievement for the Slow Learner*, p. 65) Most important is the inter-relationship of the stages: each stage becomes the foundation for the next as the child continues to develop, grow, and learn. CN1.2

are in place months before mental memory is possible; our bodies remember what our minds can't. And so the holistic development of body, mind, emotions, and spirit proceeds.

The Innate Automatic Stage: Conception Through Three Months After Birth

Immediately after birth, infants depend on a set of primitive reflex responses which have been developing since conception. These reflexes are necessary for survival and adaptation to the world outside the womb. The rooting reflex, for example, is essential for finding the nipple that delivers milk; the sucking reflex allows the infant to take nourishment. When these reflexes work properly, baby has no anxiety about her physical needs being met. Her reflexes help to teach her, from the inside out, the meaning of security.

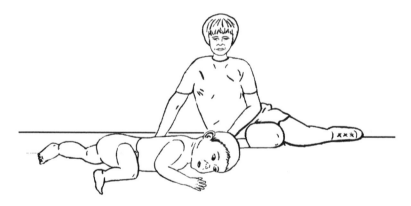

The Motor Perceptual Stage: Two Months to Two Years

Babies explore their environment through sensation, activity, and physical experience. Learning takes place gradually and each stage of learning is important for the next: rolling over is the lead-in to crawling; gurgling must come before talking; clutching teaches motor skills essential for penmanship. As babies learn to relate their internal sensations and basic movement patterns to the outside world, they learn – from the inside out – how to move efficiently in their environment.

The Perceptual-Motor Stage: Eighteen Months to Four Years

Toddlers interact with the world in ever-expanding ways as they become more systematic, more social, and more confident. Their constant activity places greater demands on their sensory, motor, and mental abilities; development requires that they feel secure – from the inside out – as they move into their expanding world.

Perceptual Stage Three-and-a-Half to Seven Years

Preschoolers are learning to perceive and interact with the world more fully. Body memory, sensory perceptions, and physical experience continue to be the foundation of learning. Ideally, the child has by this time completed the basic "inside out" learnings and his body is running itself automatically, allowing his brain to focus on cognitive learning.

Learning continues from the inside out as mental and emotional experiences affect and are affected by physical activity, such as when sharing a favorite game or adapting the game for a smaller ball or a larger playing field; when skill levels change, teams form, memories are shared, feelings are hurt.

Maria Montessori:
Pioneer of Early Education

"It is the child who makes the man and no man exists who was not made by the child who he once was."

(Montessori. *Absorbent Mind.* pp. 15-16)

Maria Montessori was a master at designing educational opportunities to enhance development of the whole child. She viewed childhood as a series of "sensitive periods" when a child's awareness is heightened specifically towards one function or ability — such as language, interest in small objects, or concern with truth and reality.

Defining education as "self-development in a prepared environment," Montessori recognized the systematic development of each sensory system. Her methods, which are still in use today, emphasize a sensory and physical basis to early education and teach systematic observation and problem-solving. Through her work, we are reminded that children learn best when they are surrounded with opportunities to explore and experience the world through their senses and physical movement. CN1.3

"It is the spirit of the child that can determine the course of human progress."

(Montessori. *Secret of Childhood.* p. 9)

The Human Matrix is Always Evolving

Human development can be viewed as the creation of a matrix: an interweaving of numerous factors and forces to establish our individuality and our connection with the human species. In human development, the human matrix weaves our genetic code with our environment and experience. The evolution of the human matrix is a life-long process, shaped by every experience, perception, capability, and discovery.

The word "matrix" has the same Latin root as "mother," "maternal," and "matter," words that all relate to the womb or origin of life. It is in the womb that the human matrix begins. Educator and parent Joseph Chilton Pearce noted that the womb offers three essentials for human growth: "a source of possibility, a source of energy to explore that possibility, and a safe place within which that exploration can take place." (*Magical Child,* p. 18) CN1.4

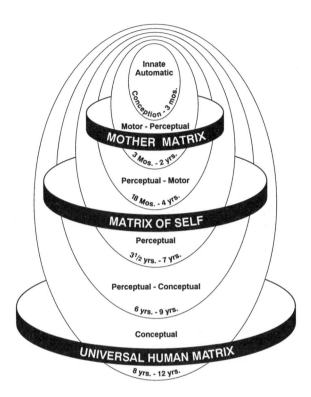

In the womb, the mother's body surrounds the developing fetus and the "mother-matrix" fully surrounds the "developing matrix" of the fetus. At birth, baby continues to depend on his mother; he knows possibilities, energy, and safety only as he experiences them through her.

Baby's matrix expands as he expands his understanding of the possibilities, energy, and security within himself. Still, his every step forward requires the confidence that mother is there for him. He will return again and again for mother's reassurance. Only when he has internalized that reassurance and incorporated mother's matrix with his own, can he move into childhood with confidence.

As children develop greater levels of skill and confidence, their own matrix separates from mother's and expands to include their environment. Eventually and optimally, the human matrix expands to interconnect each individual with all living things, becoming the ultimate source of possibility, energy, and security.

Trauma Damages the Human Matrix

The well-known anthropologist Ashley Montagu is convinced that human infants are born in a highly immature state in comparison to other species. Gestation is only half completed in the womb; the other half is completed by the time the infant begins to crawl around, about ten months after birth. Human babies depend on their caregiver, usually the mother, for survival and protective loving care for a period considerably longer than other animals. Montagu calls the period of development outside the womb "external gestation."CN1.5

> "If parents and society honored nature's purpose behind this long dependency and slow maturation, the child would discover and respond to the world without concern for the utility or value of his discovery."
>
> (Pearce. *Magical Child*. p. xi)

During this extended developmental time period following birth, children are extremely vulnerable to traumas and stresses for an extraordinarily long period of time. If their basic physical and emotional needs are met, children have the security necessary for adapting to new circumstances, and growth and learning proceed. But what happens when a child doesn't adapt? When her basic needs aren't met?

Illness, neglect, family upheavals, and other traumas can block a child's progress from one developmental milestone to the next. Learning may continue, but the sequence may be distorted if the child is missing even one tiny piece of what he should have learned at earlier stages.

Just as a pothole in the road disrupts traffic and damages vehicles, a missing piece of the developmental sequence can continue to disrupt a child's progress. Such a "developmental pothole" distracts a child's attention, slows his progress, and may damage the "undercarriage" of self-esteem and confidence. Children learn to compensate for their problems, perhaps by avoiding difficult situations or developing exceptional skills in other areas, perhaps by distracting attention from their inadequacies. Because the human matrix is constantly growing and changing, it is always vulnerable to trauma. Negative experiences can, at any time, leave permanent scars on the human matrix and may cause us to lose a portion of our potential, our security, our freedom.

"Of all purely human needs, the need for love is the most consequential, for it is the most basic of them. It is the humanizing need, the need that beyond all others makes us human....

"By being loved the power is released in the infant to love others."

(Montagu. *Growing Young.* pp. 131-132)

Children Today Face Rapid Change

Today's children are too often rushed into adult realities. Computer games mimic wartime strategies; beginning sports are organized in leagues for "real competition"; Saturday morning cartoons feature animated versions of favorite movies (often rated PG-13 or R); children's clothes are designed according to the latest fashion, with little concern for comfort on the playground.

Our modern world does little to help children be children, and research shows that today's children are not reaching their fullest potential physically, mentally, emotionally, or spiritually. Four characteristics of our modern world have a profound effect on children's growth from the inside out:

1) There's too much stress in our world.

2) Technology interferes with human development.

3) Babies are unnecessarily restrained.

4) Formal education begins too early.

1. There's too much stress in our world.

Imagine a time machine that magically transported you 80 years back in time to a world with few automobiles, no computers or fax machines, no television and few radios.

Many young couples would be living near their parents or the parents would be living with them. The workplace would be close to home. There would be no electric appliances for washing clothes, cooking, entertainment, or heat. Children would be carried until they learned to walk; then, they would be at mother's side or underfoot all day.

In today's world, life for kids is a different story. Preschool children (ages two to five) watch nearly seven hours of daytime television Monday through Friday alone. More than 45 percent of children ages three to five attend some type of educational program. Six out of ten married women with children under age six work outside the home. Twenty-five percent of working parents with young children use day-care facilities (almost twice as many as ten years ago). More than 21 percent of children under age 18 live with their mother only, twice as many as in 1970. CN1.6

The American family has outgrown all simple definitions. Many kids live in "blended families," with step-parents and half-brothers and half-sisters. Joint custody arrangements mean children may have more than one home and family. Even "traditional" families are often interrupted by split schedules, job-induced separations, layoffs, and moves.

Geography separates many children from their grandparents, thus limiting the role of the extended family to long-distance calls, mail, and occasional reunions. Careers, peers, and media (rather than family and community) now define cultural expectations and values from which children establish their identities.

Kids today live in a world that is moving and changing at an unprecedented pace. Adjusting to any change, good or bad, requires an expenditure of energy, time, and attentiveness which is then not available for other purposes. And constant change means constant stress, which may be translated into physical dysfunction, learning disabilities, social problems, loss of self-esteem.

For babies, the impact of change is profound even when the changes seem minor. It is now common practice to take newborn infants from the secure home setting into day-care centers, church nurseries, supermarkets, and other public places, where their fragile sensory systems are bombarded by noise, light, dust, germs, movement, and commotion.

Futurists expect that the pace of change will continue to accelerate. Kids need more opportunities to learn from the inside out if they are to develop the skills they need in a world of such constant change.

2. Technology interferes with human development.

Although television can expand the world in many exciting ways, it has taken the place of active play as children's primary entertainment. That means children spend less time stacking blocks, riding tricycles, coloring, pretending, reading, creating and more time sitting passively in front of a television screen.

For the eyes, television provides fast-moving colorful images. For the ears, there is constant sound, often on at least three tracks (music, voices, and background). The brain is fed information, ideas, and images of all kinds, but for the rest of the body there is no stimulation.

It's true that television introduces kids to foreign cultures, modern technology, new products, fascinating stories, and unusual relationships. But it can also promote aggression, crude behavior, consumption, poor eating habits, and quick-fix problem-solving.

Medical technology is another mixed blessing of our modern times. Thanks to neonatal intensive care units (NICUs), babies weighing just a few ounces can be kept alive through extraordinary technology. But technology can't provide loving care and the NICU provides little opportunity for parents to cuddle their newborn. The sterile, high-tech NICU environment is a stark contrast to the warm, gentle environment of the womb.

Other innovations in medical care also affect children's lives. Births can be scheduled at a time most convenient for doctor, hospital, and parents instead of at the optimum time for the baby. Medical tests can provide important information about health but details may be incomplete, inaccurate, or just plain wrong. Medications enable us to check the spread of disease, to stifle symptoms and pain, and to control behavior and escape the realities of our lives.

What we desperately need is wisdom to use technology well, to tap its life-saving and life-enriching potential without undermining the wisdom of the human body.

3. Babies are unnecessarily restrained.

Busy as we are in the fast-paced modern world, we cherish the conveniences that save us time and hassle. Among the most popular gifts at a baby shower are the portable playpen, plastic infant carrier, safety-approved infant car seat, baby swing, disposable diapers, and plastic bottles.

Certainly no baby should be transported in a vehicle today without being safely strapped into an appropriate infant car seat. And surely there are other times when infants and toddlers should be restrained for their own protection. But plastic infant seats, walkers, and playpens don't give babies the stimulation or security they need, and too often are used for the convenience of parents and caretakers.   Infant seats restrict baby's movement; walkers and jumpseats position babies vertically, prompting premature development of some muscle groups while limiting development of others.

What babies need instead is the freedom to move in a safe environment. They also need the security of being held in arms, near the sound of mother's heartbeat and near the breast that offers ready nourishment, and constantly but gently stimulated by the movement of mother's body.

4. Formal education begins too early.

Some say early childhood education is necessary to give kids a "fighting chance" for a "successful future." But we say early childhood education forgets that kids learn from the inside out.

Countless products and services challenge (or overload) the mental abilities of children with little attention paid to their child's innate needs for motor development. Few day-care programs are designed to specifically and appropriately enhance a child's developmental timeline. And many parents fear their toddlers will be sentenced to a life of underachievement without a full schedule of lessons, instruction, and organized activity even before kindergarten.

Psychologist David Elkind says such "miseducation" is robbing our kids of their personal initiative, intellectual development, motivation to learn, and self-esteem: "The miseducation of young children, so prevalent in the United States today, ignores the well-founded and noncontroversial differences between early childhood education and formal education.... Sound early childhood education is an extension of the home, not of the school." (David Elkind. *Formal Education and Early Childhood Education: An Essential Difference,* p. 65) CN1.7

Young children simply are not equipped (physically or mentally) to cope with a cut-down version of academic instruction. They don't need more years at desks with papers, pencils, rote memorization, and rules. Instead, they need time to check things out for themselves, for self-

> "Valuing childhood does not mean seeing it as a happy innocent period but, rather, as an important period of life to which children are entitled... In the end, a childhood is the most basic human right of children."
>
> (Elkind. *The Hurried Child.* p. 200.)

directed learning, free play, "reflective abstraction" (Piaget's term for the process of checking perception against reason), and exploration, all in an environment of acceptance and security.

Now is the Time to Help Today's Children

Amidst the discouraging trends just described, we see signs that there has never been a better time to help children learn from the inside out.

Currently, there seems to be growing interest in family life and children. In recent years, the U.S. Congress has struggled with mandates for better day-care legislation, parental leave, and other "family issues." There is increased support for moving beyond the guilt and pain of broken relationships, and a greater acceptance of diverse models for living together as families.

We also are broadening our definitions and expectations of health care beyond the medical arena, recognizing the role of alternative health care options. In seeking to undo the dis-ease in our lives, we can turn to chiropractic medicine, massage therapy, hypnotherapy, spiritual guidance, support groups, and a host of other helping/healing providers. And there is greater recognition of and respect for the inter-relationship of body, mind, emotions, and spirit.

Physical therapy and occupational therapy are at the forefront of holistic, preventative health care today. Although some physical therapists and occupational therapists still limit themselves to more traditional methods, many "PTs" and "OTs" are using their understanding of normal growth and development (and their medical backgrounds and professional standards) to assume a broader role in evaluation, assessment, prevention, and treatment of physical and functional disabilities. Some (like the authors) specialize in caring for children, using a holistic approach that involves the patient's family and environment.

It is exciting also to note the growing awareness of the "inner child" in all of us: the playful, spontaneous, vulnerable part of who we are. This "inner spark," the essence of being alive and free, can remain lively (and vulnerable) as we grow older. Parenting gives us a chance to rediscover the world through the eyes and experiences of our children and to better understand our own inner child.

It's Never Too Late to Have a Happy Childhood

Through self-parenting, adults can look at the background of their problems, and work at self-improvement from the inside out. In most cases, we parent as we were parented: as mothers and fathers, we look back (consciously and subconsciously) to our parents as our primary role models – even repeating abusive behavior, codependence, and discipline strategies that we most detested as children. Self-parenting enables us to break the cycle of dysfunctional parenting, and to claim healthy and loving relationships with ourselves and our children.

Any degree of abandonment, grief, fear, anger, or pain experienced during childhood will upset the developmental sequence and scar our inner child. Those wounds, visible or hidden, can be healed through self-parenting. As we develop our childhood characteristics and allow our inner child its rightful place in our lives, we can fully become the persons we were created to be.

Self-parenting begins with self-acceptance. We must recognize the inherent value and worth within ourselves "as is." How healthy is your self-esteem? Do you acknowledge yourself as a unique and wonderful human being?

The second step of self-parenting is admitting that we are imperfect – and agreeing to learn more about those imperfections. Learn what you can about your infancy, birth, and prenatal history: physical and emotional stress experienced during these early periods of your life may have had a profound impact on your development. What's keeping you from wholeness, happiness, and fulfillment? What's the problem? What's in the background?

As you uncover imperfections in your childhood, accept responsibility for your growth. Self-parenting requires a commitment to long-range goals that may seem imprecise and difficult. Problems that occurred decades ago will not disappear overnight. In fact, those childhood traumas are likely to be enmeshed in a complex "chain reaction" of the compensating behaviors, memories, and habits that won't be easily overcome. The earlier the trauma, the greater the impact on development – and the more difficult the healing.

Self-parenting – like parenting – takes time, hope, and help. Be patient with yourself. Know that you are worth the effort.

Growing Possibilities

We are convinced that providing a healthy foundation for human development is the key to the survival of the human species. Without monumental changes in modern technology, politics, and priorities, our society may be on a collision course with the master plan for human development. Understanding the miraculous sequence of human growth provides some priceless insights on who we are and where we are going, individually and as a society.

Our vision is of a world where people of all ages share joyously and spontaneously...where we prize the child-like qualities of one another...where we take time each day to explore the world, cuddle against those we love – and to "race towards destinations yet unknown."

CHAPTER TWO:
Development and Stress

As Jeff's thirtieth birthday approaches, his record for success is enviable. Five years ago, he graduated with honors from a well-respected university and soon landed a well-paying engineering job with a Fortune 500 company. With long hours, hard work, and a little luck, Jeff has received several promotions and earned the respect of his professional peers. His wife is a well-respected educator, and they have a beautiful, but fussy, baby daughter, Tami.

But Jeff doesn't feel successful. In his own eyes, his work is never quite good enough and that of his co-workers is even worse. Fits of rage sometimes overwhelm him. His ulcer bothers him and his frequent pounding headaches make it hard for him to think clearly.

At home, six-month-old Tami's incessant crying is often more than Jeff can stand. Nothing makes her happy. Jeff's mother says he cried the same way when he was a baby and that Tami will eventually outgrow it.

Sometimes when he holds Tami late at night, Jeff thinks maybe he knows how his tiny daughter feels. His stomach hurts too and he often feels like crying. He doesn't know what will take away that ache, for himself or for his daughter.

Stress Affects Us From the Inside Out

Stress is shaking the foundations of Jeff's life. Not that stress is all bad, of course. Stress activates the mind and body to face the unknown, allowing us to adapt, learn, and grow. Stress heightens our awareness, our ability to function, and our performance. But unless balanced by relief, stress will overwhelm our bodies, minds, emotions, and spirits.

> "The moment we feel threatened either from within or from without our unconscious memories will alert our survival mechanisms."
> (Stettbacher. *Making Sense of Suffering.* p. 14-15) CN 2.1

Stress has the same effect on children. Although challenges and changes are opportunities for growth, too many challenges or too much change can be overwhelming and can disrupt the developmental sequence.

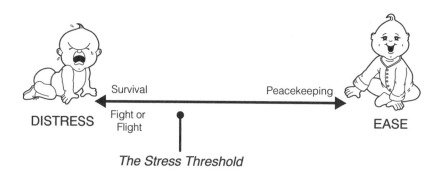

DISTRESS   Survival   Peacekeeping   EASE

Fight or Flight

The Stress Threshold

To better understand how stress affects development, let's first examine the human response to stress *from the inside out.* Our response to stress can be visualized as a continuum: a horizontal line with dis-ease (or distress) at the left end, ease at the right end.

When faced with minor inconveniences (such as a red traffic light, cold coffee, or a math error), our "state of being" moves towards the left end of the continuum. We may begin to feel some anxiety and, as a result, may decide to change our schedules, adopt new communication patterns, or learn new skills.

Major causes of stress, such as a baby's incessant crying or major life disruptions, give us a harder shove towards dis-ease and stress, and may even push us over our *stress threshold,* the point where the effects of stress become overwhelmingly negative. It is the point where kids have tantrums, parents "lose their cool," adults "blow their top." Our instinctive response is either *fight or flight.* A fight response launches us forward, ready to attack anything and everything in our path. We may swear, scream, stomp our feet, punch the pillow, slam the door. A flight response sends us running (physically, mentally, or emotionally) in the opposite direction. We may hide behind closed doors, get drunk, mumble, sleep, eat compulsively. Or we may hide from (deny) our feelings: "It doesn't matter to me," we tell ourselves.

Fight-or-flight responses were once a matter of life or death for humans. In the days of pouncing tigers and stalking wolves, human survival depended on automatic, instinctive action, either to *fight* the tiger or *flee* the battleground. Today we are more likely to be assaulted by traffic and timeclocks instead of tigers and wolves, yet the fight-or-flight response remains automatic, instinctive, and powerful. CN2.2

Normally, such reactions are short-lived, and we quickly "regain our composure" as body, mind, and feelings return to a healthy status. Each incident, however, moves us a little closer to our stress threshold, making us more vulnerable to stress overload.

At the first sign of stress, physiological changes prepare us for a whole-body response to the "tiger" or source of stress. Biochemicals are pumped throughout the body, muscles are tensed, and body functions such as digestion are put on hold until stress is relieved. If there is no tiger, no enemy to fight, no place to run, our bodies are left in a state of unresolved anxiety. The body holds a *biochemical memory* of its stress state and is more ready than ever to respond to the next stressful situation.

To maintain the appropriate balance of stress and ease, humans need to be protected from too much stress. Prenatally, the womb protects us from external threats before birth so development can proceed undisturbed. As babies, we are protected by our parents. And because our physical and mental abilities expand gradually throughout our childhood and adolescence, according to the human design, we move slowly into the larger world without being fully overwhelmed by distress.

When allowed to follow this natural plan, the human body learns how to respond to a stressful situation with appropriate excitement and energy, then move on with ease. But such behavior requires an

inner matrix of safety, confidence, and power, a matrix that
enables humans to interact with
the world moment by moment.
Only then can growth, development, and learning proceed
according to the "blueprint" of
the human species.

> "The person denied the first matrix remains grounded in that earliest stage, trying to establish some arbitrary and artificial safe place of his own making. It is a compensation that never works."
>
> (Pearce. Magical Child. p. 37)

Children who don't have such a stable matrix can only react to stressful situations with either the fight or flight response. Excitement and energy become anxiety and dysfunction and they are unable to interact fully with the world.

Like her father, six-month old Tami experiences stress each day, from bright lights, for example, and loud noises. Often Tami's stress begins internally, when she is hungry, wet, cold, or frightened.

Tami's stress is relieved when she is comforted by Mother's arms or when Father rocks her gently. Dry diapers, warm milk, and dim lights are also important for relieving Tami's stress. Without these comforts, Tami's unrelieved fear, tension, and anxiety will be remembered (stored) at a subconscious or cellular level. Each unresolved stressful experience will make her more vulnerable to future stress, leaving her less able to cope with the challenges of growing and learning.

When parents act to minimize the negative impact of stress in their children's lives, they are removing obstacles that stand in the way of their child's development. It is also important for parents to help their children learn strategies that allow them to deal effectively with stress. Because children learn best through example, parents should model healthy responses to their own stress and avoid passing it on to their children.

In caring for their children, parents often gain amazing insights into the stress situations that shaped their own development and personality. Being a parent is a unique opportunity for self-parenting: for looking into the background, or underlying cause, of current problems and developing effective strategies for growth.

For example, Jeff may recognize the symptoms troubling his infant daughter as the same symptoms he has felt all his life. With that insight, he may choose to take a closer look at his own life and to develop better skills for handling stress. These self-parenting strategies will help him recognize Tami's stress and its causes and provide him with strategies that will keep her at the "easy" end of her stress continuum.

The Stress Triad: A Holistic Look at Stress

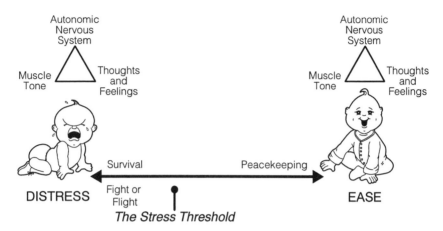

Throughout a person's lifetime, the ability to handle stress is dependent on a triad of interrelated factors: the autonomic nervous system; muscle tone; thoughts and feelings.*

The **autonomic nervous system (ANS)** is responsible for maintaining the body's autonomy and provides internal, unconscious control of involuntary body functions.

The ANS has two roles: one is to respond to stressful situations in such a way as to ensure survival; the other is to maintain the peace of our physical being. The control of the ANS is important, therefore, for handling routine situations as well as responding to emergencies.

Surviving in stress: The survival response of the ANS (technically known as the sympathetic system) prepares the body for activity by channeling the body's energy for a quick response to anger, fear, or a threat of injury. The response may be either fight or flight. Under stress, the heart rate increases, blood pressure rises, respiration accelerates, and digestion is essentially shut down. Blood is sent to the muscles to prepare them for action. The pupils dilate, saliva becomes thick, swallowing may be difficult, skin becomes cold and clammy.

Keeping the peace: The peacekeeping response of the ANS (technically known as the *parasympathetic system*) has the task of

*A more detailed and technical discussion of stress is offered in *Neurophysiological Concepts of Human Behavior,* by Margot Heiniger and Shirley Randolph. CN2.3

maintaining a state of *homeostasis* or well-being within the body: for ongoing respiration, circulation, metabolism, and other key systems. The parasympathetic (peacekeeping) response is especially important in digestion, and that's why heartburn, food intolerance, diarrhea, and ulcers are so common in times of personal crisis, transition, tension, and stress.

If our response to stress is emotional flight, we may seem lethargic, unresponsive, even relaxed. Yet the physical symptoms of stress will still be evident: pupils will be dilated, skin cold and clammy, heart racing.

The survival response of the ANS should be short and intense, allowing the ANS to quickly return to its functional, peacekeeping role. But if stressful situations are frequent, or if stress is internalized and not released, the survival state becomes the norm and the peacekeeping systems suffer. Over time, problems may develop with digestion, sleep cycles, the immune system, learning, social interactions, and general well-being. Balance can be regained by intentionally activating the opposite system. Relaxation activities such as soft music, massage, and deep breathing will de-activate the survival role and allow the peacekeepers to do their work. Vigorous physical activity uses the survival system's activation constructively, not destructively. Playing racquetball or chopping wood can be very therapeutic after a stressful day at work.

By helping their children to learn peacekeeping and survival skills needed for balancing the two roles of the ANS, parents can provide their children with lifelong strategies for handling stress.

Muscle tone is the second part of the triad that affects a person's ability to handle stress. Most of us have experienced the pain of muscle tension, the discomfort due to stress that has been stored in the large muscles of the neck, back, and legs as well as the smooth muscles of the stomach, bladder, and pupils of the eye. Stress makes our muscles less resilient and less functional. In other words, stress affects muscle tone from the inside out.

As babies grow, their internal, smooth muscles are fully operational long before the large muscles. For this reason, the smooth muscles are the first to experience the impact of stress.

When Jimmy is hungry, he experiences physical and emotional stress. When he cries, his parents respond by holding him, then feeding him. As Jimmy nurses at his mother's breast, he is comforted physically and emotionally. He stops crying and his body relaxes. Jimmy's muscle tone (beginning with his digestive tract) and his emotional tone are comforted simultaneously.

Crying activates the survival role of Jimmy's autonomic nervous system. Because he relaxes as he eats, the peacekeeping role of the ANS facilitates digestion and the muscle tone of his digestive system improves. But if his ANS is in its survival role, digestion will be difficult and inefficient. Over time, Jimmy may experience a variety of digestive disorders. The tension of his digestive system may spread to other muscle groups, interfering with function, growth, and development.

Only in the peacekeeping mode can babies ***integrate*** or coordinate the complex systems of their bodies. If integration is disrupted at one level, subsequent levels will also be affected.* Stress can disrupt integration *at any time;* prenatal stress, birth trauma, family dysfunction, or other stressors can disfigure a child's matrix and prevent her from reaching her highest potential.

Motor Integration, Stress and Learning

In their visionary work on learning disabilities, Argentine physicians and developmental specialists Julio deQuiros and Orlando Schrager studied the link between muscle tone and learning, and recognized a sequence of integration necessary for humans to function at their highest potential. CN 2.4

DeQuiros and Schrager noted that motor integration may be best understood as it relates to the evolutionary scale of development in the animal kingdom. Fish function at a very low level of integration; amphibians and reptiles at a slightly higher level; mammals' level of functioning is higher yet; and humans are at the highest level of motor integration.

As humans develop motor skills, we progress through these same levels of motor integration. Infants first become mobile using a belly crawl pattern similar to the movement of turtles, crocodiles, lizards, and other amphibians. A few weeks later, infants lift their tummies and move on "all fours," like dogs, cats, horses, cows, and other four-legged mammals. Ultimately, the child becomes upright, freeing the hands for highly skilled manipulation. No other species reaches such a high level of evolutionary integration in their functioning.

How strange that we give so little thought to the complex task of working our bodies against gravity! At birth, babies' equilibrium must adjust from an upside-down position in the womb to a horizontal position in the crib and all body processes, including digestion, must suddenly adapt to the force of gravity. (Fortunately for the human species, all baby's nutritional needs can be met by mother's milk, which is so easily digested.) In the following months baby's postural equilibrium will continue to be challenged (or

---

Integration is the automatic functioning of a body system which requires coordination of the system with itself and with other body systems.

stressed) as he learns to roll over, sit, crawl, and as he becomes a standing, walking, upright human!

Our adjustment to the force of gravity is yet another example of how we learn from the inside out. The baby's body learns to receive and respond to information about its inner world (provided by muscles, joints, tendons, and organs of balance) long before his mind can comprehend the sensory information about the outside world (provided by the eyes, ears, tongue, skin, and other sensory organs). Each movement helps baby learn to integrate the internal sensations that will enable him to position his body against the force of gravity and to function in increasingly complex ways.

Thoughts and feelings are the third part of the triad. These functions are at the highest level of development, giving humans far more self-control than any other species.

Thoughts direct our actions and reactions to life. Thoughts also enable us to analyze and respond to stress-producing factors in our lives. Memories of stress have a powerful influence on our thought patterns and on our ability to handle stress.

"When the Fight or Flight Response is activated, we begin to look for everything wrong with a situation, person, place or thing.... The mind, an incredibly perceptive and accurate tool, is looking both within and without for negativity."

(John-Roger and McWilliams. *You Can't Afford the Luxury of a Negative Thought.* p. 24-25)

Emotional feelings are the power behind our thoughts. Feelings grow from thoughts ("I get mad every time I think about it!"); thoughts grow from feelings ("Those flowers really cheered me up.") Thoughts and feelings are always interrelated.

Emotional feelings are the non-specific "gut-level" feelings that drive our actions. Emotional feelings are our primary internal response to our world and are neither good nor bad. They are different from body feelings (physical sensations) such as pain, hunger, heat, and texture that are transmitted by specialized nerve receptors and the spinal cord to the cortex of the brain for interpretation and specific response. The physical pain of poking a finger with a pin, for example, prompts the specific protective response that pulls our hand away from the pain.

The cortex also interprets emotional feelings, but in a far different way. Emotional feelings are non-specific and individualized, based on memory, physical and spiritual well-being, and other factors. Physical sensations originate at the nerve endings of the body; emotions are said to originate in the heart ("my heart is breaking"), the stomach ("a gut response"), and the head ("head trips" and "mind games").

Emotions provide us with clues about how we are handling stress. But because our culture offers little opportunity to express our feelings openly and honestly, many adults are virtually numb to their feelings. Feelings don't disappear, however, even if they are ignored.

Suppressed anger becomes rage; sadness is hidden beneath apathy; fear builds as hopelessness. Negative perceptions become our reality, and so our stress builds.

Parents often unintentionally teach their kids to ignore, suppress, or deny their feelings. Instead of helping children work through their fears, we admonish them for being "clingy" and tell them to "act your age." Instead of patiently coaching them through their anger or grief, we teach them that "big kids don't cry" and "you'll feel better later." Such attempts to help kids "grow up" actually reinforce poor stress management strategies: kids learn (at an early age) to set their feelings aside and "think their way through" difficult situations.

Children can only learn to express their feelings if they know all feelings are OK, are guided to express their feelings safely and appropriately, and are surrounded by messages of acceptance and assurance.

Stress-Busting Strategies

Fortunately, the human body has incredible powers for evaluating and directing forces within and outside itself. Harnessing these powers gives us great control over life's stressors. These effective "stress busters" are presented here for adults (parents, teachers, childcare providers, and others) who must model, teach, and guide children.

Autonomic Nervous System

Stomach aches, headaches, or general jitters often signal that your body is in a fight-or-flight response and your autonomic nervous system is in a survival mode.

Energize your peacekeeping forces with sensory pleasures such as soft music, a warm bath, herbal tea, dim lights, comfortable clothes, nourishing foods. Stay away from sugary desserts, chocolate, alcohol, and caffeine; their chemical make-up is hard on your digestive system and may be a direct stimulus to your survival system. Avoid sharp smells (such as cleansers, permanent-wave solutions, vinegar), loud music, bright lights, itchy clothing, tight-fitting shoes. Seek simple pleasures and an easy, supportive environment.

Learn to concentrate on your breathing. In any stressful situation, just taking three or four slow deep breaths will move you away from your stress threshold.

Apathy, laziness, and general lethargy may also signal that your autonomic nervous system is stuck in a survival response. Emotional flight patterns include daydreaming and forgetting that anyone else is present; your skin will be cold and clammy, pupils are dilated, and breathing and heart rate are fast. Quiet time, deep breathing, and meditation will help you relax; vigorous physical activity can help you "get back in your body" and in touch with the present world.

Your peacekeeping system is in charge when your skin is warm and your breathing is slow and even. Energize yourself with physical activity, healthy food, intellectual stimulation, and creativity. Take a walk, eat an apple, talk with a friend, paint a picture.

Muscle Tone

Feeling muscle tension? Try some deep breathing or gentle exercises. Massage your shoulders, neck, hands, feet. Take time for physical activity. Play a game of tennis. Shoot a few baskets. Go for a walk.

Thoughts and Feelings

Experiencing "brain drain"? Give your mind a rest. Sometimes a change of mental activity is the best prescription: read a book, watch a good movie, call a friend, write a letter, draw a picture.

At other times, your brain needs a more thorough "housecleaning." Close your eyes and let your mind wander for a while. Let thoughts travel through your brain without stopping. Restore your positive balance with meditation or prayer, by writing in your diary or journal, and by using healthy "self-talk" messages.

These strategies involve all three aspects of your stress triad (autonomic nervous system, muscle tone, thoughts and feelings) and are important tools for putting you in charge of your stress continuum.

Stressed Parents Raise Stressed Kids

Chapter One examined four troubling characteristics of our modern world which are affecting children's growth: the pace of change, technology, plastic childcare devices, and early childhood education. Each of these factors adds stress to the lives of parents and children today.

The stress of parenting begins before children are born and continues throughout life. Morning sickness, diapers, and bath time evolve into bee stings, immunizations, baby sitters, siblings, report cards, slumber parties, accidents, discipline, sex education, college admission, weddings, and grandkids. For parents, the stress associated with their childhood is complicated by the additional "everyday stress" of jobs, marriage, needs of elderly parents, housekeeping, health, finances, current events, and on and on.

These same factors are at least as stressful for kids as for parents. Unemployment, divorce, food additives, pollution, and war also are traumatic for children. What's more, many children today are growing up in dysfunctional family settings where their needs (emotional, physical, social, spiritual) are not met, where stress interferes with parents' ability to care for their children. As these children grow into adults, they will direct much of their energy into feeding needs that went unmet decades ago, ultimately becoming inadequate parents themselves. That's how stress is passed from generation to generation.

Expect Children to be Children

It's essential that parents and caregivers recognize children as children and that the joys of childhood are never allowed to be overwhelmed by stress.

Therapist Pia Mellody notes five characteristics of children: CN2.5

- Children are *valuable* because they exist, not because of what they do. Children learn of their value through their parents.

- Children are *vulnerable* and need protection for their physical, sexual, emotional, intellectual, and spiritual well-being.

- Children are *imperfect* and make mistakes as they learn and grow.

- Children are *dependent* on other people for their primary survival needs (food, clothing, shelter, medical and dental care, physical nurturing, emotional nurturing, sexual information and guidance, financial information and guidance).

- Children are *immature* and act like children, not like adults. Everything about children is child-like.

Parental expectations are often the most stressful factors their children face. Rigid and unrealistic expectations interfere with the developmental sequence and give children too little time just to be children.

Here are a few more realistic and healthy things parents should expect from their children:

- *Expect failure.* No skill is mastered at first attempt. Peeing in the toilet, playing the piano, riding a bike, and reading aloud are skills that take practice. Give kids a chance to try and be patient with their failures.

  Kids are heading for failure when they are pushed towards adult-sized accomplishments. Morning-to-night activity schedules, stringent training programs, highly structured contests and competition, and intense academic expectations rob children of the once-in-a-lifetime opportunities of childhood. Provide instead a balance of opportunities, challenges, and experiences to nurture their growth and fulfillment on all levels.

- *Expect movement.* Kids shouldn't be expected to sit still for more than a few minutes. Children have a short attention span and a great need for movement; they learn more from physical activity than from paperwork. Only gradually will children develop the muscle tone, movement patterns, and physical stability necessary to move or to sit still.

  When it is necessary for kids to sit for an extended period of time (such as at restaurants, church, concerts, and school), adults should provide a variety of activities to keep hands and minds busy with quiet play.

- *Expect irresponsibility.* Kids don't value money, time, and possessions in the same way as their parents do. They shouldn't be given the responsibility of caring for these treasures without patient instruction, good role models, numerous opportunities to try, and loving forgiveness when they fail.

- *Expect mixed messages.* Communication isn't easy for adults; it's even harder for kids, who don't have the verbal skills to express themselves as well as adults. Children also change their minds more often. If you want to communicate with children, listen to them. Pay attention. Care.

  The hardest message for kids to communicate is "I need you." They do. Believe it.

- *Expect stress.* It's part of life, even for kids. Helping children manage stress is one of the most valuable things a parent or other adult can offer them.

Children and the Stress Continuum

Compared to adults, children may be more likely to function close to their stress threshold. Children and teens have "mood swings" and temper tantrums more often and more visibly.

Why do children seem more volatile? In the first place, children haven't developed the ability to control their responses to stress. Reactions and recovery happen quickly.

Secondly, children are more sensitive to their environment. They are easily distracted by light, sound, odor, temperature, texture, and other sensory stimuli. For cognitive growth, they must learn how to "tune out" some of the world around them. This may be difficult in the child's early years, when the world around them is both a playground and a classroom demanding their attention.

When stress is long-term and traumatic, children adapt in age-specific ways. Infants become fussy, grumpy, irritable and restless. Toddlers may be angry, rebellious, distrustful, temperamental. A school-age child may become frustrated, aggressive, hateful, and cruel. Over time, children who are victims of excessive stress are more prone to accidents, serious illness, violence, addiction, and learning disabilities.

To minimize these risks, children need help understanding the effects of stress, and they need to acquire tools for directing their course on the stress continuum.

1. Kids need a stable home environment.

When home is a place of safety, opportunity, and possibility, children are free to develop the inner security needed to relate to the larger world.

Parents should be aware of the stressors in their child's environment that may interfere with that child's security. Pollution, food additives, loud music, weather, allergies, and other "external factors" are more distracting for some people than for others. Even household clutter, tight schedules, and anxious parents can produce a great deal of stress.

Children also need consistent times and places for meals, naps, and bed. Certain rituals are important links of security: stories before bedtime, care for injuries, responsibilities for homework and housework, reasonable discipline measures, and family vacations reinforce the stability of the family relationships and serve as reminders that each member of the family is valued.

Parents, teachers, and other caregivers may be able to minimize life's inconsistencies for kids, but children do need to learn that life is often inconsistent, unjust, and unstable, and stressful. Healthy people need healthy ways of handling stress.

2. Kids need good role models.

Children learn best by example. Admittedly, adults offer imperfect examples of such important skills as managing stress and expressing emotions. Becoming a parent provides an excellent opportunity for adults to gain some new skills in these areas.

Learn more about yourself. What are the sources of stress in your life? How do you handle them? What clues does your body give you just before you reach your stress threshold?

Look again at the stress triad. Is your autonomic nervous system dominated by your peacekeeping system or your survival system? How is muscle tone affected by stress? Do you listen to your thoughts and your feelings?

Don't be afraid to admit your inadequacies. Little messages mean a lot. Learn to say, "I'm sorry." "We'll talk about it in a few minutes when I'm not so angry." "I really need some time out now."

> "Parenting our own children will trigger our earlier developmental issues. At each stage of our children's development, our own unresolved developmental issues and unmet childhood needs will come up. Often the result is toxic parenting... Any new situation can trigger our infancy needs."
>
> (Bradshaw. *Homecoming*. p. 63)

Reduce stress in your life and take time to be a parent. You may need to cut some expectations and trim your schedule. *Give your kids priority in your life.* They deserve the best you have to give.

3. Kids need strategies for stress management.

Even toddlers need to learn healthy ways of responding to anger, fear, and pain. Older children can learn how muscle tone, thoughts, and feelings are related to stress.

Look again at the stress-busting strategies. Seek opportunities to give mini-lessons on handling stress.

"Matthew has been running around this room like a crazy man for the last hour," Mrs. Franks told Matthew's mother, Janet. Matthew had been in Mrs. Franks' preschool class for several months and his fits of temper were becoming more frequent.

"He and Jacob had a fight during the snack time, and Matthew hasn't been the same since," the teacher explained. "Every little thing seems to make him furious."

"He's gone over his stress threshold," Janet thought. She decided to try her stress-busting strategies to bring him closer to the "ease" end of the continuum.

Matthew ran towards his mother. "I don't want to go home," he yelled, then dashed for the corner of the classroom. Janet took his jacket off its hook, then sat down at a table near the door. "I don't want to wear my jacket," he yelled. "It itches."

Janet nodded. "I'll carry your jacket, Matthew. Did you do any painting today?"

Matthew and Janet were soon in the car, heading for home. Janet turned off the radio and asked quietly about Matthew's morning, seeking clues about Matthew's thoughts and feelings. He was obviously angry. He said his feet hurt; at a stop light she noticed one shoe wasn't fastened. His muscle tone was tense and he fidgeted in the carseat, kicking the dashboard and playing with the seatbelt buckle. She was sure his autonomic nervous system was operating in a survival mode.

Although it was nearly noon when they got home, Janet decided to take a few minutes to ease Matthew's stress level before he tried to digest his lunch. She held him on her lap while he straightened a wrinkled sock that was irritating him. As he worked on the shoe and sock, Janet stroked Matthew's hair and sang a little song. They then went for a short walk around the yard and collected some leaves for an art project. Janet had planned to heat some chili for lunch; instead, she fixed Matthew's favorite cheese sandwich, knowing it would be easier for him to digest. After lunch, Janet and Matthew cuddled together in the rocking chair to read a favorite book, then Matthew went to his room for his "quiet hour." By 3:00 that afternoon, Matthew was happily working on a collage of leaves; Janet laughed at the mess

*he was making – and congratulated herself on helping her son
move away from his stress threshold.*

Using stress-busting strategies to improve relationships with
others involves four basic questions:

1. Where is the individual on the stress continuum? How can
   you tell?

Janet perceived that Matthew was on the edge of his stress
threshold. She checked her perceptions with the teacher's report
and with her own observations of Matthew's behavior, body
language, and comments.

2. Does he need to move away from his stress threshold?
   How soon? How do you know?

Janet wanted to help Matthew move away from his stress
threshold so he would have more control of his behavior. She
knew that making these changes before lunch should help him
digest his food.

3. Right now, where is the optimal place on the continuum for
   this person?

Matthew's "survival response" helped him express his anger
towards his friend (though he may have paid a price for that
behavior). But for lunch and "quiet hour," Matthew should be at
the other end of the continuum.

4. Where are you on your continuum?

If Janet had been close to her stress threshold, she would have
been less able to move her son towards the "ease" end of his continuum; she may have argued with him or exploded at his behavior.
In that case, Janet would have been wise to take a few minutes for
her own stress-busting strategies (perhaps while Matthew enjoyed
some active play in the backyard). Being "at ease" allowed her to
focus her thoughts and feelings on helping her son.

The Problem Is Always in the Background

Residual stress is in the background of many common
problems including colic, poor muscle tone, and learning
disabilities. Stress takes many forms and its effects may not be
recognized until years later.

Heredity often gets the blame for problems that may in truth have their background elsewhere. What's called an "Irish temper," for example, may actually begin as a digestive dysfunction, which is then reinforced by family tradition and expectation.

If the autonomic nervous system (ANS) is locked in a survival mode, the peacekeeping force of the body is unable to maintain the balance of the body's involuntary functions. Problems may soon develop with heart rate, blood pressure, digestion, and respiration. The survival mode also keeps us locked in reactions rather than being able to interact with our environment.

In many self-help programs, participants are encouraged to search for the sources of stress that are hidden in the background of the visible problem to be overcome. Eating disorders, for example, often can be traced to a background of physical and emotional distress that began at infancy; adult children of alcoholics may find that unmet needs of their childhood triggered complex coping mechanisms.   Breaking such habits and disorders takes time and effort. Attention must be focused on the background and not just the visible problem.

Learning Disabilities and Stress

Learning disabilities constitute the most common, and most misunderstood, stress-related problems for children. Stress can impair a child's ability to receive or respond to sensory information, can disrupt the process of learning to function against gravity, and may interfere with development of motor skills. If a child's body can't function automatically and requires a mental effort to keep it in balance, there will be insufficient "brain power" available for intellectual growth, and learning disabilities may result.

As deQuiros and Schrager explain, "It is impossible to introduce human learning processes while corporal needs (physiological, survival, comfort) are not met." (*Neuro-psychological Fundamentals in Learning Disabilities.* p. 27)

Looking back, parents of children with learning disabilities often remember signs of poor sensory or motor integration long before their child's academic problems were noticed:

Elyse wouldn't let anyone cuddle her.   (Her body was confused by sensory information.)

Jeremy refused to play on swings, merry-go-rounds, slides, and other moving equipment on the playground. (The movement overwhelmed his poorly integrated motor skills.)

Suzanne always wanted to cling to Mommy. (She was afraid of moving in her environment.)

William stood in a "fatigue posture": sway back, tummy out, knees locked back, head forward. (His muscle tone was weak against the force of gravity so he had poor stability when standing.)

Frank talked as if he had marbles in his mouth. (The muscles for sucking and chewing were poorly developed.)

Monica was "accident prone." Clumsy and awkward, she was constantly bumping into things and falling. (She couldn't move her body smoothly because it wasn't fully integrated.)

Alone, such signs of poor sensory or motor integration are not an indication of learning disabilities. Most kids are *sometimes* clingy, clumsy, uncoordinated, hard to understand. If these problems persist, however, and if a child's behavior or functioning seem out of line with peers, parents should seek the advice of a qualified, prevention-minded physician, physical therapist, and/or occupational therapist. Comprehensive evaluation for learning disabilities must include observation of physical development (including eye control, left-right preference, body awareness, posture, muscle tone, movement patterns, and behavior patterns), and assessment of stress factors (physical and emotional stressors, past and present) in the child's life. Margot Heiniger's *Integrated Motor Activities Screening* is an excellent tool for identifying children who are at risk for learning disabilities. CN 2.6

The stress that learning-disabled kids experience is magnified by their inability to learn through traditional teaching methods. It's incredibly frustrating to constantly face classwork beyond one's capabilities and to know you are falling behind, not meeting expectations, and considered "different" from other students. School-age children with unidentified learning disabilities learn to avoid painful, frustrating, and difficult situations and concentrate all their energy on things they do well. Their favorite pastime may be chess or music, or it may be teasing other kids and being a general nuisance in class. These kids often develop complex coping mechanisms, and may become the class bully, the class clown, the young socialite, or the hypochondriac.

Kids with learning disabilities often live dangerously close to their stress threshold. "Fight-or-flight" responses become part of everyday life. The resulting constant tension interferes with their ability to take in new information, and stifles their curiosity, attentiveness, self-confidence, physical coordination, and other basic qualities essential for learning.

Fortunately, there is currently a growing concern about learning disabilities. Educators are introducing a variety of teaching methods to reach students with a broad range of learning styles and abilities. Parents and educators are becoming more and more aware that learning disabilities are often a result of stress, and that the learning disabilities, in turn, create additional stress.

Self-parenting for Stress-Management

For Jeff, it was an especially satisfying moment with his daughter that prompted his commitment to better stress-management strategies. Holding six-month old Tami in his arms as she fell asleep, he felt more complete than ever before. He vowed to do all he could to make those warm moments a regular part of their lives, and to free himself and his daughter from a cycle of dis-stress. He knew he needed to begin by better understanding the stressors that were shaking his life and those that might be disrupting his daughter's development.

Jeff's self-parenting began with self-acceptance. He bought a poster (a silly monkey saying "I'm OK") to hang inside his closet door as a reminder that he was worth the effort.

He learned about the stress continuum, and began to watch for stressors that pushed him towards his stress threshold. To better manage his response to stressors, he worked with his autonomic nervous system, muscle tone, thoughts and feelings.

Jeff knew that his autonomic nervous system required that a balance be maintained between its survival and peacekeeping roles; he also recognized that the aggressive character of his survival system tended to dominate his body. He made some changes in his environment that enabled him to de-activate that survival system and ease the way for his peacekeeping system to work properly. This involved:

- *Maintaining comfortable room temperatures at home and work.*
- *Using soft lights on dimmer switches.*
- *Reducing noise of equipment, radios, telephones, etc.*
- *Eating regular meals and healthy foods to ease the stress on his digestive system.*
- *Easing into transitions. Because change throws us into a survival mode, Jeff minimized other stressors when facing changes in his routine, surroundings, and expectations.*

- *Taking time out, including lunch breaks, walks around the block, weekend ventures with his family, and breaks in his on-the-job routine.*

- *Easing muscle tension with deep breathing, isometric exercises, even brief walks around the office. He took up tennis to activate his "big muscles" after work, but opted not to join a highly competitive tournament that might increase the stress level of his sport.*

Jeff also knew that the time he spent holding his daughter was a key to his stress-busting strategies. As he rocked her, he became more in tune with his thoughts and feelings. Like most parents, he wanted to spare her the pain he'd felt since childhood.

He began thinking more about his childhood. He got out the old family albums and spent an afternoon listening to his mother's stories about their family life. Memories started coming together: his frustrations on the ball field, the dunce cap he had to wear after flunking a science test, how he had been taunted by older kids at the bus stop. He learned that his parents had faced a bevy of financial and personal problems when he was just two years old. As he discovered that his mother's memories of his childhood experiences were far different from his own, he affirmed the validity of his own perceptions of childhood events and acknowledged how deeply he had been wounded by some stressful experiences.

Jeff's self-parenting gave him a new appreciation for himself, his history, and his potential. He began to cherish the times he spent with his daughter; through her eyes, he discovered his own matrix of inner security and strength that was always available to him, and a connection with a source of power greater than any stress.

THE INNATE AUTOMATIC STAGE OF DEVELOPMENT:
Conception through Three Months After Birth

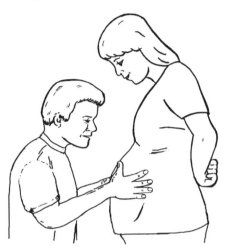

CHAPTER THREE:
Life Before Birth

For the first five years of their marriage, Suzanne and Bill were in no hurry to have children. Just hours after Suzanne's sister gave birth to her first child, Suzanne and Bill took turns holding their tiny nephew. Within a week they had agreed that it was time to begin planning a family of their own.

Becoming parents became Suzanne and Bill's most important priority, and they agreed to do all they could to provide a perfect beginning for the new life they hoped to create. They realized that their preparations must begin even before they abandoned their contraceptives.

Suzanne made an appointment with her physician for a pre-pregnancy physical exam. She enrolled in a yoga class and she and Bill began walking a couple of fast-paced miles each evening. They were more careful about what they ate, and they agreed to quit drinking alcohol and to avoid places where cigarette smoke was thick.

Suzanne and Bill also wanted to prepare emotionally and spiritually for the life-changing event of having a baby. At first, they talked mostly about the baby itself: the color of baby's hair, whether baby would have Bill's eyes or Suzanne's, if he or she would be a scientist or a chef, and whether baby would be a he or a she. In time, they also talked about the joys and pains they remembered from childhood, parents they admired, and fears they had about their new role.

Three months after making their decision to become parents, Suzanne and Bill ceremoniously stored away their contraceptives. Another six months passed before they learned that the miracle of conception had taken place: they would soon be parents.

Pregnancy is Continuing Creation

"You're pregnant!" With that announcement, the lives of a man and a woman are changed forever. Becoming parents means taking responsibility for nurturing new life and becoming a part of the unbroken human lineage. Becoming parents is participating in creation.

As potential parents, Suzanne and Bill knew their baby might be conceived weeks before pregnancy could be confirmed. They also recognized that the complex sequence of human development, which would begin immediately, must be allowed proceed rapidly and precisely, without interruption or alteration. Traumas during the first weeks of pregnancy can disrupt development of the body's most basic structures and functions.

> *"Just as a woman who wants to become pregnant must make room in her womb for the new being, she and the father must make room in their minds and hearts for the child they desire to have."*
>
> (Verny and Weintraub. *Nurturing the Unborn Child.* p. xx) CN3.1

This chapter is about the earliest months of human development, and how life before birth sets the stage for life-long functioning, growth, and happiness. Besides helping parents and parents-to-be, this information will be valuable for adoptive parents and step-parents who may have missed these prenatal months and want to better understand their children. Adults working to continue their personal growth through self-parenting also will find in this chapter information and insights that will provide them with a better understanding of early traumas which may be in the background of developmental and behavioral problems.

In functional terms, conception is the beginning of a year-long developmental stage, when the body's automatic functioning is established. Movement specialist/educator Newell Kephart referred to this as the *innate automatic stage* of development.

The developmental goal of this stage is to prepare the child for life outside the womb and to complete the physical structures and functions necessary for breathing, taking nourishment, ridding the body of wastes, maintaining body temperature, and so on. If a baby is born before these functions are completed, development must continue outside the womb.

But physiological "completion" is only part of the work of pregnancy. To be fully ready to live outside the security of mother's body, a baby must have an inner sense of security. Through bonding with its mother, the fetus experiences trust and security, and learns *from the inside out* to trust mother, self, and the world. If the prenatal experience is loving and secure, a baby expects the outside world to be the same and feels secure and competent at each stage of development. But if the prenatal environment has been hostile and frightening, the infant can only fear whatever comes next. CN3.2

Looking at the Fragile Beginning of Human Life

Pregnancy begins with the miracle of conception, when a tiny sperm (measuring about $\frac{1}{500}$ of an inch) succeeds – against tremendous odds – in penetrating the numerous protective layers surrounding the egg (which measures about $\frac{1}{175}$ of an inch in diameter, almost four times as large as the sperm). Pooling their genetic resources, these tiny ambassadors of humankind begin the sequence of events necessary for producing a human being. The combined organism contains all the genetic material needed to make each baby distinctly human, part of a human family that includes thousands of generations, and yet uniquely like the woman and man who conceived this life.

The creation of a new generation actually begins decades before conception. Men begin producing sperm when they reach sexual maturity and continue to do so for the rest of their lifetime. A woman begins preparing for motherhood just days after her own conception. Long before the female even remotely resembles a human being, her tiny ovaries are stocked with her lifetime supply of eggs, and she has stored about 100 cells of genetic material. In other words, before a mother even knows she's pregnant, her body has done the critical work of preparing for future generations. CN3.3

From the moment of conception, both sperm and egg, as initiators of a new life and carriers of genetic information, are vulnerable to a myriad of factors and forces. If, for example, one parent is intoxicated at the time of conception, exposed to radiation or environmental toxins, malnourished, or even if one parent has been under a great deal of emotional stress, the work of the sperm and egg will be affected. Such negative factors can short-change optimum development from the very beginning.

Because major body structures are developed during the first weeks after conception, this is when major problems are most likely to occur:

- The central nervous system and the heart are highly sensitive to teratogens from the third through the fifth or sixth week of development. (A teratogen is any drug, virus, irradiation, or other non-genetic factor which can cause malformation of the embryo.)

- Formation of the heart is especially sensitive to teratogens during the third, fourth, and fifth weeks of development. (The embryo's heart begins beating three weeks after conception, before the mother can even be sure she is pregnant!)

- Problems with the development of the arms, legs, and eyes are most likely to occur during the fourth through eighth weeks.

- Development of the ears continues to be vulnerable to problems through the ninth week.

Fortunately, not all traumas cause physical deformities. The sequence of human development is complex and fragile, but the tiny embryo is remarkably resistant to threats, traumas, and problems. Yet, even when physical development continues on course, prenatal traumas may be stored (remembered) at a cellular level, below the reaches of the conscious mind. These body memories may be as powerful as the memories stored in our "thinking mind," and are often expressed physically in a reflex, symptom, or reaction. How you respond to a sudden noise, a smell, or a bump on the head may be related to a body memory of a similar event that you experienced even before your birth. We'll take a closer look at the impact of prenatal and birth trauma later in this chapter.

Risk Factors and Prenatal Development

To maximize the possibilities for healthy birth and life and to enjoy pregnancy as a miraculous time, parents-to-be (mothers and fathers) should consider:

- **Environmental hazards.** Exposure to yard chemicals, on-the-job hazards, paint thinner, paint removers, local pollution, X-rays, radon, household cleaners, aerosol sprays, and permanent wave solutions may interfere with embryological development. Avoid these substances.

- **Medications (prescription and over-the-counter).** The placenta allows free passage to many medications, including aspirin, that might harm a baby. For current information about how medications affect pregnant women and unborn babies, consult with your doctor or pharmacist, or look for up-to-date resources at your library.

- **Smoking.** Each cigarette steals oxygen from baby, increasing the risk of respiratory problems, poor development, and low birth weight.

- **Alcohol, caffeine, and other mood-altering drugs.** The placenta is no barrier to these substances, and baby's tiny size makes their effects even more potent. Studies show these drugs may lead to birth defects, fetal alcohol syndrome, and nutritional deficiencies.

- **Medical history.** High-risk pregnancies are more common among mothers with sexually transmitted diseases, epilepsy, diabetes, high blood pressure, and certain other conditions. Some risks increase for women over age 35. Your doctor and other health care providers can help monitor these risks for pregnancy.

- **Genetic factors.** Cystic fibrosis, hemophilia, Tay-Sachs disorder, and sickle-cell anemia are just a few of the many conditions passed from generation to generation. Family, friends, and physicians can help assess the risks and the options available to parents-to-be facing these issues.

- **Exercise.** A regular exercise program will help parents handle the stress of the many changes that come with pregnancy, birth, and parenting, and will help prepare mother's body for the physical demands of pregnancy.

- **Diet.** Parents are "eating for two" even before their child is conceived. Baby's health may be affected if mother is underweight, overweight, a junk-food junkie, on a weight-loss diet, taking mega-doses of vitamins, on a nutrient-poor diet, skipping meals, or overeating. A healthy diet provides the nutritional security both mother and baby need for growth, development, emotional stability, and comfort during pregnancy.

- **Stress.** Having a baby is stressful, and stress can interfere with the health of body, mind, emotions, and spirit. During pregnancy, stressors in mother's life are readily transmitted to her child. Mothers-to-be can take charge of their own stress continuum by expanding their repertoire of "stress-busting techniques." (See Chapter Two.)

Pregnancy Is a Time of Constant Change

On the average, pregnancy is 266 days long, exactly enough time to complete the physiological, emotional, and spiritual foundation necessary for life outside the womb. During the 38 weeks between conception and birth, things are changing every minute. Human growth, development, and learning happen sequentially: each step requires the previous step, and sets a foundation for what's to come next.

The length of pregnancy is often expressed as gestational age, measured from the mother's last menstrual period (about two weeks before conception). In other words, five weeks after conception, the embryo has a gestational age of seven weeks and can be expected to remain another 230 days or so in the womb.

In the next few pages, we'll look at the amazing course of prenatal development, and the vulnerability of the developmental sequence at each stage:

Conception occurs when sperm and egg join forces to create new life. For the first two weeks after conception, the fertilized egg is still known as the "ovum" or egg.

The embryo is safely implanted in the uterine wall. This is when the basic foundations are set for the nervous system, the skeleton, circulation, and other body systems. Because it is growing so rapidly, the embryo is extremely vulnerable to developmental disruptions. This stage of development continues through the eighth week (about 40 days).

The fetus continues to grow in preparation for birth. The fetal period lasts from about nine weeks after conception until birth. Few new structures appear during the fetal period; this is the time for growth and maturation of tissues and organs that appeared during the embryonic period. Now recognizable as a human being, the fetus is far less vulnerable to the deforming effects of drugs, viruses, and radiation. This is also the time for practicing the basic physical functions which will sustain life outside the womb, such as breathing, sucking, and physical movements.

Birth is a process, not a stage of development. Birth may occur at any time after conception. But because every aspect of prenatal development is critical for proper functioning outside the womb, babies born prematurely are inadequately prepared for life. Development continues outside the womb but, as yet, no medical institution has replicated the ideal prenatal environment.

Conception

An hour after having intercourse, the young couple slept soundly while the miracle of conception occurred. Earlier that day, an egg had been released from one of the woman's ovaries and began to make its way down the Fallopian tube toward the uterus. During intercourse, millions of sperm were propelled into the woman's vagina and uterus. Few survived long enough to reach the Fallopian tubes; only one worked its way through the protective layers surrounding the egg. Pregnancy began the moment the sperm penetrated and fertilized the egg.

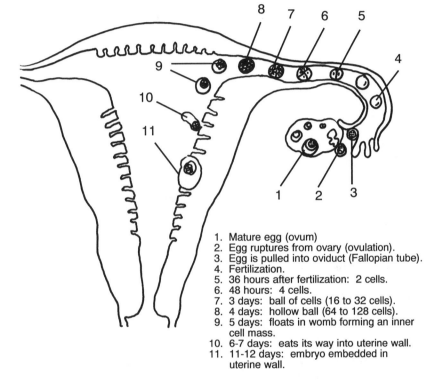

1. Mature egg (ovum)
2. Egg ruptures from ovary (ovulation).
3. Egg is pulled into oviduct (Fallopian tube).
4. Fertilization.
5. 36 hours after fertilization: 2 cells.
6. 48 hours: 4 cells.
7. 3 days: ball of cells (16 to 32 cells).
8. 4 days: hollow ball (64 to 128 cells).
9. 5 days: floats in womb forming an inner cell mass.
10. 6-7 days: eats its way into uterine wall.
11. 11-12 days: embryo embedded in uterine wall.

In the monthly rhythm of a woman's fertility, a single egg matures during the second week of each menstrual cycle and begins its journey down the Fallopian tube (oviduct) toward the uterus. Each egg contains 23 chromosomes from the mother; it also carries yolk granules which, if the egg is fertilized, provide nourishment during the first week of development.*

---

*In nature, exceptions can occur at every stage. Occasionally, for example, two eggs are released and fertilized, and fraternal twins develop. In this chapter, we describe primarily the "normal" course of events. For information on specific risk factors, abnormalities, and problems of pregnancy and birth, consult with your doctor or other specialists.

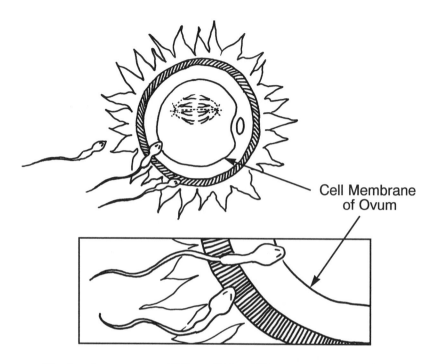

Cell Membrane
of Ovum

During intercourse, 300 to 500 million sperm enter the vagina at once; an hour or so later, only a few hundred sperm have reached the egg. That's usually the end of their journey. But if just one sperm manages to penetrate the two protective layers of cells surrounding the egg, conception takes place and the egg immediately responds by shunning other sperm. The tail of the welcomed sperm soon begins to degenerate and the head of the sperm enlarges. The "pronucleus" of the sperm merges with the "pronucleus" of the egg, and the two sets of chromosomes line up to form 23 pairs of chromosomes within a single nucleus. In the next 36 hours, the fertilized egg (ovum) will divide to form two identical cells and will continue to divide as it makes its way down the Fallopian tube towards the uterus.

The Embryo: Laying the Foundations

It takes the ovum a full week to implant itself in the wall of the uterus, where it will be "at home" for the duration of pregnancy. Now known as an *embryo,* it is surrounded by reservoirs of blood which will provide nourishment. A small *amniotic cavity* has formed outside the cell layers; eventually this will surround and cushion the embryo and stabilize the intrauterine environment.

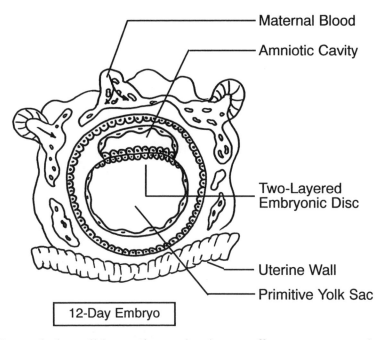

- Maternal Blood
- Amniotic Cavity
- Two-Layered Embryonic Disc
- Uterine Wall
- Primitive Yolk Sac

12-Day Embryo

Beneath the cell layers is a rather large *yolk sac;* a source of prenatal nourishment for other species, its role in human development is in formation of the gastrointestinal tract.

Three full weeks after conception, the embryo vaguely resembles a human form. It has an enlarged head at one end, and the beginning of a spine down the center back. A third layer of cells (the mesoderm) has formed between the first two. Each of these three cell layers (or "germ layers") is very specifically coded to develop certain elements of human structure:

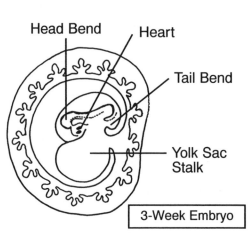

Head Bend   Heart

Tail Bend

Yolk Sac Stalk

3-Week Embryo

Cells of the top layer (ectoderm) are the "building blocks" of the skin, hair, eyes, tooth enamel, and the central nervous system.

Cells of the middle layer (mesoderm) are the "building blocks" of the skeleton, connective tissue (cartilage, ligaments, etc.), and circulatory system.

Cells of the bottom layer (endoderm) are the "building blocks" for the lining of the gastrointestinal tract, respiratory tract, and other organs.

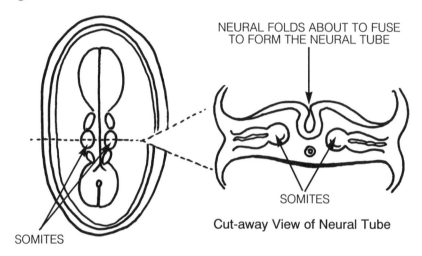

NEURAL FOLDS ABOUT TO FUSE
TO FORM THE NEURAL TUBE

SOMITES

Cut-away View of Neural Tube

SOMITES

The embryo now has a midline axis where the spine will eventually form, dividing it into two well-defined halves, left and right. Development of these two halves should happen simultaneously and symmetrically. During the third week of development, the ectoderm of the embryo forms a *neural groove* lengthwise along the embryo's midline axis. As the groove grows deeper, it fuses at the top to form the tube that becomes the spinal cord. Certain disabilities are caused by interferences to the proper development of the midline axis:

Spinal bifida or meningiomyocyle occurs when the neural tube fails to close completely.

Cleft palate or umbilical hernia occurs when the two sides don't join at the middle.

Congenital deformities of the arm or leg may result if one side fails to develop fully.

The ***cardiovascular system*** is the first system to function in the embryo; blood begins circulating through the embryo by the end of the third week. The heart, diaphragm, and liver begin to form while the embryonic disk is still flat. During the third week, the heart area begins to fold under in the area where the mouth will be; the heart takes a protected position at the center of the body.

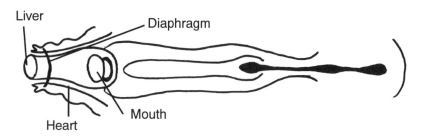

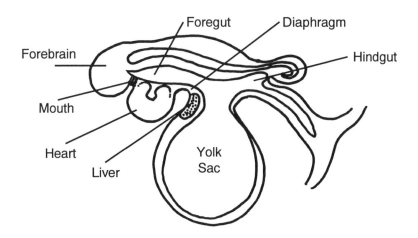

The mother has now missed a menstrual period and may suspect she is pregnant. Because of the hormonal changes that come with pregnancy, she may be feeling tired, nauseated, dizzy, or moody. Even this early in pregnancy, mother's attitude about her baby and her pregnancy is extremely important, both for her baby's development and for her own health and happiness during these months.*

---

*One excellent resource for expectant parents is *Nurturing the Unborn Child* (by Thomas Verny and Pamela Weintraub), which offers "scientifically effective exercises for relaxing prospective parents and nuturing and stimulating the unborn child up to, during, and immediately after birth."

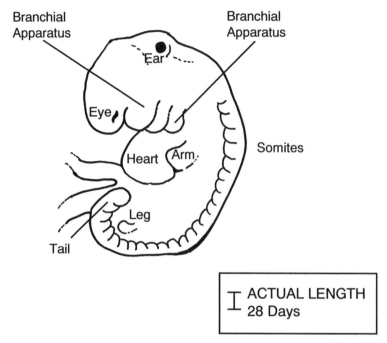

ACTUAL LENGTH
28 Days

At 28 days, the embryo measures about three-sixteenths of an inch, about triple the size it was just a week ago. The heart began to beat 22 days after conception and can be seen as a bulge by 24 days.

The neck has now formed, and the face is vaguely apparent. The embryo now has "branchial apparatus," gill-like structures which are the building blocks for the face and neck. For fish, the branchial apparatus develops as gills; human development begins with the same sequence, but continues along a lengthier timeline to form more complex human structures. Congenital malformations of the head and neck occur when this sequence is disrupted so the branchial apparatus fails to develop properly.

The fourth week is also a time for other dramatic events in human development:

- The membrane in the mouth area ruptures, creating an opening between the gastrointestinal tract and the amniotic cavity.

- The inner ear has clearly begun to develop.

- "Buds" of the arms and legs have formed.

- The body continues to lengthen and curve forward as if protecting the inner organs of the body.

- A tiny tail has formed at the end of the vertebrae, measuring about one-sixth as long as the human embryo. The tail lasts only a few weeks; the buttocks grow around it and the tail is reabsorbed, virtually disappearing by the ninth week.

Ten days after her period was due, Suzanne took a pregnancy test and learned that she and Bill had conceived a child about 24 days before. Excited and anxious, Suzanne had little appetite. She fought a craving for a beer "just to celebrate," and instead took a long walk with Bill. That night in bed, just before falling asleep, Bill kissed Suzanne's stomach. "Good night, Little One," he said.

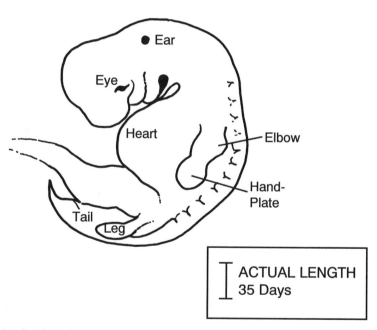

ACTUAL LENGTH
35 Days

The brain develops rapidly during the fifth and sixth weeks after conception, and the size of the head grows tremendously. This growth happens from the hindbrain forward, with the midbrain and forebrain developing later.

The hindbrain is the precursor to the brainstem. This is the earliest and most basic "command center" for the body's vital functions of respiration, temperature control, circulation, and vertical posture. The hindbrain also contains the cranial nerves which supply sensation and motor control for all the head and face structures (tongue, eyes, ears, and all muscles of facial expression). Within the hindbrain is the *reticular formation,* which is responsible for keeping the cortex in the alert state necessary for daily functioning. (That's why brainstem injuries can have such a drastic impact on basic functions, and may interfere with a person's ability to stand, breathe, even to maintain an alert state.)

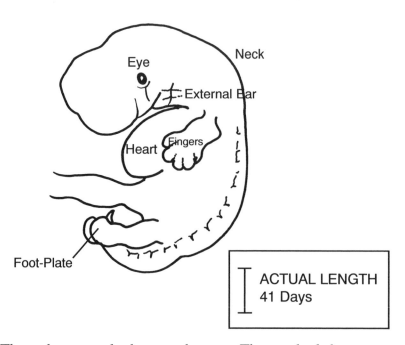

The embryo now looks more human. The arm buds have paddle-like hands and definite wrists. By the end of the sixth week, the hands are marked with "rays" that show where the fingers will be. The leg is slower to develop and may now appear only as leg buds and foot plates.

This is a good example of how human development always proceeds from head to toe, from midline to extremities: the head is formed before the toes, the arms before the legs. So, too, the shoulders are finished before the hands, the legs before the toes.*

---

*Human development proceeds in two basic directions: *cephalocaudally* (head to toe) and *proximodistally* (from midline to extremities).

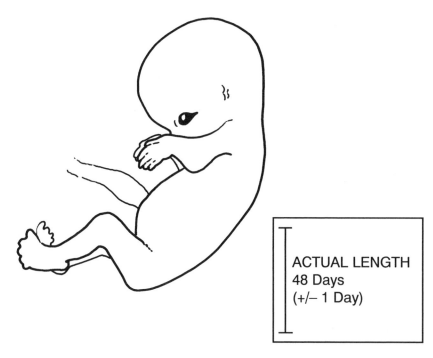

ACTUAL LENGTH
48 Days
(+/− 1 Day)

During the last two weeks of the embryonic period (the seventh and eighth weeks after conception), the head becomes erect and the body straightens. The forebrain grows so dramatically that the forehead actually bulges. The neck is now more evident, as it bends at the top of the spine. Eyelids are fused over the eyes; they will open again at about 26 to 29 weeks. The structural part of the ear is present and the ear's function can soon begin. (Notice how low the ear is on the head; in coming weeks, the ear will seem to "move up" as the neck lengthens). Fingers have separated; the toes will separate a week later. (If trauma interrupts this stage of development, toes may remain webbed.)

By the end of the embryological period, the growing life is unquestionably human, and almost all the internal organs are well established. For the remaining weeks of prenatal development, the growing human will be known as a *fetus:* the tissues and structures which appeared during the embryological period will increase in size and maturity during the fetal period. And while prenatal development follows a very specific timeline, each pregnancy is uniquely affected by genetics, maternal health, bonding, and traumas.

Prenatal Bonding is a Reservoir of Security

Through the many changes of pregnancy, the interconnection between mother and child – the bonding – establishes a reservoir of security that sustains them both, even through the emotional, spiritual, and physiological stresses of pregnancy. As Czech psychoanalyst Stanislav Grof observes, "We are so intimately connected with the mother, both biologically and emotionally, that we are almost like an organ in her body. . . . There is security, protection, and instant, effortless gratification of all needs." (*The Holotropic Mind.* p. 37) CN3.4

During pregnancy, mother's autonomic nervous system is made available to the embryo/fetus, and her physical and emotional defenses handle stressors that would otherwise upset the homeostasis (balance between stress and peace) necessary for growth and development. This is also known as *emotional entropy.*

At some point during pregnancy, the interconnection between mother and fetus reaches a unique stage known as *fusion,* when the emotional separation between them becomes nearly nonexistent. While the fetus is becoming more mature, the mother is actually regressing emotionally. At birth, then, the mother can "meet the baby" emotionally, and her emotional vulnerability gives her an incredible innate "knowing" of her newborn child.

Without healthy bonding, the embryo/fetus has no way of releasing the tension of unresolved stress and a "residue" of tension settles deep within his developing body, affecting his development *from the inside out.* The impact will be seen later in his emotional stability and his physical function.

It is important, and natural, that expectant fathers also become bonded with the unborn child as they caress mother's bulging stomach, talk and sing through the uterine wall, and anticipate the complex roles of a parent. CN3.5

"The deeper the intimacy and commitment between partners, the easier it was for a man to fully participate in the changes that pregnancy brings.... Furthermore, the origins of a father-to-be's nurturing behavior appear to go back to a man's own childhood and the nurturing he received."

(Schwartz. *Bonding Before Birth.* p. 75

During the first months of pregnancy, mothers and fathers can enhance the bonding process through activities that will help them get to know the baby before it can be seen or even felt, to love and care for the baby before it is born.

- Relaxation releases stress and opens channels for fully knowing the life that is growing in the womb.

- Imagery and visualization enhance communication with the growing embryo and fetus.

- Caressing and massaging mother's abdomen are powerful nonverbal means of communication.

- Talking and singing to the embryo and fetus build an auditory bond between parents and baby. At birth, this bond is instantly affirmed when the newborn baby hears the parents' familiar voices as her first airborne sounds.

The Fetus

Amy's second pregnancy seemed far different from her first. Her body shape began changing more rapidly and dramatically than when she had been pregnant before. She didn't have the nausea she'd had when she was carrying Michael three years earlier, but she was tired, always tired. Three years ago, she didn't have a toddler demanding her attention. There always seemed so much to do: diapers to wash, toys to pick up, childcare to arrange. . .

This pregnancy was different in other ways too; she knew a little more about what to expect and was even more aware of how seemingly minor events might affect the development of the embryo. Even her child's development in the womb seemed different in ways Amy couldn't describe.

Since her pregnancy had been confirmed, she had been keeping a journal, noting what she was feeling and experiencing each day, and collecting other information that might later show what was "in the background" of her child's development.

For weeks now, the fetus has been moving silently but freely in the amniotic fluid. It is now clearly a human offspring, functioning in ways that are distinctly human. At the beginning of the fetal period (about nine weeks after conception) the fetus is only about 3 centimeters long (1¼ inch) and weighs less than two grams. The head is heavier than the body, so the fetus is positioned head-down and fits perfectly in the pear-shaped uterus.

Because the foundations of human structures are already formed, the fetus is now less vulnerable to the effects of drugs, viruses, or radiation than the embryo. Traumas during the fetal period are most likely to result in functional problems, especially in the nervous system.

Positioned for Growth:
The Second Trimester (weeks 14 - 26)

As the embryo grows to become a fetus, its tiny body curls up in the womb in the protective fetal position. All joints of the body are bent inward as if to shield the body's most vulnerable parts (heart, lungs, stomach, genitals). From this time on, the body will remember this position as one of security and comfort. Even adults instinctively curl into the fetal position to sleep, for self-protection, and in times of stress.

From this curled-up position, the body begins to learn its first basic movements. In the gentle current of the amniotic fluid, the muscles begin to flex inward (towards the body) then let go and float out. *Flexion* is the first fetal movement, and is learned by all the muscles simultaneously. The fetus next develops the *adduction* patterns which bring the arms and legs toward the midline of the body. Next, *internal rotation* movements are established, enabling the arms and legs to roll towards the body's midline.

Gravity has minimal effect on these early movement patterns, because the amniotic fluid virtually absorbs the effects of gravity. Yet even by the tenth week after conception, the fetus perceives subtle changes in position, and changes his own position as mother moves from standing to sitting, lying down, walking, or bending over. This early adjustment to changes in position is the foundation for the *vestibular system,* which will be responsible for perceiving the position and movement of the head in relation to gravity, and for maintaining posture and balance.

By eight-and-a-half weeks, the fetus will respond to a light touch at the corner of the mouth by turning the head away, side-bending the trunk, and with flexion, adduction, and internal rotation of the arms and legs. This total body response is the first sign of the survival response of the autonomic nervous system, and is the first sign of the developing autonomic nervous system.

As we described in Chapter Two, the autonomic nervous system (ANS) has a survival role and a peacekeeping role. The survival role develops three weeks before the peacekeeping role:

not until eleven weeks does the same light touch at the corner of the mouth prompt the fetus to turn *toward* the stimulus, indicating the beginning of the parasympathetic (peacekeeping) response known as the "rooting reflex." These first movements are automatic and predictable responses, as if "prewired" in specific patterns. With practice, the fetus learns to adapt these early patterns so he can bend towards a stimulus or turn away.

Like most human development, sensation develops first at the head, then moves down the body; by about fourteen weeks, the entire body is sensitive to touch. We used to think that the top and back of the head did not become sensitive until after birth as nature's way of preparing the head to take the force as it leads the way through the birth canal.

> "The infants of mothers who were emotionally disturbed during pregnancy frequently exhibit evidences of an irritable and hyperactive autonomic nervous system."
> (Montagu. *Prenatal Influences.* p. 199) CN3.6

The fetus can hear as early as the eighteenth week. His hearing abilities become fairly sophisticated before birth, and he may respond to loud noises, familiar voices, and music. Many newborn infants recognize music they heard their mothers sing or play while pregnant.

Sometime around the sixteenth week of pregnancy, mothers experience the fetal movements known as *quickening,* the first sure sign of pregnancy. By now, the fetus has many movement patterns and mother will soon recognize how he responds uniquely to sounds, pressure, and movements of her body. These responses confirm the mother's innate feeling that she and her baby-to-be are a unit, two yet still one.

Many mothers find that quickening marks a change in their relationship with the unborn child and may be surprised to feel a break in the total fusion they have established. As the fetus moves on its own, there is no doubt that this new life is a separate being, in some ways already independent from mother. CN3.7

> "Total fusion, where the embryo is viewed merely as a content of the body, is disrupted at the first signs of quickening. The mother then begins to perceive the fetus as a separate entity and therefor begins to invest it with increasing amounts of object love. By the time of birth... the mother is able to tolerate the anatomical separation and to consider her newborn as a complete person, well separated from herself."
> (Klaus and Kennell. *Maternal-Infant Bonding.* p. 159)

Fetus at Work:
The Third Trimester (27 weeks until birth)

The last weeks before birth are a time for the fetus to prepare for the environmental changes at birth, to practice the life-sustaining functions that must soon be automatic and perfect, and to complete the "finishing work" necessary for life outside the womb.

At the beginning of the third trimester, the fetus could survive if born prematurely, although mortality rate is high and traumatic intervention by medical technology is often necessary. By the twenty-fourth week, the air sacs in the lungs are able to stay open and the fetus begins breathing amniotic fluid in preparation for breathing the oxygen that will greet him at birth. Not until 26 to 29 weeks are the lungs able to breathe air.

Weight triples between the twenty-sixth and thirty-eighth week. The fetus is storing fat under the skin and gaining weight. Blood now fills the capillaries and the skin has a healthy color.

Fetal movement is stimulated by mother's activity, which also serves to increase and enrich the blood supply to the fetus. The uterine environment has become increasingly crowded and movement is now restricted by the tight accommodations. Instead of floating in the amniotic fluid, the fetus kicks and stretches against the elastic constraints of the uterine wall. Pushing against the uterine wall is a resistive exercise for the fetus, helping him build muscle tone and expand movement patterns. By now the fetus has learned *extension* (straightening the entire body to its fullest), *abduction* (moving arms and legs away from the body's midline) and *external rotation* (rolling arms and legs away from the body's midline). These body movements are the opposite of those first learned and give the fetus far greater variety of movement.

As the uterine wall and mother's skin stretch to make room for the growing fetus, light can pass through the thinning membranes, giving the womb a warm red glow that greets the fetus when the eyes first become unsealed (about 26 to 29 weeks after conception).

During these last weeks, fathers-to-be often experience some emotional confusion, possibly feeling left out by the bonding and fusion that mysteriously connects his wife and their unborn child. He may feel neglected sexually; may be anxious about finances or the health of the fetus; and may be struggling to see himself as a father. Fathers should anticipate and accept such confusing feelings and seek the support they may need. CN3.8

In the weeks before his first child was born, Bill's concerns about being a father seemed to grow as fast as his wife Suzanne's waistline. Just lately, she had become increasingly moody and quiet and he was confused about his own feelings of rejection, anger, and fear.

At a break during a childbirth class, he overheard two other fathers joking about similar feelings. He mustered his courage and asked them if they'd like to meet for coffee later that week to "swap stories and talk about being dads."

When the four men gathered around the restaurant table, their conversation moved quickly from pleasantries to "pregnancy stories." They soon began sharing complaints and concerns about parenting. They all felt a little neglected, all worried about finances, all wondered if they would "measure up" during childbirth and as fathers in the years to come. They began to realize, too, that each of them had some "handicap" in the way of being the perfect parent, and that they wanted to do everything possible to be good fathers and loving partners.

Joe had been abandoned by his father and feared he would do no better for his own children. After Joe told his story, Pete suggested that Joe work at visualizing his relationships and interactions with his kids, beginning with his support of his wife during the last weeks of pregnancy and his role at their child's birth. "Visualization takes time," Dave advised. "Be patient as you expand your self-image to include being a father."

Pete was between jobs and was feeling the financial pressures of supporting a family. His wife was now the wage-earner and Pete was worried that the stress she was feeling might harm their baby. Bill told him of some "stress-busting strategies" (especially massage and breathing exercises) that Pete and his wife might do together.

Bill admitted he had mixed feelings about how a baby would change the lifestyle he and Suzanne had enjoyed for the past few years. Pete reminded him that the baby had already been a part of their lives for several months and probably even knew Bill's voice. Bill suddenly remembered a favorite song his mother had sung to him when he was a child, and he began thinking of other ways he could begin now to communicate with and anticipate his new child.

Birth: An Amazing Transition

Birth is the miraculous conclusion of pregnancy – and a traumatic transition from one world to the next. Considering the amazing sensory capabilities of the fetus, and the strain of the birth process, it's no wonder that babies so often cry at birth.

> *"Birth is no more the beginning of life than it is the end of gestation; it is merely the bridge between gestation within the womb and gestation outside the womb."*
> (Montagu. *Growing Young.* p. 94)

French obstetrician Frederick Leboyer has delivered more than 10,000 babies and has long been convinced that pain and suffering is unnecessary. His work on "birth without violence" has radically changed childbirth procedures world-wide through simple and gentle techniques for easing the trauma of birth.CN3.9

In most communities today, parents can choose from a variety of birth settings and philosophies, including natural childbirth programs and birthing centers. Dim lights, gentle sounds, and caring hands now greet the newborn's senses (not the loud and glaring confusion of the old delivery rooms). Moments after birth, infants are placed in mother's arms, at mother's breast, even before the umbilical cord is cut.

Parents must take the initiative for making their child's birth a loving, exciting, and perfect transition from the womb to the outside world. Their decisions include:

- *Participating in a childbirth education program* which will help them prepare for birth. These sessions should provide information about their options for labor, delivery, and maternity care. Prenatal exercises will strengthen the muscles of the back and the abdomen, in preparation for the weight of the last weeks of pregnancy, and help build the muscle control and relaxation that will ease delivery.

- *Choosing the mother's "birth partner" or coach,* who will support mother during labor and delivery and help her communicate her preferences about the environment of the birthplace, medications, monitors, medical procedures, etc.

- *Choosing the childbirth center* which can best provide the desired setting and services. Traditional hospital maternity centers, hospital birthing rooms, alternative birth centers, and home deliveries all may be considered. Parents should consider the environment of each setting; whether other family members are allowed to participate in the birth; how the newborn infant is cared for during labor and immediately after birth; what levels of medical care are available; how emergencies are handled.

• *Anticipating the need for medication, anesthesia, fetal monitors, and/or episiotomies.** Medication and surgery are invasive procedures which interfere with the natural sequence for labor and delivery, and have a negative impact on baby's entry into this world. Ideally, the pain and stress of childbirth can be handled without the intervention of any medication, technology, or surgical procedure. Yet in the height of labor, mothers often have second thoughts about their decision to "do it naturally," and medical staff may suggest drugs or episiotomies for easing the pain and speeding labor. Before labor begins, mothers and their birth coaches should carefully assess the options and their potential impact on baby and mother.

"Unless we in the medical profession take our role seriously – that of humanizing the events around labor, delivery, and, in general, having a new baby – we will have no right to criticize the trend toward home deliveries. We have forced young families to humanize it for themselves -- at home."

(Brazelton. *On Becoming A Family.* p. 41)

Four Stages of Birth

Ideally, the fetus initiates its birth only when he is ready to travel, head first, into the new world. Labor won't begin until the body's physical systems are fully prepared for functioning outside the womb, when prenatal bonding is complete, when mother and baby are emotionally prepared for the arduous event of birth.

The birth process can be described as having four stages: *engagement, a first stage of labor* (including the active phase and the latent phase), *a second stage of labor,* and *completion* (including delivery of the placenta and the period of immediate recovery).

---

*An episiotomy is a cut made at the opening of the vagina during childbirth. A local anesthetic is used; the incision is later closed with sutures and is fully healed within about six weeks.

During *engagement,* the mother's body begins to prepare for the baby to travel through the birth canal. In the first pregnancy, engagement begins about two weeks before the baby's birth as baby's head moves low in the pelvis. Pelvic ligaments begin to loosen and stretch, enabling the pelvis to shift and open wide enough to allow the baby to pass. This early "dropping" only happens once in a mother's life; once the pelvic muscles have opened to allow a baby's passage, they will be more relaxed for future pregnancies.

The first stage of labor begins with the first uterine contraction, signalling that the fetus and mother are preparing for birth. For the fetus, the first contractions are like a muscular massage as the uterus rhythmically and gently tightens, then releases. This is the *latent phase* of labor: baby is not yet ready to move down the birth canal. As contractions increase in intensity and frequency, the cervix thins (effaces), then dilates and opens to make room for baby's passage. This latent phase lasts usually about 12 hours for first-time moms but may be much shorter for subsequent deliveries. In false labor, contractions stop suddenly and may not resume for hours.

The latent phase is followed by the *active phase,* when the fetus begins descending through the birth canal and the cervix finishes dilating (opening). Contractions become strong and hard, more regular and closer together. Once the mucus plug is released and the amniotic sac of "waters" breaks, baby is no longer protected from infection and birth should take place within 24 hours.

Throughout this first stage of delivery, the mother may feel she is only an observer in the process. But that soon changes: as contractions become harder and quicker, she will need to focus intently on what's happening and concentrate her mental, emotional, spiritual, and physical energy on bringing her child into this world.

Stage two of labor begins when the cervix is fully dilated (usually to about ten centimeters in diameter). Contractions are now harder and closer together. Stage two may last up to two hours; on the average, it's about an hour for first pregnancies, only about 20 minutes for others.

The powerful uterine contractions now push the baby out of the uterus and through the narrow "obstacle course" of the pelvis and cervix. To get through this passageway, the baby must use all the movement patterns it has been practicing. The body flexes, rotates, and extends as the baby twists his way, head first, through the birth canal.

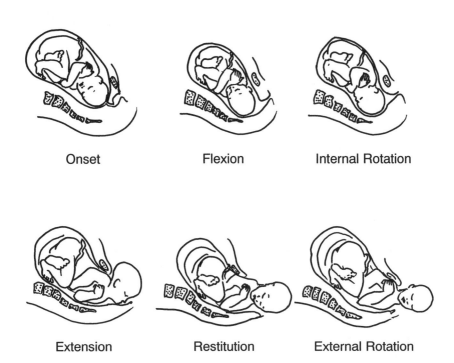

| Onset | Flexion | Internal Rotation |
| Extension | Restitution | External Rotation |

Besides pushing baby through this passageway, the forceful rhythm of the uterine contractions is an important stimulus for baby's functional systems. Each contraction gives a powerful "squeeze" on the baby's body and stimulates the skin, skeleton, and muscles. In this way, the contractions "turn on" the body systems in preparation for functioning outside the womb.

Imagine the incredible change of environment that greets baby at birth. After hours of being squeezed and pushed from all sides during labor, baby's head emerges into the dry, noisy world of the labor room. Baby's skin feels a new coolness, and her body enjoys a freedom of movement never before experienced. The talking, cries, and laughter she now hears are far more intense than the muffled sounds she heard through the uterine wall. Lights are brighter than the warm red light of the womb. As the air sweeps around baby's body, gloved hands pull her gently away from the uterine contractions that guided her journey. Then there are dry blankets, drops of medication in the eyes, more hands yet less support as her body is moved through the open air.

Now imagine the comfort and security baby feels as she is placed at mother's breast, cradled against mother, while warm and gentle hands stroke and soothe baby's weary little body. Welcome to our family. Welcome to this world.*

Completion of labor continues as mother's body recovers from the dramatic transformation required for the baby's passage through the birth canal. It will take weeks, even months, for mother's body to regain its pre-pregnancy shape, and for mother to shift her identity from pregnant woman to mother of an infant. This post-partum adjustment is complicated by the demands of a newborn.

For a while immediately after birth, the umbilical cord continues as the life-link between mother and baby. The cord is just long enough to reach the mother's breast, allowing the newborn to cuddle in mother's arms for the first time as the umbilical cord completes its transmission of oxygen-rich blood and essential hormones. This gentle welcome gives baby's body a chance to adapt to the many demands of the new world he has entered. Yet the umbilical cord also continues to transmit neurohormones which communicate stress, and also carries drugs or medications administered to mother during labor.

After the incredible trauma and transformation of labor and delivery, newborn babies have an extraordinary but short-lived sensitivity which makes them especially responsive to the loving touch of their parents. This 30 to 60 minutes immediately after birth is known as the *maternal sensitive period,* a time when newborns are exceptionally receptive, responsive, quiet, and alert. During this hour, their state of awareness is ideal for entering their new world and meeting their parents: their eyes are wide

> "The newborn infant is more fully feeling than he may ever be again; he has a wide open 'sensory window' which allows him to react wholly as he may never again; and he is born experiencing his new life without an illusory veil of ideas, which almost undoubtedly will never be the case again."
>
> (Janov. *Imprints.* p. 13)

---

*Leboyer describes birth beautifully. "The baby emerges . . . first the head, then the arms; we help to free them by sliding a finger under each armpit. Supporting the baby in this way, we lift the little body up, as if pulling someone out of the well. We *never* touch the head. And we settle the child immediately on its mother's belly" (*Birth Without Violence,* p. 43) open, they turn their heads towards voices, and seem to prefer certain sights. But this alert state doesn't last long: after less than an hour of interaction (40 minutes is the average), the newborn will sleep for three or four hours. During the brief alert state, it is critically important to:

- Use gentle, quiet movements with the newborn.
- Place the newborn at mother's breast immediately after birth.
- Have father present at birth.
- Avoid subjecting newborns to extensive medical tests and procedures except in emergency situations.

Functioning Outside the Womb

At the moment of birth, baby must be ready to perform a number of functions that were completely unnecessary in the womb:

- *Breathing.* Amniotic fluid has been squeezed from the lungs during labor, and the lungs inflate with baby's first breath.

- *Circulation.* When the lungs receive their first breath of air, major changes must occur immediately in the circulatory system. If these changes don't take place fully and immediately, the newborn may not receive enough oxygen. The effects may be obvious immediately (as "blue babies," for example) or may be so subtle that they are not evident for years (if at all).

- *Digestion.* Nourishment must now come from external sources, not from the placenta. Baby must be able to suck and swallow, digest food, retain nutrients, and eliminate wastes. Kidneys, liver, stomach, intestines, and colon must work properly.

- *Temperature regulation.* Because body temperature is no longer regulated by the uterine environment, baby must be otherwise protected from temperature extremes. A thin layer of fat under the skin offers some insulation. Baby soon learns to adapt his body temperature by changing his body position or his breathing patterns, or by crying or moving.

- *Immune system.* Newborn babies are equipped with some antibodies they received from mother but must be capable of fighting a range of viruses, bacteria, and toxins. Because these protective mechanisms are still developing at birth, babies are highly vulnerable to certain diseases and infections.

- *Behavior.* Baby soon develops patterns for sleeping and being awake, eating and eliminating wastes. She learns to process information, and begins to develop relationships with her caretakers.

- *Orientation to gravity.* In the few hours of labor and delivery, baby's body position changes permanently. Never again will he be comfortable and secure in the head-down position of the womb, insulated from gravity. Within the next several months, he will gradually learn to move his body against the force of gravity to maintain an increasingly upright position that is distinctly and uniquely human. But first (and immediately at birth), circulation and digestion must begin to work against gravity: blood must travel down to the body's extremities, back up to the heart and throughout the body; food must travel down the throat into the stomach.

- *Sensation.* At birth, the infant's sense of touch is more developed than any other sense. That's why it is so important, and instinctive, that parents caress their newborn babies.

Complications of Birth: Premature Birth

Medically, a birth is considered premature if it occurs before the end of the thirty-seventh week of gestation. Premature babies usually weigh less than 2500 grams (5.5 pounds) at birth. Premature births happen because something interrupts or rushes the timeline of development. For example, if mother's cervix is weak, it may be unable to hold the growing fetus. An accident, infection, or other trauma may set off hormonal changes and initiate labor. Some babies are born prematurely because the doctor and/or mother miscalculate the date of conception and the due date, and induce labor ahead of nature's timeline. There's reason to believe, too, that the fetus may begin labor prematurely when it perceives the intrauterine environment as hostile or unhealthy.

Because they are so small, premature babies usually have a relatively easy journey through the birth canal: it takes few contractions to push their tiny bodies through the "obstacle course" so there is less need for the body to use the flexion, extension, and rotation movement patterns. Without the pressure and sequenced movements, the body's functional systems may not be "switched on" for their essential roles. The lungs may still be full of amniotic fluid, the skin less sensitive, the muscles not stimulated for action. These babies haven't had the time in utero to "put on the fat" needed to insulate themselves against heat loss. It's no wonder that the death rate for premature infants is much higher than for full-term babies: their systems just aren't ready for independent functioning.

Emotional needs are also unfinished. Prenatal bonding has been interrupted and parents may feel anxiety and fear about the early birth. What's more, premature infants are more likely to need intensive care immediately after birth, so may not be comforted quietly and gently in their first moments outside the womb.

Parents and medical personnel must work together to face the physical and emotional effects of premature birth. Parents should participate as fully as possible in caring for the baby, even in a neonatal intensive care unit. They must take responsibility for the decisions about their baby's care and should insist on being continually informed about what's happening, consulting medical care givers, other parents, and other resources as needed. The new parents of a premature baby will need the help of friends, family, support groups – and from their own inner resources.

Medical technology can be life-saving but should be as noninvasive as possible. Medical personnel must respect the tremendous importance of bonding for both parents and infant, as well as the parents' authority as the primary caregivers for the baby. They also must respect parents' need for information, and should allow parents to be with their newborn as much as possible.

The effects of premature birth don't disappear when a baby is released from the hospital or even when a child reaches a norm on a birth chart. Often the "background" of later learning disabilities, physical dysfunction, behavioral problems, and stress reactions includes physical trauma of insufficient time in the womb or of leaving the security of the womb before baby was ready. Also in the background may be body memories of careless and invasive medical procedures, or perceived abandonment by parents during neonatal intensive care. Hypnosis, individual counseling, guided imagery, and various other techniques are being used effectively to help people come to terms with their own birth trauma and make up for losses experienced early on. Chapter Four offers more information on providing the hands-on care premature babies need.

We are also concerned about how our society cares for premature infants. Keeping premature babies alive is a big business – and big money – for hospitals and physicians. Medical technology and courageous physicians offer these tiny humans a chance at life that wouldn't have been possible just a few short years ago. But the human and financial cost of these procedures must be carefully considered, especially when these costs may be exorbitant and severely affect the quality of life of entire families. We must provide better environment for neonates, an environment similar to the womb, where the premature infant can be monitored with few invasive procedures (such as needles, bright lights) and where parents can hold, cuddle, and care for their new baby.

Complications of Birth: Induced Birth

The human timeline has a very small "window" for birth: a time when the fetus is fully ready to leave the womb, and when mother-fetus bonding is at its peak. Inducing labor (whether for medical reasons or for convenience) overrides nature's timeline. Drugs given to induce labor impair the relationship between mother and fetus, and block their full participation in this once-in-a-lifetime experience.

Of course, it is sometimes medically necessary to induce labor, such as when the fetus is in a stressed situation. But in most cases, the labor will start when the fetus is ready. Inducing labor for the convenience of the doctor, hospital, parents, or visiting relatives is compromising the importance of the beginning of life.

Complications of Birth: Drugs During Delivery

A generation or two ago, general anesthetics were fairly commonly used to "protect" mothers from the pain of childbirth. The trend didn't last long: mothers wanted to be full participants in the birth experience and sought better ways of controlling the pain and anxiety of childbearing. At the same time, research confirmed that there is no perfect pain relief medication. Each compound poses risks of possible injury, depression, sleepiness, and overdose. Any anesthesia increases the risk of death.

Medications for managing pain can be important tools for handling emergency situations. Even under the "normal" strains of labor, medications can help mother pace herself during labor and delivery. But any such medication will diminish mother's ability to bear down and push, and may inhibit baby's movement through the birth canal. Drugs also interfere with sensation, so may dull the precious "first impressions" of that moment of birth and disrupt bonding.

Because mother and fetus are still connected by the umbilical cord during delivery, any pain medication or other drugs given to the mother will be transmitted to the fetus. The earlier these drugs are given, the greater the influence on baby and mother. Drugs given towards the end of labor may never reach the baby; in fact, even the mother may receive little relief from pain, yet the chemical residue may affect her most during the "sensitive" periods after birth when being alert is most important.

Complications of Birth: Abnormal Birth Presentations

Nature designed us to take the brunt of the birth journey with the top of our heads. But sometimes the fetus tries to present itself differently: bottom first (breech), leg first, chin first, shoulder first, or other abnormal presentations. Imagine the trauma, fear, and risks that the fetus experiences in these situations! Highly sensitive parts of the body may be squeezed and stretched. The umbilical cord may get caught, blocking the oxygen supply. The body may get stuck in an uncomfortable position. Contractions may push in a direction the body can't go.

Sometimes the doctor can reach into the womb and manually turn the baby. Often a cesarean is considered the best course. Either of these options will add trauma to the birth experience, and abnormal birth presentations also will be physically and emotionally stressful for the baby. Because they haven't yet developed the mental skills for cognitive memory and reasoning, the trauma experienced by these babies will be remembered and expressed physically. Their physical memories may later evolve into coping skills and expressions of frustration: "I'm trapped... stuck...in a squeeze." "I can't breathe." "You're holding me back." "Don't push me!" The physical distress of birth may be reflected in an adult's vocabulary.

Complications of Birth: Cesarean Delivery

In the United States, nearly one fourth of all births are now by cesarean delivery; the rate is highest for mothers ages 35 and older. Many obstetricians consider cesarean deliveries to be safer, citing skyrocketing malpractice insurance rates and better fetal monitors that give more accurate information about fetal distress during labor. CN3.10

Cesarean births are traumatic for mothers and for babies. Maternal death rates are four times greater than with vaginal delivery. There are risks, too, of excessive bleeding, blood clots, and injury to bowel and bladder.

When used because labor has been "unproductive" or too difficult, the baby may already be tired or afraid, and will be further traumatized by the abrupt end of labor. When the surgery is scheduled in advance, the fetal timeline is disrupted and baby may be unprepared for birth. Without the stimulation of uterine contractions, functional systems may not be "turned on" to be operative at birth. Drugs given to mother during the surgery may reach the baby. And cesarean delivery often impairs mother's ability to respond fully to her newborn baby during the "sensitive period" immediately after birth. Disruptions may continue as the medical team intervenes to do what hasn't been done naturally: clean the lungs, prompt respiration, restore circulation, and initiate other functions normally activated by the birth process.

Infants born by cesarean section may need additional gentle pressure to make up for lack of stimulation during birth. Massage, cuddling, and swaddling in blankets are ways of providing the whole-body stimulation necessary for full functioning. Parents are wise to carry these babies with them as much as possible, so they can feel body motion. Rocking and gently manipulating the arms and legs also helps C-section babies recognize – from the inside out – their position in the world.

In later months, while babies born by cesarean section may be eager to stand up, their horizontal time (playing on the floor, rolling over, etc.) is especially important. Later, these children, even after they become adults, may sometimes feel dizzy or as if they are not "grounded." They may be easily disoriented or may suffer from an overworked "survival response" that is wrecking havoc with digestion, respiration, or other basic functions. Rolfing, massage, and other methods of body manipulation may restore some of the stability they need.

> *"The exposure to the constraints of the birth canal seems to lay the foundations for one's sense of boundaries in the world. The elective Caesareans may lack the sense of what their place is in the world and how much they can reasonably expect from others."*
> (Grof. *Beyond the Brain.* pp. 253-254)

First-line Trauma – From the Inside Out

In recent years, there has been growing interest in examining the physical and psychological effects of early traumas. In his important and startling book, *Imprints,* Arthur Janov specifically related the impact of painful experiences to three levels of brain development:

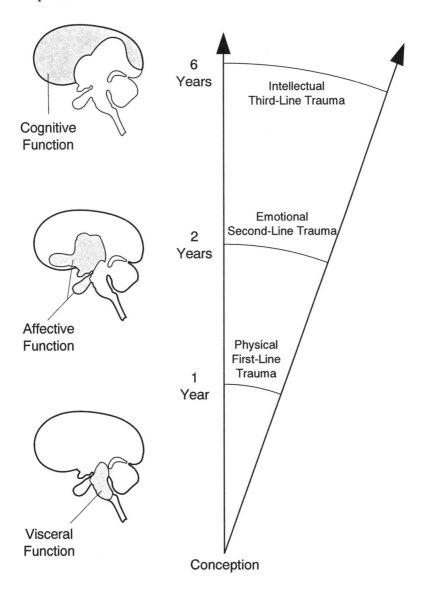

Cognitive
Function

Affective
Function

Visceral
Function

6
Years

2
Years

1
Year

Intellectual
Third-Line Trauma

Emotional
Second-Line Trauma

Physical
First-Line
Trauma

Conception

Traumas experienced before a child's first birthday (prenatally or during the first year after birth) are known as *first-line traumas* for they undermine human consciousness and functioning at the most basic level.

Traumas experienced during early childhood (between ages one and six) are known as *second-line traumas.* Because this is the time when children are developing emotionally and psychologically, these traumas may result in temper tantrums, behavior problems, personality disorders, and impaired relationships. (More about second-line traumas in Chapter Eight.)

Traumas experienced after age six affect the outer zone of brain development, the level of intellect. These *third-line traumas* may become intellectualized, or may result in obsessive or manic behavior. (More about third-line traumas in Chapter Nine.)

Because first-line traumas occur in the earliest developmental stages, they can result in physical deformities and problems with visceral functions (the heart, respiratory muscles, bladder, stomach, blood-forming organs, and hormonal regulation). Sometimes the effect is visible, as in a cleft palate. Other effects of first-line trauma are far more subtle: colic, for example, may result when prenatal stress locks the autonomic nervous system into a "fight" reaction and impairs the function of the digestive system. And because these occur long before we are able to talk (even before we are capable of cognitive thinking), we have no conscious memory of first line trauma.

The impact of early trauma can be devastating since it "secretly" affects development at the most basic level. These disruptions sometimes surface decades later, as ulcers, colitis, respiratory problems, kidney and bladder problems, heart and circulatory problems.

Severe physical or emotional distress is the most obvious source of first-line trauma. Yet even seemingly

> "After but a few weeks of life in the womb, the fetus can react to and store input.... The Pains that are stored in the womb can be 'remembered,' but not in terms of the cognitive memory mechanisms we are familiar with. Fetal recall is a body memory. The body remembers, in its own way, and that stored `knowledge' is no less valid than intellectual recall."
>
> (Janov. *Imprints.* p. 27) CN3.11

minor problems can interfere with developmental tasks. A mother's pain, due to accidents, abuse, illness, or surgery, is shared with her unborn infant. Trauma may occur if the mother is distressed about being pregnant or attempts abortion, grieves over the death of a loved one, faces the loss of a job, or is distraught about marital problems.

When any physical or emotional trauma activates mother's sympathetic (survival) response of her autonomic nervous system, chemicals are released within the body which cause irritation to the cells. When these chemicals cross the placental barrier, they irritate the fetus. The fetus is protected from the damaging effects of these chemicals in three ways:

1. The fetus dissipates irritation through movement of the voluntary muscles.

2. The fetal nervous system is also immature and the fetus may experience pain and discomfort less severely.

3. The mother's physical and emotional defenses absorb the fetus's irritation.

Even with these three protective mechanisms, development can be disrupted even by emotional factors. For example, if a pregnancy is unwanted, mother will produce chemical irritants; without adequate bonding and fusion, the fetus is not protected from irritants that cross the placenta and these chemicals may affect fetal development (or may be stored as unresolved tension in the viscera). Birth will be especially traumatic if mother is emotionally unavailable for the baby.

The unresolved tension of a trauma is stored physically as a body memory. First-line traumas go into the organs, viscera, and sustaining systems; second-line trauma, stored as the child develops muscle abilities, goes into the muscular body. When children internalize their distress during times of rapid growth, they are vulnerable to a process of genetic shifting that may have severe immediate consequences or may increase their susceptibility to future stress.

Dr. Frederick B. Levenson sees cancer as one of the most common results of first-line trauma. Researchers long ago recognized the carcinogenic affects of external irritants (such as tobacco and asbestos). Levenson recognizes that internal irritants, readily produced by the body in its efforts to control functioning, may be even more threatening and more potentially damaging. Explains Levenson, "They are produced from the body's own defensive structure, and their immediate purpose, in limited dosage and duration, is to ward off irritation. But if the reaction is too strong or prolonged, they cause it." (*The Causes and Prevention of Cancer,* p. 26) CN3.12

Levenson's understanding of the development of cancer illustrates the life-long effects of developmental trauma. Disruptions in bonding are perhaps the most common and most severe first-line traumas. Newborn infants need a gentle and loving welcome immediately upon leaving the shelter of the womb. But if tangible signs of welcome are not offered (such as when the mother is drugged, the baby is born prematurely, or hospital routines interfere) the newborn will feel abandoned.

Adoption is an enormous disruption in bonding. Studies show that many adopted children were unwelcome even from the beginning, when their mothers first learned – and grieved – that they were pregnant. The anxiety about an unwanted pregnancy, coupled with the difficult decision to "give the baby up" to be adopted, often breaks all bonds between mother and child. In fact, these mothers may strive not to bond with their child so they will have less emotional pain when they say goodbye to the child they conceived and carried.

Whenever a separation occurs between an infant and the biological mother, the abandonment and loss is imprinted on the unconscious mind of the infant. The result is what psycho-therapist and adoptive mother Nancy Verrier terms a *primal wound,* which manifests as issues of "separation and loss, trust, rejection, guilt and shame, identity, intimacy, loyalty, and mastery or power and control." (Verrier. *The Primal Wound.* p. 7) These same issues are present in infants who have been separated from their biological mothers, even when they are later reunited. CN3.13

Adoptive parents can establish healthy bonds with their adopted children through years of steady, loving care. Besides providing a stable home environment that meets a child's physical needs, adoptive parents are wise to provide daily sessions of hands-on care (massage, cuddling, and other tender touching activities) that will help rebuild a child's trust from the inside out.

Self-parenting

Most adults today were born before alcohol, smoking, and stress were recognized as having an impact on fetal development, before fathers and siblings were allowed to participate in the birth experience, before soft lights and quiet sounds become the norm in delivery rooms, before newborn babies were placed at mother's breast instead of on the cold steel of a scales. Many adults experienced the trauma of a difficult and painful birth, oxygen deprivation during labor or birth, drugs during delivery, cesarean delivery, or separation from mother. Years later, these first-line traumas may have left a physiological and emotional residue that may be in the background of a variety of dysfunctions.

David Chamberlain, Arthur Janov, Alice Miller, and J. Konrad Stettbacher are among the pioneers in helping adults connect present pain with first line trauma. For many adults, returning to the birth experience through a carefully monitored

> "Birth memories deserve close attention. What we learn from them can change how we live our lives, how we approach parenthood, conception, pregnancy, and childbirth, and how we educate each other."
>
> (Chamberlain. *Babies Remember Birth.* p. xxxiv)

"rebirthing" or "birth regression" may be the only way to get at the real problem. CN3.14

We must allow ourselves and our children the freedom to start anew, and support one another in uncovering first-line trauma. Only then can we release the trauma set in place even decades ago, and "re-parent" ourselves for full and healthy functioning today.

Innertube: Simple, Yet Powerful

A very simple and POWERFUL tool for getting in touch with prenatal trauma is to spend time inside an innertube which re-creates the in-utero environment. The tube should be suspended from a single point in the ceiling joist, a door frame, inside a closet or a specially constructed tripod (see diagram). The innertube must be of a size that puts the body into a tightly curled ball similar to the womb. For example, a small child may need a 14-inch tube, whereas an adult may need a large tractor tube.

The best time to do this activity is at bedtime in total darkness. It may be necessary to start with dim light and slowly decrease to total darkness. Children must have the presence of an understanding and supportive adult until they feel safe. If a child had a difficult prenatal time, he/she may experience very strong reactions. It is vital to lovingly and firmly hold the structure and support the child through the healing. Be positive with acknowledgement that it may be scary and the only way out is through and you are right there with them. There should be no singing, music, toys, etc., in the tube; just enough talking and touching to support being still and quiet. The ideal is for the individual to go to sleep which allows the nervous system to integrate previously unintegrated experiences. Older children 8 to 10+ years of age can get themselves out of the tube and into bed whenever they awaken in two to six hours. It is essential the tube be in their bedroom. Adults may also need a helper in the beginning for reassurance and validation of the experiences and one-and-a-half to four hours is usually sufficient.

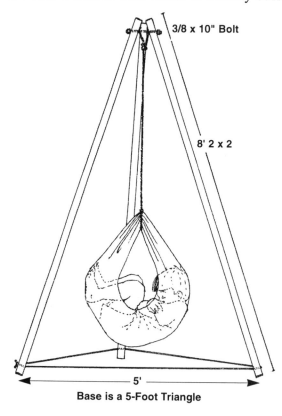

3/8 x 10" Bolt

8' 2 x 2

5'

Base is a 5-Foot Triangle

It is absolutely critical that any prenatal trauma be healed before the innertube can be used as a second POWERFUL tool in the integration of kinesthesia. Kinesthesia and how to enhance it is explained in detail in Chapter 5. The brushing and deep pressure supply essential sensory input for the movement patterns and the innertube provides the critical integration. All of these procedures are essential to re-establish the genetically encoded time line and develop a body that works efficiently, automatically and instantaneously. Be sure and refer to this section after the brushing, pressures and movement patterns ending on page 121.

THE INNATE AUTOMATIC STAGE OF DEVELOPMENT
Conception Through Three Months After Birth

CHAPTER FOUR:
The "Fourth Trimester"

Brian's first week of life is spent in his parents' arms and in his crib. He sleeps nearly around the clock; sometimes it's a deep, motionless sleep, and sometimes he is a bundle of activity even while sleeping.

Brian's four-year old sister, Mary, loves to hold her baby brother. Sometimes Brian sticks out his tongue when Mary does, and his big blue eyes follow her finger as she traces patterns in front of his face. Mary knows Brian is aware of what is happening around him: he turns his head to follow sights and sounds, and his facial expressions change and can be so funny!

Mary knows, too, that Brian is happiest when he nurses at Mommy's breast. As he relaxes against her, he rests his tiny fist on her body, as though he is giving Mommy a little hug as he nurses.

Brian can also be angry. He squeezes his tiny blue eyes tightly and clenches his fists; even his legs squeeze up as if his whole body is mad. Usually he stops crying as soon as Mommy picks him up and rocks him quietly in the wooden rocking chair.

Mary has a new doll that she takes care of just like Mommy takes care of Brian. Mary used to think tiny babies were like dolls, only noisier. But now she knows that babies are pretty smart.

Adapting to Life Outside the Womb

Newborn infants are truly amazing. Just days (sometimes even moments) after birth, they demonstrate an astounding repertoire of abilities and preferences:

- They follow movement with their eyes and may turn their heads to watch a moving object.
- They recognize visual patterns, preferring circles and stripes to plain surfaces, complex patterns over simpler patterns, curves to straight lines.
- They are especially interested in the human face.
- They move their eyes and head in response to sound.
- They prefer high-pitched voices.
- They like to be held and cuddled.
- They respond to changes in temperature, texture, moisture, and pressure – and to pain.
- They prefer sweet-tasting substances to salty, sour, or bitter flavors.
- They recognize the smell of their own mother.
- They sneeze, cough, hiccup, and gag.
- They may imitate facial expressions, sticking out their tongues, opening their mouths, pursing their lips.

Until the mid-1960s, most physicians and psychologists claimed that infants could function only at the most primitive levels, and that newborns were basically "confused" and unresponsive to their surroundings.

Researchers have now confirmed what many parents have always known: infants are astoundingly competent, responsive, and sensitive. Their many functional abilities are the natural and timely result of the developmental sequence which began at conception. In utero, the eyes, ears, skin, and other body structures were specifically formed according to a human "blueprint," and the fetus began rehearsing the functions necessary for full functioning outside the womb. CN4.1

> "The average healthy baby is born with a fairly well-established natural rhythm of functional activity, which is often only temporarily disturbed by the process of birth."
>
> (Ribble. *The Rights of Infants.* p. 71)

Even with nine months of preparation, babies face an astonishing transition at birth. The sights, sounds, and sensations of the external world require sudden, precise transformations of nearly every life-sustaining system. Baby must become instantly self-sufficient in so many ways. (This was explained more fully in Chapter Three.)

To ease this transition, and to allow the human developmental sequence to proceed smoothly, the first three months after birth should be considered *a fourth trimester* of pregnancy. The newborn is no longer protected by the womb, yet needs to have all his needs met fully and automatically as he adjusts to his new environment. The newborn baby's world should be an "external womb" that simulates the prenatal environment: a quiet place, with frequent gentle movement, instant satisfaction of physical needs, a secure position, and protection from danger. Of course, this fourth trimester world is actually quite different from the womb. But as baby finds comfort within himself, guaranteed through his mother, his matrix of comfort and security will gradually expand.

Bonding Is the Foundation for Relationships

If prenatal development has progressed as it should, if birth has been without complications, and if the birth environment is quiet and welcoming, the newborn's first hour outside the womb is a precious and sensitive time. This early hour is known as the *maternal sensitive period* (as explained in Chapter Three), when mothers and newborns have heightened awareness and sensitivity towards one another. Through subtle interactions, mother and baby establish a new reciprocal relationship of feeding, holding, gazing, hearing, caring.

For fathers, too, the first hour after birth sets the stage for a lifelong relationship with their child. Father-child bonding is immeasurably strengthened with that first "eyeball-to-eyeball" greeting as father holds his newborn child, and feels the tiny heartbeat and breath, and experiences the grasp of baby's strong fingers. Even when father talks softly, he can be sure that his baby recognizes his voice as the one that was heard through the uterine wall. Father-child bonds continue to be nurtured as father feeds and diapers baby, cares for other children, supports mother, and contributes to a happy, healthy, harmonious home.

There is, for the new mother, a curious paradox associated with the bonding process; although parent-child bonds are strengthened as the newborn is held, watched, and cared for, birth also marks a new separation in the mother-child relationship. During the last months of pregnancy, the interconnection between mother and fetus has been so tight that it is known as *fusion*, as the mother's emotional state meets her child's. Fusion is broken suddenly at birth, and the mother-child bonds are transformed through the process of ***attachment.***

Attachment defines a baby's first human relationship outside the womb. As an extension of prenatal bonding, attachment is how babies understand who they are and where they belong. Babies who feel "attached" are secure in their relationship with their primary caregiver(s), they trust that their needs will be met, and they experience the world as a positive place. Babies who are insecurely or anxiously attached will fear the larger world and their interactions may be dominated by their negative expectations.

In *Children Without a Conscience,* Ken Magid and Carole McKelvey cite research confirming that children who never experience a securely attached relationship with a primary caregiver are more likely to be fussy or hyperactive as infants and to develop a deep-seated rage that leads to severe character disturbances. Because unattachment and rage affects the autonomic nervous system and the ability to respond to stress, these children are limited – from the inside out – in every stage of development. CN4.2

This understanding of the importance of attachment can be credited to the research of Mary Salter Ainsworth and her observations of infants' responses in what she called the "Strange Situation." Ainsworth and her associates observed mothers and their babies in their homes, then in a laboratory setting where the mother was separated from the infant and a stranger brought in. Ainsworth noted that the babies responded to the "Strange Situation" in one of three distinct patterns: CN4.3

- Those who were *securely attached* cried when mother left, but greeted her happily when she returned.

- Those who were *anxious yet ambivalent* were first clingy and fearful, then became very upset and anxious when mother left. These babies greeted mother when she returned, but arched their bodies away from her and resisted comforting.

• Those who were ***anxious and avoidant*** seemed independent of mother, even when she was present. They paid little attention when mother left, and snubbed her when she returned.

Ainsworth also observed these children in their homes and recognized parallels between babies' attachment patterns and their relationships with their mothers. Securely attached babies had mothers who were responsive to their children, who returned their smiles, comforted their fears, and responded to their hunger pangs. Mothers of anxiously attached children, including those who were ambivalent and avoidant, were less consistent, less reliable, less responsive, and even rejecting towards their babies.

Ainsworth's "Strange Situation" has been replicated with thousands of children and research continues to support and extend her conclusions. Other researchers have since found that these patterns of infant attachment continue throughout life. In other words, the way mothers treat their babies establishes the patterns for how babies will relate to other people, and to new situations, decades later.

The Infant Adjusts to a New World

The first days and weeks after birth are a time of adjustment as baby learns to function in his new world. And what a different world it is! Before birth, the fetus lived and worked in a universe defined by the uterine wall. After birth, the world seems to be without bounds, full of color, movement, activity, noise.

Amidst this environmental confusion, the infant's body must now meet the demands of this new world. Hunger, breathing, digestion, and numerous other functional abilities are truly "in their infancy" at birth, yet are expected to sustain life immediately after they first become operational.

During this time of adjustment (the first months after birth), babies move between six states of consciousness, each with specific behavior patterns. The newborn has three awake states of consciousness, two sleeping states, and a transition state (drowsiness). CN4.4

Newborns sleep about 90 percent of the day and night, spending equal time in each of the two sleep states, and moving from one state to the other about every 30 minutes.

Quiet, deep sleep is baby's state of complete rest. Breathing is rhythmic and even; baby's face is relaxed, her eyelids are still. Except for an occasional startle (and very slight movements of the mouth), there is little body movement during deep sleep.

Active sleep is the newborn's equivalent of the REM sleep (rapid eye movement, or dream-filled sleep) of adults. Breathing isn't as regular as in deep sleep, and baby's eyes move beneath the closed (or open!) eyelids. The body moves, too, and baby may make funny faces as though he is dreaming – and perhaps he is!

Drowsiness is the transition state between sleep and awake, and is most common when baby is just waking up or just falling asleep.

The quiet alert state is first seen during the first hour after birth. This is when babies seem to be most attentive and curious, though not physically active.

The active alert state is especially common when babies are fussy and just before they eat. During this state, you will see little bursts of movement of baby's arms, legs, body, or face. The eyes are attentive, and baby may make tiny sounds.

The crying state is how babies communicate hunger and discomfort. The eyes may be open or closed, and the body is usually flexed. Babies often stop crying (moving into the quiet, alert state) when they are picked up.

These six states of awareness pace the newborn's adjustment and development, both physiologically and emotionally, in the first weeks after birth. Each state provides unique opportunities for parent-child bonding. Each state also plays a unique role in perfecting the newborn's life-sustaining functions, sensory systems, and early movement patterns which are the foundation for all physical development. Knowing the importance of each state, and learning to recognize when their newborn moves from one state to another, gives parents remarkable insight into their newborn baby's personality and abilities.

Respected pediatrician T. Berry Brazelton uses these six states of awareness as the keystones of his Neonatal Behavioral Assessment Scale, a tool for examining the behavior of newborn infants. As Brazelton explains, "The Neonatal Behavioral Assessment Scale is a psychological scale for the newborn human infant. It allows for an assessment of the infant's capabilities along dimensions that we think are relevant to his developing social relationships." (Brazelton. *Neonatal Behavioral Assessment Scale*. p. 2) CN4.5

Babies Need Time-in-arms

Mothers throughout human history have known that babies are happiest and healthiest when they spend most of their early weeks cradled in the security of mother's arms. Even today, infants in many cultures spend nearly 24 hours a day cradled against mother's body. But in the "modern" world, parents may need to be reminded that it's OK to hold a sleeping infant, that many chores can be done one-handed, that cuddling a baby may be more important than cleaning the house.

The benefits of time-in-arms have been documented by numerous scientific studies. More than 30 years ago, studies by Dr. Lee Salk confirmed that mothers prefer holding baby on the left side; since most mothers are right handed, this position frees the dominant hand for other work. And in this position, baby's ear rests over mother's heartbeat, the familiar rhythm of prenatal times. The importance of that rhythmic sound should not be underestimated: Salk's research showed that even recordings of the human heartbeat improved the breathing patterns of newborn infants and resulted in less crying, fewer digestive difficulties, and better weight gain. CN4.6

The rhythm of the heartbeat is just one benefit of time-in-arms. Through baby's remarkable sensory system, time-in-arms also gives messages of touch, pressure, temperature, and position, as well as providing the sights, sounds, and smells of the environment. Through mother's movement and activity, the infant begins to experience changes in total body position. This movement provides the first integration of information about body position and orientation to the force of gravity. Best of all, this stimulation is all on a background of the security of the mother-child bonds. And for fathers, siblings, adoptive parents, and grandparents, time-in-arms is the best way to establish the mutual and intuitive "knowing" with an infant.

Rocking also is an excellent and important way for parents to interact with their infants. To a baby, the rhythmic motion and in-arms security closely resembles the prenatal environment. Rocking is also a powerful tool for easing the survival role of the autonomic nervous system; many babies learn to rock themselves while standing, kneeling, or lying in bed. Adults, too, often find comfort in repetitive, rhythmic motion of a rocking chair, or measured pacing, gentle swinging, swimming, or dancing slowly.

The soft "snuggli" infant carriers make time-in-arms more convenient for modern parents. Made from soft fabric with long straps that fasten around the neck and/or waist, these versatile carriers position the infant quite close to the womb and are far better than the rigid plastic "bucket" seats or carriers that isolate babies from mother. Sling-style carriers allow infants to hear parents' heartbeat and voice, and to feel body warmth, movement, and security. Of course, infant seats should be used for safety reasons (always in automobiles) but not as a replacement for time-in-arms.

Whether baby is supported by a band of cloth, a custom-made fabric carrier, or simply by mother's arms, the body-to-body contact between mother and baby nurtures development in countless complex and subtle ways. During this fourth trimester of baby's development, time in a parent's loving arms provides the security of the womb amidst the stimulation of the outside world. Time-in-arms is baby's first experience of family, of being valued, and of belonging. Time-in-arms is the birthright of all infants. CN4.7

> "Each stage of development is a step toward the full ripening of adulthood. If the child's needs are not met at the proper time and in the proper sequence, he moves on without the resources necessary to meet the tasks of the next stage."
>
> (Bradshaw. *Homecoming.* p. 34)

Sensation and the Skin

A baby's skin is notably softer and smoother than an adult's, and plays a key role in teaching him about the world. For it is through his "baby-soft" skin that baby first receives messages of temperature, pain, texture, comfort, and distress. The skin is the body's protective covering, and is essential for regulating body temperature, metabolizing and storing fat and other substances, allowing passage of gases, forming vitamin D, and as an elimination organ. CN4.8

Developmentally, the skin grew from the ectoderm, the same layer of the embryo that formed the nervous system. The skin, then, can be considered an "external nervous system" that requires efficient functioning of its other roles. If circulation of the skin is inadequate, the cells will be poorly fed and their functional abilities will be diminished. When we're under stress, for example, the autonomic nervous system's survival response pulls blood away from the skin, allowing it to receive messages that signal a need for protection, such as pain or temperature extremes. And although skin is naturally more sensitive in some parts of the body than others, and at certain times more than others, long-term problems with sensation will affect movement, stability, and security.

Hair patterns have a surprisingly important role in skin sensitivity. The phrase "he rubs me the wrong way" originally referred to the physical discomfort of having hair patterns disturbed, such as when the hair on the arm is combed up. People who are hypersensitive may be irritated by socks that pull the hairs on the legs, or a sleeve that rubs against the hair on the arms. A baby's hair pattern (or cowlick) may be irritated by a crib sheet or blanket, yet baby has no way to tell his parents why he's so upset or to explain that a soft bonnet, tied in place, can protect his head from irritation. Washing baby's hair or gently massaging his scalp can bring comfort by activating the peacekeeping response of the autonomic nervous system. As adults, hair patterns are the reason we feel more irritable when hair is dirty or disarrayed, and why a shampoo or a head massage has such a calming effect.

By providing proper care, parents can enhance baby's sensation, parents can heighten their child's enjoyment of the environment, and communicate love through their touch.

- *Massaging baby* gently stimulates the skin as well as the muscles and is a wonderful experience for baby and parents. The effects can be varied by using baby lotion, dry hands, or a soft towel. Babies need frequent massage of their entire bodies, as well as their hands, feet, scalp, and face.

- *Bathtime* is more important for skin stimulation than for keeping baby clean. Make this a relaxing time by using warm water, dim lights, a quiet voice, soft singing. Bathing with baby (with one or both parents in the tub with baby) simulates the warm, wet, and peaceful environment of the womb. Dim the lights; keep the conversation quiet and the mood tender.

Sensation and the Mouth

Like the skin, the mouth is a sensory organ that was formed from the ectoderm (the outermost layer of the three-layer embryonic disk). In the early weeks of prenatal life, the tongue develops extraordinary tactile abilities; salivary glands and tooth buds form to equip the mouth for its role in digestion. At birth, the mouth becomes essential for eating and is the connection between inside and outside. Hunger is a new experience for the newborn; not until birth do we feel the awful gnawing of an empty stomach, our "innermost inner." When her physical hunger is appeased quickly and lovingly, her emotional hunger is also relieved and baby learns to trust her caregivers. Then she can begin to realize that she has an inside (where the hunger is) and an outside (where relief comes from). Digestion is at the forefront of her learning – *from the inside out.*

Babies discover that the tactile sensation of the tongue and mouth (assisted by the lubrication of the saliva) also make the mouth a delightful way to explore the environment. This oral exploration is especially important before baby has the motor skills and visual acuity for exploring with hands, eyes, and movement. In these early months, the mouth's ability to feel is as important as its ability to taste. When a baby puts her fist, a block, a piece of paper, or other objects in her mouth, her intent is to feel each object, not to taste or eat it. In fact, parents should be concerned if a baby doesn't put things in her mouth: the sensory-motor control of lips, tongue, cheeks, and jaw must be developed as the foundation for speech.

Prewired Circuits: The Innate Automatic

Development of baby's first motor skills begins shortly after conception when the "wiring" for some highly specialized "circuits" is first established. At birth, several of these "prewired circuits" enable the newborn to respond to the environment in some critical ways. This "wiring" becomes less specialized as baby grows.

The rooting reflex is the "prewired circuit" that makes the fetus turn towards a "tickle" at the corner of his mouth. This reflex response was practiced prenatally. At birth it has the specific purpose of telling baby in which direction to turn his head when it is time to eat. Just moments after birth, when the nipple is touched to the corner of his mouth, the newborn infant turns his head towards the breast.

A few weeks later, the rooting reflex prompts him to try turning his head from side to side when lying on his stomach. When the blanket touches one cheek, he reflexively turns his head toward the stimulus. Soon, of course, this reflex becomes integrated as baby learns to control the movement so he can rest and provides the background for head movement and neck stability.

The rooting reflex

Sucking begins when baby's lips are stroked. It, too, is a prewired circuit but often needs more assistance to become functional. Mothers may need to put the nipple inside the newborn baby's open mouth, then gently and rhythmically move baby's chin up and down.

Baby quickly realizes that sucking (and rooting) are rewarded with the satisfaction of a full tummy and the security of mother's or father's arms. Sucking also stimulates circulation of blood to baby's head and face, gives a deep rhythm to breathing, and provides the *background* for feeding, breathing, and speech.

> *"Many infants in the first weeks of life nurse quite contentedly without getting any quantity of milk. The mouth activity has relieved tension, and a beginning relationship with the mother is forming."*
> (Ribble. *The Rights of Infants.* p. 23)

The suck-swallow-breathe sequence is a rather complex "prewired circuit" that must be properly coordinated for taking nourishment. Like the other innate automatic functions, this sequence involves numerous smaller skills. The lips must be able to purse and seal the corners of the mouth, or milk will run out. The tongue must have appropriate sensitivity (a hypersensitive tongue will spit out the milk) and sufficient muscle tone (an underactive tongue is unable to pump the milk for swallowing). The jaw must not lock shut, nor can it be so weak that it hangs open during feeding. Breathing must be even, deep, and coordinated to occur after swallowing, so baby doesn't choke.*

---

*Sucking problems are an early warning that something isn't right structurally or functionally, and immediate intervention is necessary. See a developmental specialist (occupational therapist, physical therapist, or speech therapist) who works with oral development of infants.

With *the positive supporting reflex,* newborn infants are able to support their body weight when placed on their feet. Actually, a "prewired circuit" tells the legs to straighten (extend) whenever pressure is applied to the ball of the foot. Although the muscles and joints of baby's leg are not responding to voluntary control, he will continue to "stand" as long as his feet feel pressure. This reflex is in the background for standing.

The positive supporting reflex

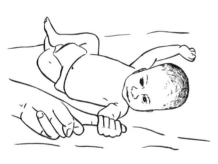

The grasp reflex

An infant's grasp is a strong "prewired circuit" at birth: whenever the palm of baby's hand is even lightly touched, she will respond with a tight grasp that is strong enough to support her body. *The grasp reflex* provides the *background* for hand function, dexterity, manipulation, and sensory exploration.

Because this reflex is so strong, it is a fun way to interact with tiny babies. Through the grasp reflex, baby discovers his sensation as a tool for exploring the world. But until baby learns to control this reflex, it may be a source of confusion because she will not know how to let go!

At six months of age, Carrie pulled herself up to a standing position in her crib. Her parents were delighted with their daughter's accomplishment – until Carrie suddenly started screaming. For although her legs and arms weren't really strong enough to support her body, her fingers were unable to loosen their grip on the bed. Her troubles were over when her father reached down to uncurl Carrie's tiny fingers and lift her out of her predicament and into the security of daddy's arms.

The fencing reflex positions baby's body comfortably for breastfeeding: with one arm flexed and one arm extended, the head is turned toward the straight arm. Legs may or may not be positioned similarly.

This is also known as *the asymmetric tonic neck reflex,* and begins to show how the position of the head and neck can dominate the rest of the body. These movements are important for establishing the body's midline as an innate "reference point." With time and practice, baby learns to control the "fencing reflex" and use it as a basis for many other movements. But the pattern never disappears: as adults, this pattern is what makes us reflexively turn the steering wheel to follow our eyes or swing a tennis racquet as our head turns.

The fencing or
asymmetric tonic neck reflex

The "fencing position" keeps baby from rolling off the couch and enables her to rest comfortably against mother while breastfeeding. The fencing reflex provides the background for left-right preference and dominance and eye-hand coordination.

Response to fear is also "prewired" at birth. Only two basic fears are present at birth; all other fears are actually learned. A newborn infant is equipped for predictable, whole body responses to *loss of support and loud noise.* Both fears set off the "survival system" as a protective response.

Loss of support means falling – or even the fear of falling. The response is *the Moro reflex:* the body goes into complete extension (arms stretched out, head back, back arched), then draws back into the fetal position of complete flexion.

The Moro reflex

The startle reflex is a response to a loud noise and begins as the infant becomes more sensitive to sound (about two weeks after birth). The body curls into the fetal position as if returning to the security of the womb while protecting the body's most vulnerable organs.

At birth, an infant will react predictably to loss of support, and soon responds also to loud noises. Within just a few weeks, she learns to screen out some of these disruptions. She may sleep through noises that once awakened her and will be comforted by mother's voice even before she reflexively jolts in response.

The reflex responses to loud noises and fear of falling remain powerful throughout our lives. As adults, a sudden loud noise makes us cringe inward, while we'll reach outward in the Moro reflex ("to catch ourselves") when we fall. These fears will send us instantly into a survival response that is best broken with peacekeeping strategies: breathing deeply, counting slowly, or taking time to relax.

Innate automatic reflex responses develop sequentially. As humans grow from infancy to adulthood, we become capable of increasingly complex and skilled movements. It takes years of physical development and practice before we can type, kick a ball, whistle, or wink. The newborn baby's random movements of her arms and legs, and her innate automatic reflexes, are the beginning of a developmental progression that prepares her for a limitless variety of motor skills.*

The rooting reflex, for example, is first an automatic response: the newborn has little control of this action, but soon realizes that she receives a "reward" of milk if she turns her head when her cheek is touched. She learns to move her head in either direction at will, and to use her tongue efficiently as she nurses. As a result, her tongue and neck become stronger and more useful for eating and making sounds. But if there is no milk (due to an inverted nipple, for example) and her rooting reflex is repeatedly ignored, she will have no incentive to practice this necessary movement.

There are many ways parents can help their infant develop motor skills without expensive toys, elaborate activities, or dazzling surroundings. Human interaction is the best way to stimulate a child's development: loving daily care – not "age appropriate curriculum" – is what is most important. In fact, the latest research indicates mobiles have little effect on a child's mental development,

---

*As with prenatal development, growth proceeds cephalocaudally (head to toe, or from the upper part of the head to the lower parts of the body). Infants have control of their neck before their arms, their hands before their toes.

music doesn't enhance hearing, and exercise classes for infants may actually interfere with a child's individualized timeline for development. Even newborn babies love simple "games." Playing touch-my-nose, grasp-release, find the nipple, and other interactive activities encourage babies to discover their bodies and explore their relationships with the world.

Parents should be concerned if a reflex is absent or doesn't become integrated with other movements and functions. Trauma or stress may mask or delay development of a reflex. Relieving the stress and breaking dominance of the survival response through peacekeeping strategies, including a quiet environment, time-in-arms, and gentle massage, may allow the reflex to emerge. If the problem persists, there has likely been some interruption to sensory-motor development and parents should seek the help of a physical therapist, occupational therapist, or speech therapist specializing in developmental intervention. Remember that a difficulty with any prewired circuit will be in the background of future developmental problems.

Babies on the Floor

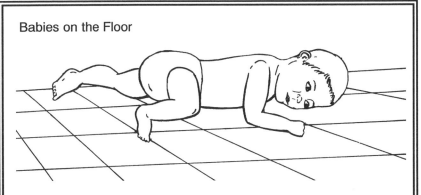

Until just a few years ago, every human generation spent its infancy in two positions: nestled against mother's body, and on the firm ground or floor. In mother's arms, babies experience sensation and security; on the ground, they learn to use their bodies freely, easily, and naturally.

A clean floor or other flat, uncushioned surface is the ideal place for babies to practice flexing and extending, rotating in and out, lifting and turning. On the floor, children are unrestricted by gravity, cushions, carpeting, or barriers. The floor gives babies a two-dimensional opportunity to learn the movements they soon will be performing against gravity in the third dimension of space.

Time on a smooth surface is especially important for the development process that leads to walking. In Chapters Five and Seven we will examine this process in detail.

Breastfeeding is the Ideal Meal

Imagine a single food that provides all nutrients necessary for health and growth. Imagine mealtime that is convenient, comfortable, and shared with your dearest friend. For the infant, breastfeeding is both: human milk is the perfect food, eating at the breast the ideal meal. Not even a master chemist could create mother's milk. In fact, no two mothers produce identical milk and each mother's milk changes from day to day, even from one feeding to the next. CN4.9

The unparalleled qualities of breast milk include:

• The protein in breast milk is easy to digest.
• Breast milk is rich in vitamins: compared with cow's milk, it has twice the amount of some vitamins, up to ten times as much of other vitamins.
• Breast milk is high in lactose (an easily digested sugar) which provides quick energy, improves digestion, and gives the milk a deliciously sweet flavor.
• Breast milk is ready-to-serve and needs no mixing, measuring, sterilization, or heating. And the cost is minimal!
• Breast milk contains antibodies which protect against diarrhea, allergies, and infection.

Besides its physiological benefits, breastfeeding is probably the most powerful means for enhancing mother-infant bonding. At each feeding, the mother-child interaction involves four factors which have been specifically noted for their importance in bonding: CN4.10

• Holding the infant's body against mother's.
• Prolonged and steady eye contact.
• Smiling.
• Soothing sounds.

Immediately after birth, breastfeeding is especially important in helping mother and baby recover from the strains of labor and delivery. Baby's sucking stimulates the muscle fibers of mother's uterus to contract and prompts constriction of uterine blood vessels, reduction of the uterine size, and release of the placenta.

Newborn babies don't need food for three or four days, yet they still "hunger" to suck at the breast. The "early milk" they receive isn't milk at all, but colostrum, a remarkable protein-rich fluid which contains antibodies for fighting infection and preparing the digestive tract for functioning. Colostrum also reduces diarrhea, jaundice, and allergies.

As babies grow, breastfeeding plays an important role in reinforcing motor skills:

- At the breast, baby practices the innate automatic reflexes of rooting, sucking, sequential sucking-swallowing-breathing, grasp, and the fencing position (asymmetric tonic neck).
- Sucking exercises the lips, tongue, and jaw, and enhances development of lips, teeth, jaw for speech.
- Holding baby against mother's body eases baby's stress. This secure and comfortable position is the "trademark" of the peacekeeping system.
- All five senses are involved in breastfeeding (vision, hearing, touch, smell, taste).
- Because baby feeds at both breasts, body position and patterns develop bilaterally (on both sides of the body).

Although breastfeeding is an important and precious time for parents and babies, it is not a guarantee of health or security. What babies need most is a healthy diet, a secure world, and loving relationships. The breast may be the best opportunity for babies to receive these things but it certainly isn't the only opportunity.

Bottle-feeding at Its Best

For mothers unable to breastfeed, bottle-feeding should be done carefully to offer as many of the advantages of breastfeeding as possible:

- Feed baby whenever he is hungry, and allow him to eat as much (or as little) as he wants. Don't worry about how often is too often, how much is too much; babies know how much they need to be satisfied.
- Hold baby as if you were breastfeeding. It's the natural position for infant feeding and is important for sensation, neck stability, visual development, and other growth.
- Hand-hold the bottle so you can respond to baby's movements as she eats.
- Hold baby on alternate sides while feeding her, just as if she were nursing at your breast. This is necessary for balanced development of both sides of the body.
- Don't increase the hole in the nipple, even if baby doesn't seem to be sucking properly (or if you fear baby isn't getting enough milk). Babies need to work at sucking for normal development of lips, jaws, and teeth. Stressed babies may have difficulty sucking; massaging baby's face may stabilize sensation and activate the sucking reflex. Sucking also will be enhanced by minimizing environmental distractions, and by cuddling baby in your arms, rocking, and offering other expressions of care and security.

The Infant's Continuum for Stress

There's no such thing as a stress-free world, even for a newborn baby. Consider the traumas of traveling the birth canal, the shock of air on baby's wet skin, the first hunger, the fears of abandonment after being sheltered in the womb, the fear of falling, and later the startle at a loud noise.

Like humans of all ages, newborn babies automatically respond to stress and excitement with a survival response of their autonomic nervous system (the ANS; see Chapter Two). Yet the ANS must be in its peacekeeping mode for the body to work efficiently and effectively. When the survival response is dominating, there is a disruption to digestion, circulation, respiration, and other basic body functions. With continual or repeated stress, these disruptions become cyclical and one problem leads to another.

Babies also "share" any stress their mother is experiencing. Not only will anxiety affect mother's ability to care for baby, but stress can also cause hormonal changes that may be transmitted to the baby through the breast milk and may diminish her milk supply.

Babies are individuals, and each responds to stressors in a unique way. Some babies experience stress through their skin, others through their digestive system (See colic later in this chapter.) Still others may develop disorders of their most basic functional systems (breathing, circulation, immune responses, etc.).

Personality also affects how babies respond to stress. One baby might ignore a noise (or a flavor, smell, sight, or sensation) that sends another into a screaming frenzy. And, as any parent knows, once a child's ANS is provoked into a survival response, he will be much more easily distressed by stressors that otherwise seem irrelevant. That's how the stress cycle builds and why minor problems can become serious dysfunctions.

By watching for certain warning signs, parents can be alerted when stress is taking its toll on an infant's health. Disruption of baby's sleep cycle, the inability to suck, or frequent choking or gagging when feeding are among the most common signs of excessive stress. Stress may also interfere with the body's sustaining systems: breathing, digestion, and the skin.

Even with the most loving and attentive care, babies will occasionally be uncomfortable, frustrated, unhappy – and stressed. The effects of stress are minimized when babies are provided with a peaceful and secure environment, loving care, a regular schedule, and have their physical needs (food, warmth, baths, dry diapers, etc.) met. Parents can use some baby-sized stress-busting techniques to move infants from the stress-filled survival mode into the peacekeeping state:

- Baby's autonomic nervous system will respond to the warmth of parents' embrace and quiet voice. Soft music and dim lights also help set a peaceful mood.

- Baby's muscle tone becomes more relaxed with the rhythmic movement of a rocking chair, or when riding in the car (although the necessary security of an infant car seat doesn't allow parents to cuddle a distressed baby while traveling).

- Baby and parents can play quietly together in a warm bath, or cuddle together in the parents' bed. Sometimes the most peaceful activity is a quiet walk outdoors with baby snuggled close against mommy or daddy's chest.

Parenting a Premature Infant

The first months after birth may be surprisingly traumatic for parents of infants born prematurely. Underdeveloped physically, some premature infants seem less attractive than those born after a full nine months gestation; they are small and without the body fat that is gained at the end of pregnancy. Premature infants are also likely to seem more passive – not because they aren't interested in life, but because they aren't ready to function fully. Parents may find it hard to bond with a premature infant; they may feel disappointment or guilt about the "imperfect birth," or simply feel unprepared for the arrival of their new family member. Premature babies and their mothers haven't fully experienced the emotional fusion that is essential in the bonding process.

It's a stressful time for the premature baby also. A birth that may have been traumatic is often followed by isolation in a neonatal intensive care unit (even during the early postnatal hours) where babies don't receive the vital time-in-arms during the sensitive period immediately after birth. Born before they finished the normal tasks of prenatal development, premature babies often have difficulty with breathing, digestion, and other sustaining system functions; each meal, each breath may be stressful.

The fourth trimester environment is especially important for premature babies and their parents for it must allow continuation of the development that was interrupted by the early birth. The post-natal environment should closely resemble the womb, a quiet, warm, dark place, where physical and emotional needs are met promptly.

Babies born prematurely often develop more slowly than those born after a full nine-month gestation. Yet if we compare their development to their gestational age (beginning at conception), however, premature babies usually follow the "normal schedule" for growth and development.

> *Emily was born three months early. From the beginning, she was small and underdeveloped. She may never "catch up" with her peers. But when her parents compare her growth and accomplishments according to children three months younger than Emily (i.e. those conceived at the same time Emily was conceived), they can see that their daughter is developing quite normally.*

Although premature infants may be slow to develop, they should acquire all normal functional abilities according to the basic timeline for human development. If parents perceive there is a developmental delay or dysfunction, they should consult with a pediatrician and/or developmental specialist.

Colic Means Distress

With knots of tension and distress in their stomachs, colicky babies can only cry. The tension builds, crying makes babies feel worse, so they cry more. Parents of colicky babies often feel helpless and inadequate; nothing seems to comfort baby enough to end the tears. And so parents lose sleep, lose their temper, lose their confidence.

Physicians continue to debate the causes of colic. Certainly such digestive distress is both cause and symptom of a variety of physical and emotional discomforts. Digestion is the first neuromuscular system to be coordinated and is often the "front line" for pain. The pain may be due to diet (cow's milk for bottlefed babies; caffeine, vitamins, or other factors in the diet of a nursing mother) or may be an expression of baby's anxiety.

Colic tends to disappear by the third to sixth month as baby's digestive system matures. But the effects of colic may be long-lasting; babies with colic are more susceptible to allergies, earaches, asthma, and other problems with basic functioning. The stress of colic may begin a progression of developmental disruptions that leads to chronic earaches, audio-perceptual problems, social problems.

Because colic can have such far-reaching effects, parents should do all they can to break the cycle of disruptions and provide comfort and development.

- Reduce baby's stress and discomfort. Maintain a regular schedule, a quiet home environment, a comforting lifestyle. Read again the "baby-sized stress-busting techniques."

- Hold baby often, even if he continues crying. Your loving embrace and physical contact, and even the familiar rhythm of your heartbeat, may comfort your baby more than you realize.

- Make sure baby's diet is easy to digest. Breast milk is most likely to agree with baby's digestive tract. Nursing mothers may find that their babies are sensitive to certain flavors, chemicals, and foods. Some babies may have an allergy to cow's milk, even when it is received only through mother's breast milk.

- Take care of yourself. Parental stress is readily transmitted to baby. If possible, mother and father should take turns caring for the crying infant so each can sleep, eat peacefully, and take time to relax.

- Encourage baby to suck. As an innate automatic skill, sucking may relieve physical and emotional stress. Colicky babies can suck on a rubber nipple pacifier or a parent's clean finger.

- Offer frequent, small feedings. Some colicky babies take in more milk than they can readily digest, which then leads to more digestive pain. Smaller feedings give baby's digestive system a more manageable amount of food and more time to cuddle with Mom. Breastfeeding mothers should offer just one breast at a feeding if baby is colicky.

- Review baby's development: Is some prenatal trauma or birth trauma "in the background" of the colic? How might such stress be relieved?

- Consider the long-term implications of colic. If baby's sleep habits have been disrupted by colic, parents may need to give baby extra attention at bedtime even after colic has subsided. If once-colicky babies develop allergies, earaches, asthma, or other problems with basic functioning, the stress in the background of these problems must be addressed. These children may have internalized the stress of their first weeks of life. Parents can break the disruptive survival system patterns by providing a peacekeeping environment and hands-on care.

Infants in Today's World

In the first months after birth, it is critical that infants learn from the inside out that they are safe in this world, even as they grow in competence and independence. Too often, however, the agenda of today's world interferes with what infants most need. CN4.11

- *Infants need to stay home, where they are secure in familiar surroundings.* Considering how abruptly their world changed at birth, it makes perfect sense that babies need time to adapt their awareness to their new surroundings. Yet many parents today are eager to resume their daily routine, or "show off" their babies, and they fail to consider the "sensory overload" their newborn faces in any new setting. Bright lights, loud noises, new faces, strange smells, unexpected movements, and other realities of the world can be extremely stressful for an infant. At best, such experiences only distract him from the secure and peaceful state of mind that is so important in establishing trust.

- *Infants' eyes should not be expected to respond to bright lights or visual stimulation.* Although their pupils constrict and dilate appropriately, babies prefer dimly lighted rooms, where their eyes are sheltered. As they grow, vision will become a primary stimulus for curiosity, coordination of body position and movements, and learning. Yet for now, infants have other needs, which early visual stimulation interrupts.

- *Infants should interact with people, not things.* Mobiles, toys, books, and other objects should only be used to enhance relationships, not to replace person-to-person contact or time-in-arms.

- *Infants should be sheltered from television.* Although some infants may seem to "enjoy" the sights and sounds of television, it distracts their attention away from their own internal awareness and fosters discontent with the quiet, peaceful setting that is so necessary for growing.

- *Infants need human milk.* Breastfeeding clearly provides babies the best possible diet and interaction with mother. Mothers should feel no embarrassment or discomfort about nursing their babies. Instead, they should be given encouragement, information, and guidance for proper breastfeeding. Of course, breastfeeding mothers must eat a nutritious diet that will provide optimal nourishment for their babies and themselves.

- *Mothers need to take time to be mothers.* Three months of maternity leave is simply not enough time for mothers and babies to fully adjust to their new relationships. Too many babies spend most of the day in "institutional day care" because their mothers feel trapped by financial pressures, societal expectations, and inadequate day care options.

When a mother must return to work when baby is small, it is especially important that she continue to meet her baby's needs for physical and emotional security. Some working mothers may be able to ease back to the job by working part-time. Some mothers employ a family member, nanny, or other at-home care provider to minimize the disruption to baby's schedule and environment. A few find childcare close enough to the workplace that they can drop in during the day to breastfeed, play, and interact with their children in other ways.

For working parents today, the options are less than ideal. We look forward to a time when our society affirms the importance of children by providing:

- Realistic maternity leave policies.

- Greater support for mothers and fathers who choose to stay home with their children.

- More support for parents who share parenting responsibilities, even when it means working less than full time.

- Fewer newborn infants in shopping malls, social gatherings, and other hectic surroundings.

""The reason we have failed our children is not because we cannot afford to look after them, but because they have been at the bottom of our list of priorities."
(Hewlett. *When the Bough Breaks.* p. 263)

Self-parenting

As she drove across town on a cold January morning, Leslie was mentally reviewing her infant son's latest achievements. Now three months old, Brian was becoming so much more responsive and playful than he had been just weeks before. Even four-year-old Mary had noticed how much her brother was growing. But for Leslie, the demands of a second child were greater than she had imagined. Most days seemed a blur of activity – with a constant whirl of jobs still unfinished.

Lost in thought, Leslie was startled back to reality as the car lurched to a stop when she drove into the ditch. She turned off the ignition and sat for a moment, her hands shaking and her heart pounding, before climbing wearily out to assess the damage.

A week later, Leslie's neck and shoulders remained sore from the accident, but her mind still couldn't recall what had happened. She remembered passing an historic barn about two miles before the accident occurred, but could remember nothing after that until she landed in the ditch minutes later.

Although she hadn't been severely injured, her sore muscles slowed her activity considerably. Laundry didn't get folded as quickly as usual and other jobs simply went undone. She discovered that she was most comfortable sitting in the well-cushioned rocking chair, and so spent more time than usual rocking Brian in her lap.

As she rocked, her mind wandered back to the days before the accident when Brian hadn't been sleeping well, Mary had had a sore throat, and Leslie's husband, Jim, had been out of town. Leslie was sure that stress was partly responsible for the accident by interfering with her concentration, perceptions, and reaction time.

Hoping to hasten her recuperation, Leslie made an appointment for a massage. Her skin and muscles seemed to come alive under the touch of the masseuse, and Leslie felt relaxed, and yet more energized, than she had felt for months. Towards the end of the session, as the masseuse worked on her shoulders, Leslie felt her arm twitch in a strangely familiar way. Suddenly she remembered seeing a bird dart out of a tree stump across the road and then, in her mind, saw her own car heading towards an all-too familiar ditch.

Just that quickly, Leslie remembered the accident. Surprised by the bird's sudden movement, her eyes had impulsively followed his flight across the road as her hand instinctively pulled the steering wheel in the same direction. When the masseuse finished her work, Leslie turned her head to the right, flexed her right arm down by her side, and felt her left arm swing up. It was a reflex movement she had seen Brian do thousands of times, the fencing reflex, an innate automatic movement Leslie had been doing since she had been an infant some 30 years ago.

As she rocked Brian later that evening, Leslie was filled with a new appreciation for his many abilities. She felt a sense of awe for the miraculous sequence of human development directing her son's ever-growing capabilities and interconnecting his generation with past and future generations.

THE MOTOR PERCEPTUAL STAGE OF DEVELOPMENT
3 - 24 Months

CHAPTER FIVE:
The "AHA!" of Kinesthesia

At nine months of age, Angela sits on the kitchen floor surrounded by her toys: plastic containers, a blanket, and a doll. The uncarpeted floor is her favorite place to play, and the wide open space is a firm foundation for all kinds of movements.

Suzanne and Bill, Angela's parents, now talk proudly about their daughter's great personality. She's good-tempered, curious, independent, and smart. And she's growing so fast! Just last week, she learned to stand up all by herself from a squat position without holding on to anything; now she goes from squat to stand, up and down, again and again. Her sense of balance is far from perfect and she frequently falls over.

Daddy Bill is her best friend. Their favorite games are peek-a-boo and airplane, and they read books together every evening before bed. Daddy also takes turns giving Angela her bath, dressing and diapering her, and watching her play.

Angela is still nursing at Suzanne's breast, so spends time every day in Mommy's arms. It's there that she feels most secure, and it is to Mommy that she's most likely to turn when she is tired or afraid.

Movement in the First Two Years

At three months of age, Angela could lift her head but not roll over; she knew her mother's voice but not her own name. At nine months, her world is horizontal; her perspective of the world will change to a vertical orientation as she learns to sit, stand, and walk. By her second birthday, she will be walking and talking. Becoming upright and mobile will place new demands on her digestion, circulation, and other functional systems.

Major steps in development are achieved through a progression of smaller steps, with each new skill building upon what has already been learned. By the time an infant is three months old (at the end of the "fourth trimester"), she has developed some control of her innate automatic reflexes, and is beginning to learn about her body, to move and control its different parts, and to explore her world.

The key to coordinated movement is *kinesthesia:* our internal awareness of tactile (sense of touch), proprioceptive (from within), and vestibular (gravitational) sensation. This chapter explains these terms, and examines how kinesthesia develops and relates to vision, hearing, and other sensory systems.

As Angela gains voluntary control of her movements, she begins the *motor-perceptual* stage of development, defined by movement specialists/educators Clara Chaney and Newell Kephart as development between the third month and second birthday. Through this process, babies "sort out" (differentiate) their arms and legs, shoulders and elbows and wrists, thumbs and fingers. Differentiation proceeds from head to toe, from midline to the ends of the extremities: baby first discovers that the head is separate from the trunk; arms are "discovered" before legs; shoulders before wrists, knees before toes. CN5.1

"In normal development a child differentiates his movements in sequence and integrates each with the next in an orderly way, thus developing organization in development."
(Chaney and Miles. *Remediating Learning Problems.* p. 28)

Baby's first and most basic movements are building blocks for the child's body image, her sense of who she is and where she is. Body image is the starting point for every human function and movement and the point of origin for spatial relationships. This internal understanding of body image is critical for walking, talking, seeing, eating, writing, and all other activities. Taking a step, for example, requires a quick determination of how far to move the foot, and judging how slippery, rough, or steep is the ground. In eating, we collect cues that tell us how wide to open our mouths, where to direct our forks and whether to prepare for sweet or salty, hot or cold, liquids or solids.

A newborn infant, of course, doesn't pay much attention to the sensations she is receiving. But as innate automatic functions are perfected (and her physical needs are met), she begins to notice external sensations such as texture, temperature, pain, and pressure. In time, she will organize these sensory cues into patterns that allow her to identify mother, anticipate mealtime, and to begin to communicate her needs. This sensory information will be integrated with her first body movements and become the foundation for the first voluntary movement patterns. But first, baby must have the freedom to gradually become aware of internal sensations so she can establish her body image and enhance her internal awareness.

Movement Patterns and Motor Planning

It's common knowledge that the head of a newborn baby must be carefully held as the neck simply isn't strong enough to support the weight of the head. Within just a few weeks, the neck will grow stronger, so baby can move her head towards the nipple. As neck stability increases, she will have more control of the head and will learn to hold it herself. This simple skill indicates she has reached the stage of stability necessary for sorting out the neck from the body (the first stage of differentiation). Stability of the neck is essential for eye movement and vision, and so baby becomes more responsive as she nurses at mother's breast.

Babies develop these skills best when lying on their tummies. (The muscle skills necessary for lifting the head while lying on the back are not developed for several months.) The horizontal position is fundamental for proper circulation of blood, digestion of food, visual orientation, and orientation to gravity, as well as for the internal orientation of muscles. When baby first voluntarily picks up her head, it is because she has mastered a cluster of smaller movements which she now can use in combination to form patterns of movement. In turn, these first movement patterns become building blocks for more complex and coordinated movement patterns. Her growing repertoire of movement patterns will equip her for spontaneous, coordinated movement; when she perceives a need, she will be able to automatically respond with controlled and sequenced movement. As she moves, she will continue to receive feedback about her actions and adjust movement accordingly.

The specific word for movement patterns is *schema* (not to be confused with body scheme or body image). The technical term for the sensory-motor-sensory process is *praxia,* or motor planning. If sensation is inadequate or abnormal, the motor response and sensory feedback will also be poor; movement is likely to seem awkward and uncoordinated. This is known as *dyspraxia:* impaired ability to plan movements.

Dyspraxia is when Jenny is unable to estimate how far she must reach to grasp the spoon on the table: her hand will move jerkily towards the spoon before grasping it. She will have lots of spills and will learn to move quickly so others won't notice her clumsy movements.

Dyspraxia means that Peter must concentrate on each movement of the spoon just to eat. ("Touch spoon with fingers. Curl fingers around handle. Lift spoon to mouth; watch bowl of spoon to keep it level. Open mouth...") When his mind wanders even to think about the taste of the food he is eating, he is likely to drop the food or the spoon.

Dyspraxia occurs when:

- Sensation is impaired (the brain receives poor information about the task to be done and/or the task as it is carried out).

- Motor skills aren't developed adequately (muscles, joints, and tendons haven't perfected the schema).

- There's too much stress (the mind is over-loaded, attempting to run the body, so can't tend to the task at hand).*

Kids get frustrated when they can't move their bodies smoothly and spontaneously. Their heads know how they want to move, but their bodies just aren't cooperating! They may withdraw ("I can't do this, so I'll just hide"), lash out in anger ("It makes me furious that you think I can do this!"), or distract

---

*Inadequacies in this developmental process are especially critical at age eight, when children are at the threshold of cognitive development. Eight-year-olds who aren't comfortable with their body image or are unable to move smoothly and spontaneously may have trouble with academics and behavior and their autonomic nervous system may initiate a survival response that brings physical and emotional distress.

attention from their inabilities ("If I keep talking – reading – watching television – you won't notice my clumsiness").

The seeds of dyspraxia are sown in these first months after birth, as babies are developing their body image, schema (movement patterns), and praxia (motor planning). Babies need time and space for learning from the inside out.

- Babies need to lie on their tummies so they will learn to pick up their heads.

- They need time on a clean, slick floor (without carpeting) so they can practice moving their arms, legs, and bodies. Movements are easiest on a surface that is smooth, firm, and slightly slick, such as in a wet bathtub or on the kitchen floor (especially when baby is dressed in a one-piece "crawler"). This reduces the restraint of gravity and enables freer movement of the head, arms, legs, and trunk.

- They need freedom from sensory distractions so they can tend to their work. Too many dangling mobiles, crowded rooms, cooing strangers, or other amusements will assault baby's senses and interfere with developmental tasks.

- They need time in arms to reinforce parent-child bonds, security, and affirmation, and to provide the very best sensory stimulation possible.

"Behavior develops out of muscular activity, and so-called higher forms of behavior are dependent upon lower forms of behavior, thus making even these higher activities dependent upon the basic structure of the muscular activity upon which they are built."
(Kephart. *The Slow Learner in the Classroom.* p. 79)

Kinesthesia and Kinesthetic Figure-ground

Like any newborn baby, Angela developed her first movement patterns by repeating the innate automatic reflexes (such as sucking) which brought her nourishment, comfort, security. Knowing those needs would be met, she began to pay attention to sensations of her body: the feel of the blanket on her arm (tactile), a bend in her elbow towards mother's breast (proprioception), the position of her head when she lifted it away from the crib (vestibular). In time, she began matching these sensations and establishing a profound awareness of her body movements.

Moving her arm across mother's skin, Angela became aware of the familiar smoothness of skin-on-skin as she recognized the way her arm felt as it moved. Touch matched movement, movement matched body position, body position matched touch; all three levels of sensation are matched at the same instant.

This simultaneous matching is the "AHA!" of kinesthesia: the discovery that gives us control of our movements. Kinesthesia allows us to initiate, maintain, change, or stop movements instantaneously, spontaneously, and automatically.

Kinesthesia has been called the "sixth sense," putting it right beside taste, touch, smell, sight, and hearing as a means of perceiving our surroundings. But unlike those five senses, kinesthesia is primarily about our *internal* awareness. Kinesthesia requires matching sensations of movement/stability, body position, and touch (or more specifically proprioception, the vestibular system, and tactile sensation). Kinesthesia is not a single sensation (like vision), but a complex combined message arriving through numerous internal sensory channels.

Proprioception provides an inner sense of muscles, tendons, joints, and pressure. Proprioception gives constant knowledge of the movement and position of our bodies as a whole, and of individual parts (arms, legs, fingers, toes...).

The vestibular system perceives the position and movement of the head in relation to gravity. The vestibular system is especially important for keeping us in a vertical position, maintaining posture and balance. (Remember "vestibular: vertical orientation to gravity.")

Tactile sensation is delivered through the skin. Clothing, temperature, skin health, moisture, and numerous other factors affect tactile sensation. (Remember "tactile: touch.")

Together, these sensations (proprioception, vestibular, and tactile) give messages about our body position, activity, and stability. Kinesthesia develops as we learn to make sense of these sensations; only then will we have a reliable framework for body image, movement patterns, and motor planning.

Everyone agrees that Karen is "such a good baby." Babysitters find her easy to care for; she is content to just watch television for hours. Visiting her grandparents for the holidays, she prefers sitting quietly on grandpa's lap while he reads the newspaper, just within view of the active play of her young cousins. Back at home, Karen almost always cooperates with the daily schedule without a fuss.

Yet, in some ways, Karen seems a little slow. Perhaps, her parents reason, it is because she is somewhat large for her age. Although other children her age are slightly ahead of her developmentally, Karen is never much behind and hasn't really missed a stage. Yet she never mastered crawling; instead she learned to roll or scoot on her bottom to get from place to place. At age four, Karen still loves to cuddle with her parents and isn't easily distracted like some children her age. But recently her parents have noticed that Karen still has trouble sucking through a straw, and her speech is less articulate than her classmates at the preschool. She still seems clumsy, awkward, and a little lazy. And she still seems to need a lot of assurance, especially when doing something for the first time. "But she seems pretty happy, doesn't she?" her parents ask each other.

Karen has yet to discover the "AHA!" of kinesthesia. For whatever reasons, she is not making sense of the many sensations about her body's position and movement. Perhaps, like so many of today's children, she never had the appropriate environment and encouragement to practice basic motor patterns. Perhaps she has not integrated many of her innate automatic reflexes, hasn't differentiated body parts or developed praxia (motor planning). Now, she seems unable to use her body efficiently.

Karen's two-year old cousin Jacob is constantly in motion. Since he never takes a nap, he is on the go from morning to night. He runs. He talks. He wiggles. He's small for his age, but has enough energy for three kids. And his frequent temper tantrums are violent and virtually unstoppable.

Last month, the day-care center called Jacob's mother in for a conference. Jacob's active and destructive behavior was simply too disruptive for the teachers and the other children. They were sorry, they said, but Jacob would no longer be allowed to attend their center.

It wasn't the first time. Jacob had been dismissed from another care center six months ago for similar reasons. His parents both work full time and there are no grandparents or close friends available to provide care. When he was a tiny baby, his mother, Mary, tried bringing Jacob with her when she needed to work after-hours, setting him up in his infant seat or playpen near her desk. But he was always so active and fussy that she never accomplished much. Mary had hoped Jacob would "grow out of it" and "settle down." But now she isn't so sure.

Sharing her despair with some of her co-workers, Mary learned of a nearby child development center with a reputation for "nurturing the bodies and minds of growing children." She decided to see for herself.

Mary was amazed that the application process at the center included not only the usual stack of forms, but also an hour-long personal interview with the director of the center who seemed quite interested in Jacob's entire life (favorite toys, temperament, eating habits, etc.) and the lifestyle of their family. Touring the center, Mary noticed that large areas of the floor were uncarpeted, and there were no playpens, baby walkers, or infant seats.

At the end of Jacob's first week at the center, Mary was asked for permission for Jacob to be evaluated by the developmental therapist. Mary agreed and was soon contacted about Jacob beginning a regular program of "body work."

Mary wanted to know more and made an appointment to meet with the therapist. "We are convinced Jacob's behavior problems are actually expressions of a physical need," the therapist explained to her. "His sensation is poor, so his skin is giving him all kinds of mixed messages. Being touched, even cuddled, actually irritates him. His sense of muscles and tendons (his proprioception) and balance (vestibular sensation) is poor. All together, that means Jacob can't match the essential components of kinesthesia. He is less able to know automatically where his body is and what it is doing."

The therapist correctly guessed that Jacob had been born prematurely and that his development had been slow. She outlined a program for enhancing Jacob's kinesthesia. "I'd like to work with Jacob twice each week," the therapist told Mary. "I'll also teach you and your husband some basic activities to do with Jacob. Together, we'll be reprogramming Jacob's body -- just like reprogramming a computer -- so it will work the way it should. We anticipate that Jacob will learn to use his body more efficiently, freeing up more of his mind for learning about, and relating to, his world. I think you will soon see a dramatic change in his behavior as he discovers that his body does what he wants it to do."

Like Karen, Jacob doesn't have good kinesthesia. Without kinesthesia, Karen was unable to move her body; without kinesthesia, Jacob is never still. They both lack the ability to spontaneously control body movements. Karen doesn't try to move her body; Jacob never quits trying. With good kinesthesia, they will be comfortable with their bodies, will know how to use their bodies efficiently, and will have the mental and emotional resources for exploring and enjoying the world around them.

In other words, kids with good kinesthesia don't pay much attention to their bodies, they know just what their bodies can do. Their kinesthesia gives them reliable information about their bodies and enables appropriate responses to sensory information. They have established *kinesthetic figure-ground:* an innate awareness of body movement and non-movement. Stability of the trunk (known as the holding muscle tone, or ground) is the reference point for movement of the head, arms, and legs (known as the movement muscle tone, or figure).

Only with kinesthetic figure-ground can children sit still as easily as they can move quickly and smoothly. Kinesthetic figure-ground enables the body to run itself, so kids can put all their attention on learning new skills. Once mastered, these new skills become integrated into the "background" of their kinesthetic figure-ground, adding to the ever-growing repertoire of physical abilities. Kinesthesia, then, is *in the background* of kinesthetic figure-ground – which is *in the background* of praxia (motor planning).

The critical time for developing kinesthesia is when babies are just beginning to explore their worlds (from birth to six or eight months). But development of kinesthesia will be impaired without the proper environment (slick surface, freedom to move, time to practice) and encouragement (time in arms, cuddling, breastfeeding, love). Here are some ways parents can enhance their child's kinesthetic development:

- Don't keep babies in infant carriers and strollers where they can't move freely.

- Don't put babies in jump seats, swings, walkers and other moving things that put them in an upright posture before they have the stability and movement to achieve the position on their own.

- Give babies time to play on a slick surface. On soft surfaces (cushioned play mats, carpets, mattresses, etc.), arms and legs must overcome the "give," friction, and texture which inhibit free movement.

- Don't expose babies to bright lights, mobiles, and televisions, which "turn on" the eyes and distract babies from using their bodies.

- Don't encourage babies' "intellectual development" prematurely. Developmental stages will be interrupted if babies are prompted to walk at six months or to read before they are two years old; the body won't have a chance to develop appropriately.

• Give babies time-in-arms. The loving stability of parental arms provides an unequaled foundation for physical, emotional, and spiritual development, and gives them tactile, proprioceptive, and vestibular stimulation.

Enhancing Kinesthesia

Under optimum circumstances, kinesthesia develops as an integral part of every developmental stage. But when kinesthesia is impaired, the impact also affects every aspect of development and function. Enhancing kinesthesia requires "re-programming" the internal sensory channels of tactile sensation, the vestibular system, and proprioception.

This re-programming can be done at any age, but becomes more difficult with age, as more complex habits and patterns must be changed. School-age children without kinesthesia may have learned to compensate physically, mentally, and socially. In adolescence, compensation becomes even more complex. By the time we reach adulthood, compensation mechanisms are integrated into all aspects of behavior and we have learned to accept our poor body image and dyspraxia.

Enhancing kinesthesia requires time, effort, training, and commitment, so that old patterns can be set aside and new patterns can be learned. Is it worth it? Yes! Enhancing kinesthesia (at any age) frees the body and mind to work at the fullest potential.

On the next few pages are three specific techniques for enhancing kinesthesia, developed through our professional experience as therapists working with hundreds of children, youth, and adults. CN5.2 Refer to page 75 for the innertube section.

The information is provided to show parents how to help their child, themselves, their spouses, or loved ones. These techniques should enhance the adult's relationship with the child, and should be introduced gradually in an encouraging and gentle way. Any reluctance on the part of the child usually disappears quickly as he begins to feel the benefits of the technique. If parents find themselves forcing their child's participation "because I say so," or if these techniques (used over a period of time) seem to be harming the parent/child relationship, parents may wish to seek help from a therapist. A therapist also can help if, after weeks of practice, the child seems to be making no progress. The Appendix includes information about working with therapists.

Enhancing Tactile Sensation with Dry Brushing

Kinesthesia requires reliable tactile information. Tactile sensation is distorted or inadequate when the skin is unhealthy, especially if circulation is poor. The best way to enhance tactile sensation is by gently stimulating the skin with dry brushing.

How to Use Dry-Brushing to Enhance Tactile Sensation

Dry brushing enhances kinesthesia because it improves the general health of the skin, establishes healthy channels for tactile sensation, and provides a foundation for appropriate proprioception.

All you need is a natural bristle brush (nail brush), a flat surface, a quiet place and time, and a few simple instructions.

Choose a brush that is comfortable in your hand. Natural bristles are essential. If you plan to do dry brushing on your own body, choose a brush with a removable long handle. Remember, though, that the benefits of dry brushing are enhanced by a partner; it is difficult to be both giver (loving, attentive, gentle) and receiver (relaxed and focused).

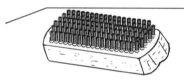

At first, dry brushing may take 20 to 30 minutes per session. With practice, the process should take only about ten minutes.

- Have your child (or partner) undress and lie face-down on the flat surface. Make sure the room is quiet so your child can relax. Television, music, and conversation will only distract him/her.

- Hold the brush firmly. Begin with the trunk, brushing in circles up and away from the midline of the body (the spine). Keep your strokes gentle. Use only enough pressure to stimulate the skin without causing an abrasion. The skin should turn a healthy pink as brushing stimulates circulation. You may see flakes of dead skin, dried lotion, and other waste products.

- After brushing the trunk (back and front), brush the arms (beginning with the hands) and legs (toes to thighs). When working with someone who has acne or super-sensitive skin on the face, begin there, so the brush is completely clean.

- As you brush, you will discover areas of skin that are extremely sensitive, even ticklish. Some areas of the body, of course, are naturally more sensitive: the stomach, inner arm, and inner leg, for example. Other areas may seem to be numb or asleep. You may be asked to "skip" certain areas. For now, do your best to brush the entire body (except genitals), even if some areas receive only the lightest stroke of the brush.

Uneven tactile sensation is a reminder of the importance of brushing. Over time, sensation should improve greatly, and the skin will respond much more evenly when it is touched. More vigorous brush strokes will then be important for increased stimulation.

- After brushing the entire body, a bath or shower may be necessary to remove any debris, and to reduce any lingering "tingling" of the skin.

The skin is the body's largest organ, an external nervous system and baby's first line of communication with the outside world (see Chapter Four.) Dry brushing cleanses the skin by removing layers of dead skin, soap, and lotion. The stimulation brings blood to the surface of the skin and enhances the blood supply to skin cells (especially the sensory receptors). Because circulation is improved, waste products are more efficiently removed from the skin.

For dry brushing, use a small, hand-held brush with natural bristles, and use it without lotion, soap, or water. Gentle, smooth circular strokes will minimize the survival response of the autonomic nervous system and diminish ticklishness, startling, or annoyance responses.

Enhancing Proprioception with Deep Pressures

Children with poor proprioception don't sense the movement, stability, and position of their muscles, tendons, and joints. They can't move their bodies efficiently and they can't hold still. Poor proprioception is the missing piece of kinesthesia for many children.

From our experience, providing specific deep pressures to key areas is the most efficient way to enhance proprioception and kinesthesia. Applying finger-tip pressure to specific points deep in the body "awakens" the proprioceptors to internal sensation and provides the link in the sensory channels necessary for kinesthesia.

Because skin sensation is so closely related to proprioception, the benefits of deep pressures will be greatly enhanced by beginning each session with dry brushing (explained on the previous pages).

Remember that it will take time to replace the missing sensory information. Expect to repeat the pressures daily for weeks, even months. First, the body may respond in any of six ways, with different parts of the body responding in various ways.

1. There may be no response, as if the body doesn't notice pressure is being applied.

2. There may be a body response: the skin reddens, muscles twitch, large muscles contract, the entire body moves.

3. There may be pain: any amount of pressure may hurt.

4. There may be acceptance: any amount of pressure feels good.

5. There may be ticklishness.

6. There may be accurate and immediate information about pressure. This is our goal: we should be able to tell if the touch is light or heavy, when touch turns to pressure, and when pressure becomes painful.

Our techniques for deep pressure use many of the principles of acupressure, reflexology, and shiatsu. Studying these related techniques may enhance your understanding of the effects of deep pressures.

How to Use Deep Pressures to Enhance Proprioception

Deep pressures improve proprioception and thus kinesthesia by establishing healthy channels for proprioceptive sensation. These techniques are also effective for easing sore muscles, relieving stress, and enhancing relaxation.

All you need are clean hands (fingernails clipped short), a quiet place and time, and a few simple instructions. Giving deep pressures involves three factors: patterns, pressure, and speed.

- Have your child lie face-down on a flat surface. Make sure the room is quiet so he can relax. Television, music, and conversation will only distract him from his body sensations.

- If desired, begin with dry brushing.

- Use your fingertip to find the bone at the top of the spine; move your finger just to one side of the bone and press firmly straight down at that point – not on the spine, but in the narrow space just beside it.

- Continue applying pressures down the groove next to the spine, as indicated on the diagram below; don't leave a space between pressure points but slightly overlap each pressure with the last. Make each pressure firm and direct; push straight down into the muscle.

- Turn the head so it is always directed to the side where you are working.

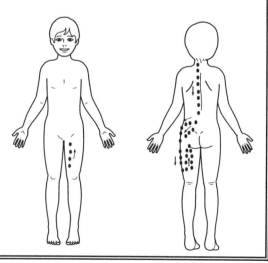

- Start with mild pressure. As you get to know your child's body, increase pressure gradually.
- Take your time. Working too quickly gives the nervous system too little time to respond. Go especially slowly in areas that are ticklish. Be patient; the body needs the messages provided through the pressures.
- Repeat, doing a total of three "trips" along each side of the spine.
- Follow the diagram to continue doing pressures on the buttocks and thighs, three trips in each area.
- Feet can be done at the same time or at a different time, following the diagram.

Always start with the top of the spine; always do three trips. Vary your "route" to maximize the impact of the sensory messages. One day, you might make one complete trip on the right side (back, buttocks, and thighs), then the left side, then repeat to make a total of three trips. The next day, do both sides of the spine, then both sides of the buttocks and both thighs.

Refer to page 75 for the use of the innertube.

Enhancing Kinesthesia with Patterns of Movement and Nonmovement

Each smooth, coordinated movement of the human body is actually a perfectly synchronized pattern of movement and non-movement: one set of muscles moves, then stops to allow other muscles to move in the opposite direction. For stability of a joint, the muscles around that joint must contract simultaneously. Movement must stop for stability to occur, and stability must stop for movement to occur.

These patterns of movement and non-movement were first learned prenatally and affect physical, emotional, and cognitive function throughout our lifetime. If our muscles don't work together for stability and for movement, we may be unable to sit still, unable to concentrate, unable to move our bodies automatically and efficiently.

Children who have been labeled "hyperactive" often find it difficult to stop moving. Their muscles haven't coordinated movement with non-movement, so their bodies have no stability, especially in the midline of the trunk. The muscles around their joints don't contract simultaneously, so they have no stability of their ankles, knees, hips, shoulders, elbows, or other joints;

something is always wiggling. These kids haven't learned *from the inside out* how to move and not move.

Ideally, the belly crawl is one of the first integrated movement patterns that babies learn. It is best learned during baby's first weeks after birth, before they are stimulated by auditory and visual activities. To learn the belly crawl, babies need the right environment: a slick surface and dim light, provided several times each day when baby is alert, but not just before or after mealtime.

Because the belly crawl is done on a flat, slick surface, it allows freedom of movement with minimal resistance from gravity. With this simple movement pattern, babies differentiate muscle groups and establish the kinesthetic matching of internal sensations. As a coordinated movement of the head, arms, and legs, the belly crawl is the beginning of orientation of the vestibular system (because of the turning of the head), and provides a fundamental awareness of proprioception. As babies grow, this movement/non-movement pattern becomes the basis for learning to sit, stand, walk, and run, and using their bodies efficiently.

Babies can't learn the belly crawl if their movements are always restricted by carpeted floors, infant carriers, baby walkers, or cushioned playpen mats. Learning basic movement/non-movement patterns may also be blocked if children are under constant stress, lack the security of bonding, or live in an environment that is inadequate and non-supportive.

Learning this simple coordinated pattern is an excellent way for persons of any age to enhance kinesthesia and to improve stability, coordination, and learning.

How to Use Patterns of Movement and Nonmovement to Enhance Kinesthesia

The belly crawl is a rhythmic pattern of movement and non-movement. It is best learned as a series of steps or "pieces," and must be done in a completely horizontal position so gravity has little effect on the pattern.

Rhythmic movement requires perfection of each "piece." Learn one piece at a time. Perfect each piece before adding it to other pieces. Learn each piece in position before using it in a movement pattern.

As an adult, you can teach yourself the proper belly crawl patterns, but only with patience and honest self-evaluation. Remember that it will take time to un-learn inefficient movement patterns. You may find that mirrors and video recorders help you monitor your progress.

All that is needed to help children practice the belly crawl is a clean floor, patience, and some basic instructions. Dress your child in soft, comfortable clothing that covers the arms, legs, and feet (such as infant sleepers, or sweatshirt and pants with socks). Dim the lights to minimize visual distraction. A quiet room will help you and your child focus on the task at hand. Keep talking to a minimum.

Have your child lie face down on a smooth surface: a vinyl floor is ideal. Turn the head so the ear, not the cheekbone, is on the surface. Arms should have the elbows bent, the palm of each hand flat on the surface at eye level.

Many children at first resist movement, have trouble relaxing, or want to "help" by consciously moving their bodies. That's why it is best for the parent or therapist to begin by moving one joint at a time.

1. Begin with the legs

These movements enable the child to experience one joint or one leg moving all alone, and to feel movement in the correct position.

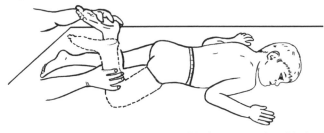

Begin by bending the right knee to a 90 degree angle with the foot in the air; hold the knee and move the thigh out to the side (abduction), then in (adduction), with the foot pointed at the ceiling. Repeat eight to ten times, making sure the child is relaxed at all times. Repeat with left leg.

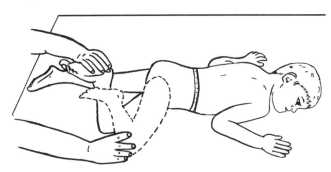

Then, with right knee bent as before, move the thigh out to the side, and lay the foot flat on the table beside the opposite thigh (external rotation). Pick the foot up and return the thigh to the midline (internal rotation). Repeat right leg eight to ten times, then practice with the left leg. It's essential that the child be totally relaxed: give her plenty of time, and don't scold or nag.

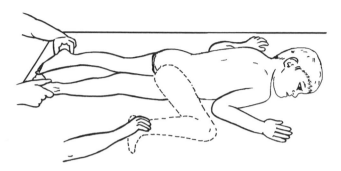

Now straighten legs so toes are touching at the midline. Roll the right leg out so toes are now pointed out (external rotation), then move leg out to the side, flat against the table (abduction) so knee goes up to touch the elbow, knee and ankle both flexed at 90 degrees, and the foot directly below the knee. Be sure the toes are not doing the movement. As the leg comes down, be sure the foot goes down only at the very last moment, to be easily rolled in: the toes must touch in the middle and everything must stop before the next movement starts. Repeat eight to ten times with the right leg, then practice with the left.

Make sure the child is relaxed by stopping her movement periodically or reversing a short section of the pattern. Coach by saying "Let go," "Don't help," "Relax." As she becomes more relaxed with these patterns, allow her to assist you. At first, make sure you are still in charge, moving the body smoothly in the correct patterns. As patterns become smooth and automatic, she can take more control and eventually do them on her own.

Usually when children begin doing patterns by themselves, it is helpful for an adult to give simple commands, such as "up" and "down." This adds another dimension, as the child must listen and move the body only on command. Children may also now begin counting the patterns, saying the numbers exactly as they begin the movement. Start with ten repetitions, then build to fifty or even 100 repetitions on each leg.

2. Practice head movements

When each leg is smooth and perfected (and the child can do about fifty repetitions on each leg), start turning the head when the toes touch. To turn the head, raise it just enough to clear the nose and/or chin. Lift the head without pushing up with the arms, moving the head towards the shoulders, or "humping" up with the bottom. Practice turning the head on command until it can be done smoothly and properly. Be sure the head is resting flat on the ear.

When head turning is perfected, incorporate it with the leg patterns, so that the head action initiates movement of the legs: the leg comes down, turns in, and the toes touch, then the head immediately turns in the opposite direction while the rest of the body is non-moving, then the other leg begins its movement pattern. Repeat this alternating leg-head-leg pattern up to 100 times.

3.   Practice the arms

Once the leg and head patterns are working well, begin moving the arms. It's best to put long stockings on the hands and arms so they slide more freely. Place the hands, palm down, on the surface; elbows

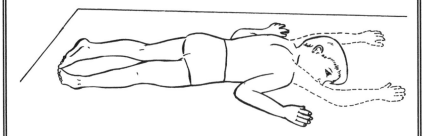

should be against the chest, the arm flat against the surface. Turn the head to the right. Gently grasp the hands and move them slowly along the surface until the arms are fully extended and the elbows are fairly close to the ears or head. Keep the palms of the hands flat against the surface, fingers still. Then guide arms back down to the starting position, elbows bent, arms and hands flat, shoulders flat against the surface. ***The eye should watch movement of the hand up and down.***

Repeat this pattern several times with the head turned to the right, then several times with the head turned to the left. You can then turn the head between each arm pattern to make an alternating pattern. Expect to spend numerous sessions just on the arms. At each session, review the leg patterns independently.

4.   Put arms and legs together

Once the leg, head, and arm movement are smooth and coordinated, begin putting them together:

As the leg rolls out and comes up, reach up with both arms, while the eye watches the hand. Bring arms and leg down; turn the head as soon as the toes touch at the midline. At that moment, begin the sequence with the other side.

Even well-practiced patterns often fall apart when something is added or changed. Perfect arm movements may become awkward when done with the legs. Stationary patterns may no longer be coordinated when they become a movement pattern. Encouragement and support, and continued practice, is essential. In time, the sequence should become increasingly smooth and coordinated. If there continues to be difficulty when pieces are put together, it's a sign that the previous step isn't yet perfected. Practice the previous step until it is completely automatic.

After each session, take time to "put the body back together." Invite your child to curl up in your arms. (Older children and adults can curl up into the flexed position and roll back and forth, then side to side. Loop the arms under the knees to keep the knees tight to the chest, and forehead down on knees.)

Vision and Visual Figure-Ground

Vision is, without question, a primary source of information about our world. But in our earliest weeks of life, our eyes give us only generalized sensory information.

Newborn babies are unaware of three-dimensional space. They are very nearsighted and see best what is seven to nine inches away from their eyes (about the distance of mother's face while baby is at the breast). They have little peripheral vision and see only what is directly in front of them. Yet they are able to recognize "basic unity": they can perceive one object, shape, or color as separate and different from other objects, shapes, or colors.

Most babies can track movement during the first day after birth and prefer to watch moving objects more than non-moving objects. During the first year of life, the eyes develop ever-increasing abilities not only to watch the world, but to direct movement:

- During the first two months, one eye may seem to be staring into space while the other eye looks at an object. At about seven or eight weeks, the eyes converge; vision is now clearer and baby begins recognizing nearness of objects and major spatial relationships.

- By four or five months, babies are watching their hands move. In the next few months, some movements are directed by the eyes: he sees the rattle, picks it up, and watches himself play with it.

- By the third birthday, children can focus briefly on tiny objects (letters on a page) but can't systematically scan a series of tiny objects until age six.

As visual skills progress, children should develop *visual figure-ground:* the immediate and spontaneous recognition of the primary object in a visual field. Looking out a window, for example, you might see a hillside, trees, a road, a car, sky, and dozens of other recognizable objects. The eyes will be immediately drawn to a moving car, and the appearance of a large bird might distract attention, while small stationary objects are likely to remain unnoticed.

Visual figure-ground provides reliable information about body position and our environment, and is confirmed by kinesthesia. It's important to remember that kinesthesia, not visual perception, is the foundation for expanding our perception of the world.

Hearing, Listening, and Auditory Figure-ground

Like vision, sound also provides important information about the world. Our ability to hear provides the foundation for speech, our primary means of communicating with the world. The ability to make sense of the sounds we hear, and to use sound to communicate, evolves gradually through a developmental sequence.

Sound provides important sensory information even before birth. Babies whose parents talked and sang to them before they were born will recognize their parents' voices at birth. The intensity of sound increases at birth; sound waves are no longer muffled by the uterine wall, and are carried by air, not water.

The newborn infant fixates on the sound of mother's heartbeat and voice, turns his head in the direction of a sound, and is startled by loud noises. Within the first few weeks after birth, he will begin to respond differently to different sounds. Heartbeats, lullabies, and familiar voices are comforting messages that remind baby of the security of his world.

As babies grow, their ability to locate a sound becomes even more accurate, as any tip-toeing parent knows! Turning their heads in the direction of a sound, babies show they are comparing the relative loudness in each ear. If the sound is equally loud in both ears, the noise must be straight ahead (at the midline). Before their first birthday, most babies are babbling -- an early form of speech -- in response to sounds. Within a few months, and with encouragement, they will respond when asked what sound a cow makes, a doggie makes, and so on.

As auditory discrimination becomes more refined, babies begin to use subtle sounds as clues about the world. Their ability to "tune in" to certain sounds requires *auditory figure-ground:* the immediate and spontaneous recognition of what sounds are primary and what sounds are in the background.

Babies won't develop auditory figure-ground if they are continually bombarded with loud noises. Babies need the opportunity to sort out the soft, soothing sounds of mother's heartbeat and voice, to hear the sounds of their own bodies, to match subtle sounds with the simple movements of feeding, moving, breathing.

The Tomatis Method of Auditory Stimulation

"The voice contains only what the ear hears."   A.A. Tomatis

Long before a child speaks his first word, he is surrounded by words and sentences, conversations and outbursts, lullabies and newscasts, and hundreds of other means of communication. These sounds of language will be his building blocks for speaking, writing, and reading. Children who are unable to hear and understand sounds properly won't have the background for developing language. Even without a physical impairment to hearing, communication will be stymied when listening is inadequate.

The auditory stimulation methods of French physician Alfred A. Tomatis are based on learning to listen. "If you make the ear work to its full potential, it acts as a charging dynamo for the cortex," Tomatis explained in a radio interview (Nov. 1986) "The more the listener knows how to listen, the more he is stimulated." CN5.3

Tomatis makes an important distinction between listening and hearing: in listening, we actively "focus" the ear so we can precisely analyze the sounds that we hear. It involves neurophysiology as well as motivation: the mechanics of the ear must be intact and functional, and the individual must have a desire to listen and communicate.

Researching prenatal development and communication, Tomatis recognized that the fetus has both the ability and motivation to listen just four months after conception. The ear is fully functional by this time and hears a symphony of sounds from within the mother's body: her heartbeat, breathing, digestion, and so on. Because these sounds are filtered through the amniotic fluid, only sounds of the highest frequency are heard. Mother's words, then, are undiscernible, but her speech rhythm and intonation come through. Tomatis believes the higher frequencies of mother's voice literally nourish the fetus: the fetus recognizes the unique sound wave patterns of her voice and is calmed and relaxed by them.

As we grow, listening can be impaired by a variety of physical and psychological factors. An unpleasant uterine environment will distort the earliest connections between sounds and relationships. Chronic ear infections affect the ability to process sounds. Birth trauma, childhood disruptions, and other psychological factors will interfere with the motivation to listen.

Children unable to listen are prime candidates for a variety of learning disabilities. If they can't hear the sounds of language, they will be unable to integrate sounds for speaking, writing, and reading. If their bodies can't respond adequately to auditory stimuli, their physical coordination may be poor, as will their body image.

The Tomatis Method of auditory stimulation has proven effective for children, adolescents, and adults. The program works simultaneously at three levels:

1. Improving the *function of the ear.*
2. Re-encountering *emotional factors* which may have interfered with the desire to listen and communicate.
3. *Counseling* to help participants integrate their new skills and anticipate the impact of proper listening and communication on their daily lives.

The Tomatis Method is offered through The Listening Centre in Toronto, Ontario (Canada); professional centers and schools around the world use Tomatis's methods. For more information on the Tomatis Method, see Appendix G.

Stress Interferes with Motor-perceptual Development

Stress is the most common obstacle to children's progress on the developmental timeline. Instead of moving towards new abilities and new learnings, kids under stress are forced to deal with painful disruptions in their lives. Stressed kids may not develop the necessary foundations for movement, kinesthesia, visual and auditory perception, and emotional stability. Over time, their bodies must learn to compensate for what isn't working properly.

Babies and young children are unable to ask for help, and parents may be oblivious to the stress in their children's lives. Yet stress breeds more stress. The impact of today's unresolved stress is sure to be evident eventually, and someday may be found "in the background" of Johnny's short temper, Joan's ulcer, or Sarah's lisp. If parents take time to see the world as their children do, they are apt to discover a myriad of factors unnecessarily complicating their children's lives and increasing the stress they face daily.

Here are some tips for easing stress during the motor-perceptual stage of development (ages 3 months-2 years).

1. *Speak softly.* The parental voice has amazing power and it can provoke a child's startle reflex as quickly as a fire whistle. When Mom is angry or excited, her voice becomes high-pitched and shrill. Dad roars and booms his words. And the kids may cower or rebel. Wise parents work to control their voice; they know that lowering the volume and tone has a calming effect on kids and adults.

2. *Play for fun.* Playtime is a necessary – and fun – way for parents to support their children's development. But playtime also can be stressful; parents often forget to see things from their child's perspective. Tickling and teasing can quickly get too rough for a child, and the resulting tears and fears can temporarily damage trust. Parents should work to maintain eye contact during play; eyes are usually the first communicator of anxiety.

3. *Swim gently.* Believing infants have an innate love of water, some parents put their babies in swimming lessons before they can crawl. Although water can be a wonderful playground for children, it is an environment far different from what they usually experience: movement is distorted, there's no firm surface to support their bodies, and their eyes, ears, and mouths fill with water. Parents need to recognize the fear infants may feel in this new situation and provide the time-in-arms (even while in the water) and other support to help their children adjust to the water.

4. *Enjoy the darkness.* For babies who are healthy and secure, a dark room can be a safe and comforting place. In the dark, they aren't distracted by the sights of their environment; awareness of their bodies becomes more important than visual cues. In the dark, they experience security within themselves as an extension of the security they receive from their parents.

5. *Hold your children.* Even toddlers need time in parental arms. As they grow, hugging and cuddling with parents continues to be essential for self-concept and security.

Self-parenting and Re-patterning

As Angela approached her first birthday, Suzanne and Bill were amazed by how much she learned each day. Individually, each new learning might seem rather inconsequential. But her daily discoveries were constantly moving Angela towards remarkable abilities.

One day, for example, Suzanne noticed Angela was pointing with her index finger. Until then, her tiny fingers had worked all together. But now she was using her finger to point, poke, even to push pieces of food across her plate.

Thinking back to her own childhood, Suzanne wondered if anyone had noticed the day she first used her index finger. Suzanne was the youngest of six children. Their mother had died shortly after Suzanne's birth and the children's father had been assisted by a loosely organized team of neighbors and relatives. Suzanne's earliest memory was eating sandwiches at a long table with numerous other children in a room she now couldn't identify.

Bill's parents had divorced just before he was born. He had been raised by his mother, an admitted super-achiever who was determined to provide a comfortable income for herself and her young son. Bill was two when his mother graduated from law school; he was six when she became a full partner in a prestigious law firm. Bill's first memory was of falling off the slide at the day care center. Watching Angela, Suzanne sometimes felt a twinge of envy, wishing she had received the love and attention that she was giving Angela. She was astonished when Bill quietly admitted he had the same wish. Within a few days they had made a pact to begin to be more intentional about their parenting, not just with their young daughter but also with one another.

After listening to a physical therapist talk about how children develop movement patterns, they began to watch Angela more carefully as she learned to move her body. They soon realized their own movement patterns and kinesthesia weren't all they could be – or should be. To enhance their kinesthesia, they agreed to begin doing deep pressures and dry brushing on each other. They started with two sessions a week, but soon realized that the twenty minutes they spent on these treatments made a significant difference all day. They agreed to get up half an hour earlier for daily "self-therapy."

In the meantime, Suzanne and Bill had been talking in more depth about their own childhoods. More memories emerged, some good and others quite painful. Suzanne remembered feeling lost and abandoned, feelings that could still overpower her today. Bill, too, remembered feeling abandoned when his mother didn't have time to help him with his math, or wasn't there to comfort him when he cried. If only he were a little smarter, a little faster, a little more confident... or needed a little less. Now that he was a parent, he pledged to "be there" for his daughter, his wife, himself.

Most adults carry the residue of an imperfect childhood. We can't change the past. But we can come to terms with imperfections, and often we can restore the "missing pieces" of our development. It is never too late to improve our ability to enhance kinesthesia, build movement patterns, establish kinesthetic figure-ground, audio figure-ground, and visual figure-ground. It's never too late to pursue our fullest potential!

THE MOTOR PERCEPTUAL STAGE OF DEVELOPMENT
3 - 24 Months of age

CHAPTER SIX:
Moving Up in the World

Just ten months old, Jerry can't quite stand by himself. He loves to creep on his hands and knees, and that's how he moves and explores. He'll soon be walking, his parents tell themselves; after all, his sister was walking when she was ten months old. Yet they know that Jerry's timeline is all his own and perfectly correct for him.

Jerry has things to do before he can walk. Right now, he is working to stand up. And what work it is! From lying on his tummy, he can easily get himself on all fours. Then he awkwardly pulls one leg up and puts a foot flat on the floor. He puts his other foot up, leans back a little, and slowly pushes his chubby body into a squatting position so his diapered bottom is just barely off the ground. He pushes himself up into perfect posture in a standing position and, for a moment, his back is ramrod-straight, his tummy in, his head held high. Then, he loses his balance and sits down with a plop.

Jerry never stays down for long but quickly pushes himself back onto his hands and knees and moves forward on all fours. He can pull himself up by holding on to the edge of a table or chair and uses the furniture for stability as he cruises around it.

It hasn't been long since Jerry first learned to roll over, then to sit up. Step by step, stage by stage, Jerry is working to perfect each stage of his developmental sequence even as he begins the next.

The Motor-Perceptual Stage: Every Step Is Important

Jerry has discovered that his body is the ideal tool for exploring his world. With his arms and legs, hands and mouth, eyes and ears, Jerry is constantly learning about, and interacting with, himself, his world, and society. As a newborn infant, Jerry's movements were controlled by reflexes (innate automatic movements); repeated use of these simple movements allowed him to "discover" his body and learn to use it for a wide variety of tasks. CN6.1

Now Jerry is mid-way through *the motor-perceptual stage,* from the third month to his second birthday, and is learning to use his body as the reference point for all movement. Kinesthesia gives him a constant internal awareness of his position and movement in relation to the world around him so his body moves with coordination and spontaneity. Without kinesthesia, Jerry would be unable to use his body efficiently.

Jerry's parents are wise to provide the best environment, and just enough encouragement, to allow their son to perfect each stage of development while continually reinforcing his growing sense of kinesthesia.

The Prone Progression Moves Us
From Horizontal to Vertical

Standing independently is one of the six steps of *the prone progression:* the sequence of skills (milestones) that take us from the horizontal (prone) position to the vertical (upright) orientation of sitting, standing, and walking. Each step is important; each step requires the background of the previous steps, plus the correct environment – and lots of practice!

The prone position is the baseline for the prone progression. In the prone position, on their stomachs, babies are completely horizontal. Within hours after birth, they begin moving out of the prone position as they lift their heads.

Belly crawling is baby's first movement pattern. It is a coordinated movement that requires stability and control and is the foundation for all other movement patterns.

Rolling over begins with a reflex action (innate automatic movements) of the neck. In time, babies integrate this reflex so they can roll over when and where they want.

On all-fours, babies have even more head control. Now they are also able to shift their body weight up and down, forward and back, from side to side, and diagonally.

Sitting is a milestone only when baby can move into a sitting position by herself. To sit, her body must be stable: her arms and legs work together and her trunk rotates.

Creeping is moving on all-fours on a horizontal plane. It is a coordinated, reciprocal pattern using arms, legs, eyes, and hands.

Standing, like sitting, is a milestone only when baby can move into this position by himself. When babies are physically ready to stand independently, their posture is perfect: straight backs, chin and tummies in.

The prone progression takes months; each stage provides unique and necessary opportunities to differentiate ("sort out") the parts of the body. For each stage, babies need the background of the previous stage plus the correct environment and lots of practice. Only then can this step-by-step learning be perfectly sequenced to develop increasing levels of flexibility, stability, strength, and coordination.

This sequenced learning also expands baby's sense of *space* and *time.* With their bodies, they experience space as they move from here to there, and time as they compare moving and non-moving. This physical understanding of space and time enables rhythmic, controlled, efficient movements of the body. (We'll explain more about learning space and time *from the inside out* later in this chapter.)

As babies gain control and confidence in the upright position, their bodies become a measuring device and reference point for understanding the world around them:

- Where is the cracker – and how can I get it into my mouth?

- If I lean this way, can I reach far enough to touch the rattle?

- How far away is the ball – and how long will it take me to get there?

In this way, the prone progression forms the background for translating motor action into mental action – in other words, for making sense of our actions. Posture confirms our position; legs give us mobility, stability, and movement; arms are tools of exploration; kinesthesia frees the brain for cognition and thinking.

Although the prone progression is monitored by its milestones, even more important is the progress *between* each stage. Each stage requires a stronger foundation of sensation, kinesthesia, differentiation, movement patterns, problem-solving, flexibility, hand-eye coordination, and physical development (including bone density, maturity of the neuromuscular system, and visual acuity). Instead of emphasizing the milestones, parents should recognize the importance of steady practice and gradual learning. Children will suffer if they are pushed through the progression; too much encouragement can distract children from their innate timeline. Children also suffer if their progress is restricted: when infant seats, carpeting, baby "walkers," or jump-seats limit their physical movement.

Let's take a closer look at what Jerry must learn to reach each stage, and how his parents can support his progress.

In *the prone position,* the horizontal orientation affects function of the vital systems of circulation, respiration, and workings of the inner organs. Newborns have little control or stability of the neck and head. They often bring their knees under their bodies to sleep in a flexed position much like they were in utero. Soon after birth, they learn to turn their heads from side to side to clear their noses.

The prone position is the natural position for babies and gives them the essential orientation, stability, and freedom they need in their first weeks of life. The only other natural, nurturing position for a baby is in human arms. Propping babies in plastic infant carriers or in the corner of the sofa will weaken the foundation necessary for proper orientation, full stability, and the ability to move freely.

With *the belly crawl,* babies move like lizards across the floor, reaching with the arms, pushing with the legs. This is the beginning of mobility – and an essential link between horizontal and vertical, space and time. Like walking, the belly crawl evolves into reciprocal movements, with the right arm and left leg moving together. Done efficiently, the motion is smooth and rhythmic, and highly effective in getting babies where they want to go. The belly crawl offers unique opportunities to work on differentiation of arms, legs, and head, as well as to build trunk stability and enhance hand-eye coordination.

Babies learn the belly crawl before they can roll over. When they are propped up or lying on their backs, babies are physically unable to move in this new and exciting way. To learn the belly crawl, babies also need time on a firm, slick surface. (For tiny ones, a two-by-four foot strip of smooth linoleum can be placed in their cribs or on the carpet. Clean vinyl or hardwood floors are ideal for older children.) It's not enough to put babies on the floor for just five or ten minutes a day; only with extended periods of time on nearly unrestricted space can they perfect this essential skill. Be sure to keep the light dim. Boundaries can be established with gates and other barriers. Once babies learn to belly crawl, their coordination (and enjoyment) will thrive when they have opportunities to belly crawl on large expanses of floor.[*]

Learning to *roll over* gives babies control of the fencing reflex (asymmetric tonic neck reflex), one of the innate automatic reflexes present at birth. For newborn infants, this reflex automatically positions baby's body comfortably for nursing: one arm is flexed, one arm is extended, and the head is turned toward the straight arm. As neck muscles become stronger, baby learns to stabilize the head in midline, thus integrating the asymmetric tonic neck reflex.

Babies first roll over by accident: while lying on their tummies, one day they lift their heads, arch the back and – plop – over they go. This "accident" happens again and again, and gradually babies learn to integrate another innate automatic reflex.

Rolling from the back to the tummy is a much more complicated task. (Try it yourself and see why!) First baby must flex both arms and legs close to his body. The head turns, then the shoulder and hip, and the body turns to the side as the rolling motion continues until baby is lying on his tummy. At this point,

---

[*]The basic movement pattern of the belly crawl was explained in detail in Chapter Five. The belly crawl as the first mode of locomotion is in Chapter Seven.

baby can either straighten his legs to lie flat on the surface, or keep his knees bent so he lies in a flexed position.

At first, a baby can only roll over in one direction, either to the left or right, and only from front to back. With time and practice, this once-accidental movement becomes fully integrated, enabling baby to roll over whenever she chooses, in whatever direction she wants.

Rolling over is initiated by movement of the head. As a movement pattern, it involves both *flexion* and *extension* of the arms and legs and *rotation* of the body around the midline. Babies don't learn this controlled movement until they have "sorted out" (differentiated) their head, arms, and legs. They also need adequate stability and strength of the neck. And, of course, they need a place where they can roll over easily and safely.

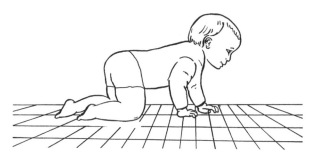

On all-fours, the trunk of the body is lifted off the security of the floor and baby has reached a major milestone towards the upright position.

Reaching the all-fours position is a logical next-step in the prone progression. Once babies have learned to roll over and crawl on their bellies, they learn to prop themselves up on elbows. This quickly becomes a favorite position: babies spend hours leaning on one or both elbows, shifting their weight to reach and play with one hand, then another. Soon they push their bottoms back over their heels and up they go into the all-fours position.

This bottoms-up position isn't that different from the comforting prenatal flexion position. But now baby has control of his head and arms, and can support and shift his body weight over his legs, arms, and hands. Soon she learns to push back with the arms while flexing the legs, and to push forwards with the legs while flexing the arms. She can flex with her right arm and leg while pushing with the left, then flex with the left and push with the right. The result is a rocking motion that shifts the body weight forward and back, side to side, and diagonally. Besides being a great way to exercise the arms and legs, rocking is a powerful stimulation to the vestibular system and helps establish orientation to gravity and balance. In addition, this vigorous movement increases muscle tone and alerts the mind, and so provides a powerful body-mind connection.

Sitting puts baby's head in a fully upright position for the first time ever. With body stable, head lifted, and arms free, she is now much better positioned to explore her world. Moving smoothly into a stable sitting position is evidence that baby has developed a healthy body image, has differentiated her arms, legs, and head, and has developed kinesthesia.

> "It is wrong to order a child to sit up. If he does not do so himself, he has already been thrown out of proper development, and something must be done to make him feel right only in the proper posture."
> (M. Feldenkrais. *Body and Mature Behavior.* pp. 96-97)

As a continuation of the prone progression, learning to sit incorporates what baby has been learning and practicing on all-fours, in rolling over, and in the belly crawl. Some babies first move from all-fours into a sitting position; others move from side-lying into sitting.

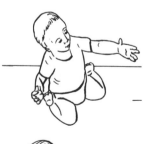

From all-fours, babies may sit in a "W" position: knees together, heels to each side. Starting on their hands and knees, they push back, first to sit on the heels, then moving their legs out so they can sit fully on the floor. By keeping their feet together, they also should be able to "side-sit," rotating the body to sit at one side of the legs, then holding their bodies upright without propping themselves up with their arms.

From a side-lying position, babies sit up by rotating the trunk over their hips and off the floor. The neck is flexed as the body rotates and moves forward and upward; one leg rotates out, the other rotates inward, allowing the pelvis to move from horizontal to vertical position.

After they first sit on their own, babies should soon be able to move in and out of each position: from sitting to all-fours, from all-fours to sitting to side-lying to sitting, and on and on.

Babies can't learn these sequenced movements when they are propped into a sitting position. If their stability is always provided by furniture (such as pillows, couches, or infant carriers), babies won't develop the internal stability needed for proper progression towards full use of their bodies. Instead, other sensory systems (especially vision and hearing) will be prematurely "turned on," distracting them from the necessary sequence for learning from the inside out.

Creeping on all-fours increases babies' mobility far beyond the reaches of the belly crawl. Just as the belly crawl is a lizard-like movement, creeping resembles the movement of cats, dogs, and other four-legged mammals. With heads up, bodies stable, and increasing strength in the legs and arms, children can creep across great expanses of territory in a very short time.

The trunk of the body is stable as baby creeps; the arms, legs, and head are working together. At first baby can move only one limb at a time but he quickly learns the typical cross pattern: the left hand moves forward, then the right leg; the right hand, then the left leg. Once this pattern is coordinated he will be able to lift his head while creeping; until then, the head remains down, watching his arms and legs move. That's why babies are often likely to bump into things when they first begin creeping. Then, for a while, they will creep a ways, then stop and look before creeping further.

As he creeps across the floor, baby has a long list of things to practice. Through creeping, he gains stability of the trunk, learns to lift his head and to work arms and legs in a coordinated and reciprocal pattern, practices hand-eye and eye-hand coordination, experiences moving in space and time, practices flexion and extension, and matches sensations from inside and outside the body. Mastering so many concepts requires, time, practice, space, and encouragement.

Parents often unintentionally make creeping difficult for their children:

- Baby girls can't creep if their dresses catch on their knees when they crawl.

- Feet can't flex properly when restricted by high top shoes.

- Legs can't move as easily on carpeted floors as they can on a slick surface.

- Children won't go far if furniture and clutter are always in their path, or if small rooms restrict their journeys.

- Children can't move their bodies efficiently without the AHA! of kinesthesia that connects sensations within the body with sensory information about the world.

It's usually relatively easy to adapt the home environment to provide kids with a safe space for creeping. It's not so easy later on to change the past or to correct errors and imperfections that may have damaged the background of a child's growth and development.

If children have trouble proceeding through the prone progression, it may be because they don't have the adequate background of posture, balance, kinesthesia, or sensation and/or because their skill development has been thwarted by stress or first-line trauma. The previous chapters of this book can help parents discover problems in the background, and begin to make the changes necessary. CN6.2

When babies are ready for *independent standing,* they can pull themselves up from the all-fours position in one of two ways. Some babies push themselves backwards over their feet into a squat position before lifting themselves up into a vertical position. Others put one foot flat on the floor, then lean forward to shift their body weight over their foot so they can stand. In either case, babies should have perfect posture when they first stand up. When babies are following their developmental sequence, their trunks are strong and stable when standing. The abdomen is strong enough to support the body as weight shifts. The neck has the stability and flexibility to support the head as the body moves.

Even before children are able to stand independently, they pull themselves up by grabbing the nearest object. Soon they are "cruising," walking themselves around tables, chairs, and other furnishings, and feeling perfectly stable as long as they have one hand on solid support. If baby can walk around a table, isn't she about ready to take her first steps by herself? No! Cruising isn't walking, but an important step in establishing stability in the upright position. Coaxing children into standing or walking before they have the necessary stability and strength is like expecting children to spell before they know their alphabet. First things first!

The sway-backed posture of many toddlers should never be considered normal or acceptable. With tummies sticking out and knees locked back, this posture indicates children don't have the necessary internal stability for proper movement and haven't had the necessary time, space, and encouragement for working their way through each of the steps from prone to upright position.

What about kids who never creep? Who have spent hours, even days, in baby swings? Who grew up on carpeted floors? It's never too late to "re-program the computer" and restore proper sensation and function. But because early problems set an imperfect foundation for development, intervention is best done as soon as possible. Patterns of compensation may be difficult to re-program.

Intervention may mean changing baby's environment or schedule to provide more time-in-arms. Intervention may mean looking at the background of the problem, then working to enhance kinesthesia with dry brushing, deep pressures, and/or patterns for movement/nonmovement. (See Chapter Five.) Intervention may include the "stress-busting strategies" explained in Chapter Two.

Because intervention means changing existing patterns, it is always somewhat stressful. Encouragement, support, and love must always accompany any intervention strategies. Intervention requires commitment and persistence by the parents, and the firm belief that change is possible and worth the effort.

Creating the Ideal Environment
for the Prone Progression

Ideally, all babies would begin life in a loving, supportive, healthy environment where they could move steadily along the specific human timeline for development. But in the real world, there is always need for improvement and it's never too late to make positive changes.

Hazel was six months old before she was allowed to play on the kitchen floor. Until then, she had seemed happy enough sitting in her plastic baby seat where she could see her mother or watch television. The baby seat was certainly convenient: it kept Hazel out of danger and was easy to move from place to place, even when Hazel was sleeping. And Hazel was certainly happy in her chair. In fact, her mother, Marilyn, had recently noticed that Hazel didn't seem nearly as happy anywhere else.

In the church nursery, for example, Hazel looked rather forlorn when left on her favorite blanket, even though other children her age seemed to be playing happily. Marilyn noticed one child in particular: although she was about the same age as Hazel, this little girl was busily scooting across the linoleum floor on her tummy.

After naptime one afternoon at home, Marilyn dressed Hazel in a stretchy one-piece jumpsuit and placed her on her tummy on the kitchen floor. At first, Hazel just lay there, motionless, and then she started to wail. Marilyn quickly picked her up and cuddled her. "Don't panic, Honey," Marilyn said quietly. "I'm right here." When Hazel stopped crying, Marilyn put her back on the floor and the crying resumed. Marilyn picked her up, quieted her, then put her back down three times before she gave up.

The next day, Marilyn tried again. This time she dimmed the kitchen lights so Hazel wouldn't have so much to look at, and turned off the radio and television. Hazel again cried as soon as Marilyn put her on the floor, but her cries were weaker. Marilyn picked her up and consoled her wordlessly, holding her close and stroking her head. When Hazel was calm again, Marilyn lay down beside Hazel on the floor. Hazel lay quietly for a while, then cautiously lifted her head. An arm came up, then down, then up again. She rubbed her hand across the floor. Her legs flexed and straightened. Hazel played quietly on the floor for several minutes. But when the doorbell rang, her body tensed and she wailed in dismay. Marilyn picked up her daughter and held her lovingly as she answered the door.

An hour or so later, Marilyn put Hazel back on the floor, and again after dinner. At bathtime, Marilyn watched carefully as Hazel played in the tub while the water was draining out. Hazel delighted in jerkily moving her arm back and forth across the slippery surface.

After Hazel went to bed that night, Marilyn stretched out on the floor alone, and gently moved her body against the hard surface just as her daughter had done hours before. With the lights dim and the house quiet, Marilyn found herself listening to her body. "Move me," it seemed to be saying. "Use me well, for I am your life."

There's truly no place like home for learning basic movement patterns from the inside out. Marilyn recognized that Hazel was not making adequate progress along her developmental timeline and took the initiative for making needed changes. She realized that being on the floor would, at first, be stressful for Hazel, so used "peacekeeping strategies" to calm her daughter. (See Chapter Two.) Marilyn set the stage for internal learning by modifying the environment: reducing sights and sounds that might be distracting, communicating with body language (not words), and offering repeated opportunities for experimentation and practice on the firm, slick floor.

For Hazel to continue developing according to her developmental timeline, these opportunities should be continued daily: happy, stress-free times on the floor, with minimal distractions and maximum space for playing.

Motor Generalizations

By their second birthday, children should have completed the prone progression. They also should have begun to establish five *motor generalizations:* generalized areas of movement that can serve as landmarks of a child's growth and development. As therapist/educator Newell Kephart explains, motor generalizations "permit the type of exploration which the child needs to develop adequate information about the environment which surrounds him." (*Slow Learner in the Classroom,* p. 97)

These five skills should develop spontaneously, building and intertwining with each other in complex ways. CN6.3

Posture and maintenance of balance establishes the body's stable frame of reference in the upright position.

Locomotion (moving the body through space) provides the opportunity to explore and interact with the environment. Locomotion includes rolling, scooting, belly crawling, and creeping as well as walking, running, jumping, hopping, and skipping. (Explained in Chapter Seven.)

Contact includes reaching, grasping, and releasing. (Explained in Chapter Seven.)

Speech allows us to express ourselves using a common language. (Explained in Chapter Seven.)

Receipt and propulsion enable us to relate to moving objects: to deflect or catch objects coming towards us (receipt) and to give motion to an object by pushing, pulling, kicking, throwing, or hitting (propulsion). (Explained in Chapter Nine.)

Each of the five motor generalizations equips the body for different skills and stages of growth. If the natural unfolding of these skills is altered by parental interference (such as if babies are pushed to become early walkers) the developmental timeline will be short-circuited. The resulting chain of com-

pensations will compromise movement, behavior, and potential.

Posture and the Maintenance of Balance

The village women stand tall in the hot sun. Many carry a jug of water, a basket of food, or a bundle of clothing on their heads. Their movements seem especially graceful as they manage heavy and awkward loads with perfect posture and balance.

The infants are bundled in bright-colored cloths which hold them snugly against their mother's bodies. Older babies crawl, creep, walk, and play on the vast areas of open ground. Under the supervision of all the village, these children are not expected to follow a textbook chart of developmental milestones. By spending their first months of life in the security of mother's arms, then playing freely and actively in the fresh air, the children grow healthily according to their own timeline. Growing up in a primitive culture, their health may be threatened by disease, malnutrition, poor sanitation, or war. But for now, unrestricted by clocks, infant carriers, strollers, plastic toys, and televisions, the village's youngest residents are free to enjoy the work of being a child.

Our technological society has had a phenomenal impact on human development and on human posture. Modern civilization gives too little opportunity for postural development and the results are seen in the weak posture and poor motor skills of today's children.

The motor generalization for posture and maintenance of balance gives our bodies stability and a consistent orientation to the world around us. Gravity is our reference point; maintaining our posture means always having an immediate, internal awareness of the body's position in relationship to the surface of the earth. This awareness and stability allows us to move our bodies quickly and efficiently while sitting, standing, walking, and for an endless variety of tasks and in countless body positions. We can maintain our balance while prone, upright, moving, or still.

Perfect posture takes little effort to maintain. Each part of the body is perfectly balanced over other perfectly balanced parts of the body. Movement in any direction is graceful, fluid, and nearly effortless.

In perfect posture, the arches of the feet are strong and stable, and toes are pointed straight ahead. When standing, the knees may be slightly bent, and the pelvis is straight, directly above the thighs. The lower back is slightly curved, and the arms hang in

---

"We cannot conceive consciousness without fixing the position of our body in relation to the outside world. More precisely, we cannot appreciate any sensory experience, emotion or feeling without presenting ourselves to the vertical."

(M. Feldenkrais. *Body and Mature Behavior.* p. 81)

line with the body. The upper back is straight, the chest elevated, and abdominal muscles are firm and flat. The head is positioned so the ear is directly over the shoulder. In this position, our posture gives us the head-to-toe stability we need to move against the constant force of gravity.

We first experience some level of postural stability in the womb. As infants, we find postural stability in a horizontal position, as we lie on our stomachs on a firm surface. Through the prone progression, postural stability gradually becomes vertical through belly crawling, then rolling over, pushing up to all-fours, sitting, creeping, and standing independently. The result is the stable posture and maintenance of balance that give stability to all movements.

Perfect posture should be the birthright of all humans; it is nature's design that we establish upright posture as the culmination of a carefully sequenced process of development. Such a developmental sequence can be nurtured in our modern society as well as in a primitive village if infants receive the necessary time in arms and if babies have adequate opportunity and activity for the prone progression.

> *"Posture is the basis from which any type of skilled movement must take place."*
> (A. Jean Ayres. *The Development of Sensory Integrative Theory and Practice.* p. 68) CN6.4

Orientation in Space and Time

Babies first experience distance and spatial relationships in terms of their body position. Through movement and stability, babies learn to use their bodies as a reference point for understanding top and bottom, this side and that, front and back, also known as the vertical, lateral, and transverse dimensions.

These terms for organizing space are based on Euclid's spatial system depicting three straight lines running in the three directions through space; time is the fourth dimension. Therapist/educator Newell Kephart used the same understanding to explain how children organize their world. Kephart explained that the force of gravity is at the center (origin) of a child's spatial system, and simultaneous muscle action around a joint is the origin of the time dimension. A child's orientation to space and time is established in all directions by stopping or fixing the body position. CN6.5

> *"Motion enables the body to learn the most about its relation to space, for motion elicits the greatest number of proprioceptive impulses."*
> (A. Jean Ayres. *The Development of Sensory Integrative Theory and Practice.* pp. 19-20)

The vertical dimension is the direction of the line of gravity, which pulls us towards the earth in a constant direction. Because body learning happens cephalocaudally (head-to-toe), we learn to move our heads against gravity before the arms, the arms before the legs.

Eventually, the body learns to move and position itself vertically, relying on the perfect matching of proprioceptive, vestibular, and tactile sensations. This match of sensory and motor information sets the stage for understanding up and down, above and below.

A child's understanding of *the horizontal/lateral dimension* begins as she recognizes the distance from the spine (as the body's midline) to the ends of her extremities (fingertips and toes). This new-found internal measuring device is used when she first reaches for an object just an arms-length away and is checked by kinesthetic information as her hand moves.

Laterality develops from the realization that there are two sides of the body. Children first learn to work these two sides of the body together in a bilateral pattern; then they learn to work them in opposition and separately.

Gravity is the constant for developing midline stability and an important factor in establishing laterality. Babies learn that they can lean only so far in any direction before falling over and will try to maintain their stability and vertical position by extending the head, reaching with one arm or leg, or leaning with the body.

The horizontal/lateral dimension is the foundation for understanding left-right directionality. But it is far too soon to think about left-right preference. The lateral dimension isn't about "left" and "right" as much as it is the body's *internal* understanding of distance from the midline.

The transverse dimension begins at the center of the body and progresses forward and backward. Eventually, this is how we "divide the world" into front and back. This also is the foundation of depth perception.

Again, the force of gravity is the constant as it defines the midline of the body. Leaning forward too far, the body will work to realign itself with gravity by extending the head, shoulder, and back. This is why, when a parent reaches to pick up a child, the child's head remains aligned with gravity while the body flexes toward the adult.

Our bodies' internal and automatic understanding of the vertical, lateral, and transverse dimensions of space give us – from the inside out – our three-dimensional orientation to the world. Movement also leads us to understand time as the fourth dimension. Moving our bodies through space and time, we experience the present as different from the past and the future.

"To locate a point permanently, you must consider the variable of time... Time is a fourth dimension of space."
(Newell Kephart. *The Slow Learner In The Classroom.* p. 172)

The "zero-point" of our orientation in space is postural stability. It is from our stable, upright posture that we measure distance and direction. In the same way, the "zero-point" of our orientation in time is an internal awareness of *now* as the physical moment when muscles around the joint act simultaneously, stopping movement and producing non-movement. If children are always in motion, they don't have an innate understanding of non-movement and will be unable to integrate the space-time dimension.

Movement and non-movement teach us about now and then, past and present, and require that we integrate all four dimensions to work together. Correct orientation in space and time enables us to see the components of a whole, so that we can break things apart and put them back together: lines to form squares, movements to perform a task, syllables to make words, steps to reach a destination. Integrating space and time allows us to draw a square: we move the pencil in *space* to draw one line at a *time* to form the correct shape. Integrating space and time as we look around us, we see a panoramic view of the world. But if we are unable to integrate what we're seeing at different moments in time (even from second to second), our eyes will bring us a series of separate images instead of a single, expansive view.

Our orientation to time expands as our movements become more complex. Three components of time are evident: rhythm, pace, and sequencing.

Rhythm is obvious in our breath, in the beating of our hearts, in the contractions of the digestive tract. Rhythm is the smooth and steady regularity of movement in time. Rhythm gives flow, fluency, and smoothness to our actions.

Pace is the ability to change the tempo of an action without changing the rhythm. Whether we breathe fast or slow, our breath still goes in and out, in and out, always in the same rhythm. We walk fast or slow, stepping with left foot, then right foot, left and right.

Sequencing is the ability to coordinate muscle groups in posture and movement. Kinesthesia is essential for sequencing. Unless we can accurately match sensory information within the body (from tactile, vestibular, and proprioceptor sensations), we will be unable to coordinate the movement and position of our bodies in time and space.

Our orientation in space and time develops gradually as we progress from infancy to adulthood. More specifically, it is the prone progression that leads us through the necessary stages for developing orientation in space and time *from the inside out.*

As a newborn infant, Amy's world seems to be in perfect rhythm with her breath. Even while feeding at the breast, she usually sucks at a perfect beat. Her mother sits in the rocking chair for hours, holding her tiny baby close to her heart.

Joseph is just a month old. His first free movements (unsupported by the womb or parental arms) are a powerful symmetrical motion using both arms exactly together as if they were controlled by a single switch.

Katie is now crawling on her belly, using perfectly sequenced, rhythmic movements of her arms and legs. With her body weight resting on the horizontal plane, she can wiggle her body in all directions or hold it perfectly still.

Michael has just learned to roll over. Like the belly crawl, this new skill requires a sequence of movements. Watching him, his father realizes that rolling over didn't change how Michael sees the world as much as it has changed how he feels in the world: lying on his back changes his body's orientation to gravity. Front and back don't look different, they feel different.

Until Leah moved up onto all fours, her head had always been level with the ground (except when she was in someone's arms). Now Leah can lift her head high enough to look at the world vertically. Positioned on her hands and knees, she can rock her body in all directions, in a forceful rhythmic motion that is highly sequenced.

Matthew is now sitting, and his head and eyes have adjusted to his new vertical orientation. Because his trunk is now positioned vertically, there are new and different demands on his digestive tract, breathing, and circulation. Yet his legs are still on the horizontal plane, and Matthew frequently moves from vertical (sitting) to horizontal (prone) positions and back again. He falls backward, leans forward, sits upright, leans sideways. He can quickly move from sitting to lying or crawling, and from lying or crawling into a sitting position. Each transition involves a different sequence of movements of his head, trunk, arms, and legs.

When Dawn began creeping, she seemed to discover a new pace for her life. Sometimes her hands and knees barely inch her forward. Other times she races after the cat or towards her daddy. Fast or slow, this movement requires an even higher level of sequencing and rhythm, and more control to vary the pace. Her body knows how to move by itself in an efficient and complex manner.

Travis has just begun to stand independently, and his posture is perfectly vertical. Now his head, trunk, legs, and arms, and his internal organs, are functioning in the vertical plane, not the horizontal. He is most intrigued by what is directly in front of him, most afraid of what's behind him. He can't yet walk independently, but cruises around the furniture in all directions. When he wants to explore something across the room, he quickly drops to his hands and knees to creep in that direction.

If children are unable to deal adequately with space and time, learning disabilities are likely to result. Because their bodies lack orientation to space and time, they will have poor kinesthesia, problems with balance and coordination, difficulty organizing themselves in their environment, and difficulty with timing and sequencing the movements of their bodies through space.

Without the consistency of the space-time dimensions within their bodies, children can't develop a systematic method for organizing things in their environment. They reverse letters when writing, can't sequence letters on a line or words on a page or cards on a rack, and often have trouble sequencing their movements.

The problems intensify in the classroom, because reading and writing involve time and space dimensions simultaneously. To read smoothly, children must be able to move their eyes across the line in a lateral direction, holding each image while recognizing the next. The task becomes more complicated when reading aloud. Talking and walking simultaneously is an extremely complex task for it involves integrating mental concepts at the same time that space and time must be coordinated for body movement.

Self-parenting

The precise sequence of the prone progression offers numerous opportunities for development to get sidetracked. Instead of perfecting a skill, we may leap forward ahead of schedule or "get stuck" doing things imperfectly. Without adequate muscle strength, for example, we may lock our knees backwards to support ourselves while standing, an inefficient postural position. This may begin a cycle of compensation that continues forever, or until we take the initiative to correct the imperfect patterns.

In the ten months since the birth of her second child, Lynn had been nearly overwhelmed by the joys and challenges of parenting two small children. At her husband's urging, she had taken a little time each week for herself to take a walk, to have coffee with a friend, to visit an art gallery. Even so, there were times when her self-esteem hit bottom. She knew she shouldn't expect a lot of acknowledgement for her efforts at home, yet she felt lonely, unappreciated, and unattractive.

After talking with her sister one evening, Lynn decided that getting her body back in shape might improve her attitude. With a few phone calls, she found an evening aerobics class for beginners at a nearby health club and signed up for the upcoming six-week course.

Lynn was nervous when attending the first night of class and more than a bit embarrassed about her pudgy figure in the form-fitting dancewear she'd bought. She took a place in the back row and then listened carefully to the instructor's words of welcome. When the music and movement began, the instructor explained each movement quickly and simply.

But the movements were far from quick and simple for Lynn. The music went too fast and her body seemed to be always going in the wrong direction. Even when she heard the instructions clearly, her feet and arms wouldn't cooperate. She felt like an octopus, a clumsy octopus. Only during the cool-down period of gentle floor exercises did she feel in some control of her body.

When she got home, Lynn stood in front of a full-length mirror and looked at her body. She watched carefully as she did some of the simple moves slowly in front of the mirror. "Right-step-clap-hop, left-step-clap-hop," she said quietly. Even in the quiet of her bedroom, her movements seemed awkward. Standing up straight, she saw a crook in her neck, a sag in her shoulders, a flabby stomach, and locked-back knees. It wasn't just that she was out of shape, she realized, her body simply didn't line up the way it should.

The next morning, she watched her young son Jerry move easily around the floor. Although he sometimes lost his balance, he moved smoothly from lying on his tummy to lying on his back, from sitting to all-fours, from all-fours to standing. She got on the floor with him and began mirroring his movements. Just like in the aerobics class, her movements felt awkward and uncontrolled, as if the parts of her body weren't fully connected. "I think I need to parent myself," she said aloud.

Lynn couldn't remember ever enjoying how her body worked. Even as a child, she hadn't been able to jump rope or hopscotch very well. Growing up, she always had considered her body rather unreliable for all but the most basic activities. She had many memories of times when she had been embarrassed about her physical imperfections – not just adolescent dissatisfaction with her appearance, but misery and dismay at her poor coordination. She knew her body image was intricately intertwined with her self-esteem and confidence.

Continuing to watch Jerry, Lynn decided to let her young son teach her to use her body efficiently. After all, his developmental timeline was destined to maximize his abilities; it was only logical that he could guide her to improving her coordination, muscle tone, even her body image.

She withdrew from the aerobics class and, instead enrolled in yoga to learn more about breath, awareness, physical control, and relaxation. At home, she spent time each day watching her son, mirroring his movements while "tuning in" to the myriad of sensations within her own body.

Lynn also began attending a parenting class where she learned that Jerry was following the prone progression, a series of skills important for establishing postural stability, developing orientation of space and time, and learning to walk.

A few months later, Jerry was walking and running exuberantly and Lynn was busier than ever just monitoring his progress. She had continued with the yoga class and took time daily to practice simple movement patterns of the prone progression. Comparing Jerry's developing skills with her own,

Lynn became convinced that she had never fully learned even these basic movements and that those "missing pieces" of her development were the reason she had never felt confident about the way her body worked.

Lynn was determined to improve her coordination by relearning basic movement skills. Her progress wasn't nearly as quick and steady as her son's but in time she, too, gained strength, stability, and coordination. Her progress came more quickly after she learned the importance of sensation and kinesthesia and began using dry brushing, pressures, and movement/non-movement patterns to enhance her kinesthesia.

As Lynn's coordination improved, she discovered new reservoirs of strength within herself and a new enthusiasm for her roles as parent and self-parent. Never before had she felt so capable, so alive, and so wonderfully human!

THE MOTOR-PERCEPTUAL STAGE OF DEVELOPMENT
3 - 24 Months of Age

CHAPTER SEVEN:
Making Contact

It's just a month before her second birthday and Beth loves being the center of attention. Energetic and curious, she plays happily by herself. She makes a tower of plastic containers, climbs in and out of cardboard boxes, then pulls a string toy across the room. Later she will cuddle her dolly in her chubby arms as she "reads" a favorite book aloud.

She's been walking now for months. Being upright and mobile has given her amazing freedom to explore the world: to move in for a closer look, to chase a moving object, to avoid something frightening. Now that her arms and hands are no longer supporting her body, they are free for grabbing, touching, playing, carrying.

As she explores her world, she is also learning about her environment. Every movement provides sensory information about where her body is and how much space it occupies.

Beth's new abilities come so quickly that her parents can't celebrate them as they'd hoped. Even taking her first step wasn't the landmark occasion they had envisioned. It happened before dinner one evening, while her parents were busy in the next room. Beth just walked across the living room as if she had done it hundreds of times before, as if she were doing exactly what she was ready to do, as if she had her own schedule, her own timeline, for perfecting each skill and stage.

Developmental Milestones Mark the End of the Motor-perceptual Stage

The second year of life is a rapid succession of achievements. This is the time when children master walking and talking; when they learn to play and pretend; when they "sow the seeds" for social skills, intellectual growth, and personality development. It's the end of *the motor-perceptual stage,* and the completion of key stages of physical development that form the background for lifelong growth.

The motor-perceptual stage spans the development between the third month after birth and the second birthday, as babies learn to interact in meaningful ways with their environment. Motor-perceptual development involves expanding innate automatic reflexes, developing kinesthesia, learning movement patterns, and beginning the mastery of five motor generalizations: posture and maintenance of balance, locomotion, contact, speech, and receipt (catching) and propulsion (throwing).

These learnings are often seen as a series of milestones or stages to be remembered; we proudly note the date of baby's first smile and send grandparents a photo of her first step, as though these can somehow measure a child's progress against some universal standards. But developmental milestones are only markers along the way, not destinations unto themselves. Given the right environment and the adequate background, children proceed along their developmental timeline at the pace necessary for optimum growth. If parents focus only on the milestones, children may be pressured to move on to the next stage before they are ready, developing problems that may stay "in the background" and affect future learning.

The complexity of the human developmental sequence includes countless variables, and each child's development proceeds at its own pace. Developmental milestones simply show us that we are moving forward in the right direction and the proper sequence. Parents should be alarmed only if a child's development is substantially different from that documented on any developmental chart. Reaching each milestone requires concentration and practice. For that reason, other skills may temporarily falter. While learning to walk, for example, children may seem to lose some of the dexterity of their hands. While learning to talk they may seem more awkward on their feet. Rarely, if ever, can a child make great progress towards two motor generalizations simultaneously.

The developmental milestones reached at the end of the motor-perceptual stage are unique to the human species. One of these is dexterity of hands and arms, and independent movement of the thumb. At the same time, the cerebellum assumes its role as the principal organ for coordinating muscular activity and the cerebral cortex expands to enable audio, visual, and spatial perception, and language. These learnings (walking, grasping, and speaking) are the focus of this chapter.

Locomotion: Moving Through Space

The human ability to move through space is far more advanced, flexible, and controlled than in any other species. Only humans can belly crawl, roll, scoot, creep, walk, run, hop, skip, or use other methods of *locomotion* to get from one place to another.

The word "locomotion" actually means movement (motion) from place to place (loco). Locomotion, of course, is one of the characteristics that separates animals from plants; only the more evolved animals are capable of complex methods of locomotion. Human locomotion is upright, coordinated, rhythmic, and adaptable. It is the second motor generalization and it can only be perfected if the first motor generalization, posture and the maintenance of balance, is well established.

"Locomotion comprises those activities by which the child moves through space. His knowledge of overall space and of the relationships between objects in space, beyond arm's reach, develops out of exploration through locomotion."

(Clara Chaney and Nancy Miles. *Remediating Learning Problems: A Developmental Curriculum.* p. 112)

Through the stages of the prone progression, these two motor generalizations develop gradually, first on the floor and eventually in the upright position.* This progression allows babies to gradually stabilize posture and balance against the force of gravity while maintaining the flexibility to move freely and appropriately. The end result of this prone progression is the human ability to walk: a coordinated, upright movement that involves a rhythmic heel-toe pattern.

There is no doubt that baby's first step is something to celebrate. But, in truth, it is the logical thing for children to do, according to the timeline for human development, because they are ready *from the inside out* to take that next step forward. Babies will walk when they are ready *if* they feel good about themselves, if they have confidence in their movement patterns, *if* they have opportunities to practice:

- Cruising around furniture, children begin to pursue what is within their visual range as they practice maintaining stability while upright and mobile.

- Rocking the pelvis back and forth, they discover the body's balance point.

- Stepping forward and back, they practice shifting their weight from leg to leg, from heel to toe.

- Squatting, they gain stability while moving up and down.

If locomotion is firmly established as a motor generalization, the body will be capable of running itself without the help from the conscious mind. Movement has coordination and rhythm, and the body can overcome obstacles such as a toy on the floor, can change directions quickly when chasing a ball, can adapt to changes in terrain when running across the driveway to the lawn, and can respond quickly to commands such as "Don't touch!" or "Stop now!"

Locomotion also changes how children learn about the world. Moving their bodies from place to place (and from one thing to another) gives them an innate understanding of how things compare and relate. But this is possible only if they are able to concentrate on gathering information, not on moving their bodies.

---

*Chapter Six explains the prone progression in more detail: from the belly crawl (like reptiles) to crawling on all fours (like many mammals), to walking and running in a vertical position (like only the most advanced members of the animal kingdom).

If locomotion is only a collection of skills and not integrated as a motor generalization, or if kinesthesia is impaired, children must learn to run their bodies with their heads. They "figure out" how to climb stairs, step over an obstacle, or run across the yard. If every simple movement requires mental planning, less "brain power" is available for thinking, exploring, and discovering. CN7.1

Babies can't learn to walk if their movement is restricted by tight clothing, cluttered rooms, or infant seats. Baby walkers place children in an upright position before their bodies are ready, and force developmental functions out of sequence. Televisions and video games preoccupy children's eyes and minds without regard to any developmental timeline while actually discouraging physical movement.

Locomotion and other milestones of physical development can also be blocked by a background of traumas and inadequacies. When stress overloads the autonomic nervous system, children may be using all their energy just to survive with none left over for discovering how to use their bodies.

Backaches, poor posture, poor coordination, clumsiness, and even learning disabilities are indications that the motor generalization of locomotion has not been mastered. Improving locomotion requires returning to the basic stages of learning and repairing any damages in the background. This re-learning begins with the first pattern of locomotion: the belly crawl. As explained in Chapter Five, babies learn to belly crawl in the first two or three months if they have time on a smooth, slick surface and the correct environment. As babies grow, the belly crawl becomes the base for learning to sit, stand, walk, and run. But if the belly crawl pattern is not well-integrated and coordinated, children are unable to move smoothly and automatically and the body learns to compensate for imperfect movement patterns. Over time, imperfect patterns build upon one another to bring greater stress and dysfunction.

As baby's first mode of locomotion, the belly crawl helps them to differentiate muscle groups, focus on kinesthetic matching, and use their bodies efficiently. The force of gravity is minimized because movements are done on a flat, slick surface, and so require little stability of the neck and extremities. Babies, children, and adults can learn these movement patterns to improve coordination, relieve bodily aches and pains, and begin to resolve learning disabilities.

Using the Belly Crawl to Enhance Locomotion

As a movement pattern, the belly crawl is actually a coordinated sequence of steps or "pieces." When children can smoothly do the belly crawl in position (as a stationary pattern), the pattern becomes a keystone of locomotion.

Step-by-step instructions for the stationary belly crawl are in Chapter Five, where it is explained as a tool for enhancing kinesthesia.

Below are instructions for using the belly crawl to enhance your child's locomotion. The instructions can be easily adapted for adults. Note that children under age five should not do the same-side pattern (homolateral) or cross-pattern belly crawl. Older children and adults will find these advanced patterns to be excellent tools for enhancing coordination and endurance.

For the belly crawl, all you need is a clean floor, patience, and some basic instructions. Dress your child in soft, comfortable clothing that covers the arms and legs, such as infant sleepers or sweatshirt and pants. The feet and hands should remain bare.

Dim light and a quiet room are important for minimizing distraction. The crawling space must be at least 16 feet long for children, over 30 feet for adults. The surface must be smooth and relatively clean: a vinyl floor is ideal.

Have your child lie face down. Turn the head so the ear, not the cheekbone, is on the surface. Arms should be bent at the elbows, with the palm of each hand flat on the surface next to the shoulder.

1. The two-arm belly crawl (basic pattern)

    *   Start each session by doing five to ten repetitions of each leg pattern, then five to ten repetitions adding the arms to each leg pattern, then turning the head and alternating sides. (These patterns are explained in detail in Chapter Five.)

    *   With both arms and one leg in the "up" position, pull with the arms and push with the foot to move the body forward. The hands should stop at shoulder level, with elbows against sides of the chest. Be sure the eye is following the hands' upward and downward motion. As the leg finishes pushing, continue the motion by rolling the leg in so toes touch as in the starting position. Then hold everything still and flat while turning the head to the opposite side and bringing the arms and leg up together in preparation for the next push-pull.

    *   Coach your child to perfect each piece of the pattern in a smooth, coordinated manner. Trying to move too quickly or cover too much

distance will only distract her attention from the precision of each piece of the pattern.

- Practice this pattern until it is perfectly smooth, automatic, and rhythmic. Build endurance to cover at least 500 feet at a session (adults can cover at least 1000 feet per session).

- After each session, take time to "put the body back together." Invite your child to curl up in your arms; older children and adults can curl up into the flexion position and roll back and forth, then side to side. Loop the arms under the knees to keep the knees tight to the chest.

2. The same-side belly crawl (homolateral pattern)

Children under age five should not do this pattern.

- Once your child has mastered the basic belly crawl using both arms together, practice the homolateral pattern (using the right arm with right leg, left arm with left leg).

- Begin the session with five to ten repetitions of basic crawl in place on each side, then alternating, then two or three lengths of the basic belly crawl pattern.

- When the head has turned to the right, reach forward with the right hand as the right leg comes up; bring arm and leg up together so arm is fully extended when leg is fully bent (abducted). Each push-pull brings the body forward, so the arm and leg return to the starting position. Then turn the head to the left side and repeat with left arm and left leg. Be sure the hand on the non-working side stays with the palm flat on the surface. If the hand is coming up on fingertips or flopping over (palm-side up), they are moving too far with their push-pull. The pulling hand should stop at eye-level.

- Practice this pattern until it is perfectly smooth, automatic, and rhythmic. Build endurance to cover about 1000 feet in a session.

3. The cross-pattern belly crawl

Children under age five should not do this pattern.

- Once your child has perfected the homolateral belly crawl pattern, practice the cross pattern.

- Begin the session with two or three lengths of basic crawl, five lengths of the homolateral crawl, and at least five cross-patterns on each side (in place) and alternating before starting to move.

- When the head has turned to the right, reach forward with the right hand as the left leg comes up; arm and leg come up together so arm is fully extended when leg is fully abducted. As they push-pull, the pattern will return the arm and leg to the starting position. Then turn the head to the left side and repeat with left hand and right leg.

- Practice this pattern until it is perfectly smooth, automatic, and rhythmic. Build endurance to cover at least 1000 feet in a session.

Contact: Reach, Grasp, and Release

Learning to sit, stand, and walk puts children in an upright position that frees their hands for the motor generalization of contact: reach, grasp, and release. Contact includes our ability to use our hands to grab, squish, point, push, pull, drop, and literally to be in touch with our surroundings. The hands become tools of exploration.

As the third motor generalization, contact requires a firm foundation of what has come before: kinesthesia, stable posture and maintenance of balance, and coordinated locomotion. Essential to the development of contact is differentiation, which begins at body's midline and progresses outward to the fingertips. The shoulders must be differentiated from the back, the arms from the shoulders, hands from arms, wrist from hands, fingers from palm of the hand, thumb from the fingers. Only with full differentiation will these extremities be able to work together to do the tasks of reaching, grasping, and releasing.

As a newborn, Chelsea's hands automatically close tightly around anything pressed in the palm of her hand. This is the **grasp reflex,** *with just the fingers clenching tightly anything in her hand.*

Since birth, Dylan has favored the fencing position (due to **the asymmetric tonic neck reflex)** *with his head turned toward his outstretched arm. Now four weeks old, Dylan fixes his gaze* *on his own hand or on the rattle or blanket grasped by that hand. Watching the movement of his hand has fueled his self-awareness and the realization that he can interact with the world.*

Bonnie's first attempt to reach for an object was a clumsy "swipe" that represented the beginning of a purposeful and useful ability. At three months, her head, neck, and back have stability enough that she can lie on her tummy, using her arms and clenched hands to support her body. With her body weight resting on her arms, she feels a different pressure on her upper body and discovers a change in muscle tone as she turns her head from side to side. This **rotation and differentiation** *of the shoulders prepares her learning to use the upper body in new ways.*

At four months, Brad loves to explore objects by putting them in his mouth. Reaching with his arms, he uses his hands like a rake, scratching things towards himself using his outstretched fingers. **Extending and flexing** *his arms and fingers repeatedly, he is continuing the process of differentiation.*

Five months old, Brenda lies on her back while holding things directly over her head where she can best see them. Her reach is more accurate than it was just weeks ago: now she uses her outstretched fingers to pat something she sees. This new-found **control of her hands** *is a natural outgrowth of differentiation and stability of her upper body.*

At seven months, Alex **creeps** *around the house on his hands and knees. His shoulders and arms now have enough strength to support his body. He often stops to get a closer look at something. Studying objects takes full concentration: he examines things visually, then looks away as he uses his hands or his mouth to explore the same objects.*

Nine-month old Lucia has just discovered how efficient her **index finger** *can be. She pushes food across her plate and pokes holes in her bowl of cereal and can sometimes work index finger and thumb together to pick things up.*

At eleven months, Sally uses her thumb and first two fingers fairly efficiently for **picking up** *all kinds of things. Now begins more specific exploration and manipulation.*

Learning to match visual perceptions with body movement is an essential part of the motor generalization of contact. As babies become aware of the sensation received through their hands, they watch their hands explore the world. This is hand-eye coordination, which forms the base for eye-hand coordination, especially important for writing. Only at age seven or eight will the eyes be able to work together to follow what is within arm's length. Until then, the eyes can only focus on work at least an arm's length away.

Working at the blackboard or on an easel is ideal for preschoolers, as their eyes can easily focus on what their hands are creating with their whole arm movements. When the eyes must focus together for precise eye-hand coordination at close range, at a coloring book, perhaps, or a notepad and pencil, young children can only see their work clearly if they turn their head to follow with one eye. If they do this type of work frequently before age seven, children learn to use one eye for close work, the other eye to see things at a distance, and won't develop normal binocular vision or depth perception. CN7.2

"As long ago as the turn of the century, famed American philosopher John Dewey quoted eye specialists in noting that children's eyes are made primarily for distant vision or for looking at large objects. To require the child to concentrate on near work or upon small objects for any length of time, he reasoned, would create undue nervous strain. He estimated that children should not be required to make these refined and cramped adjustments until about age 8. Otherwise, he noted, there would be a sad record of injured nervous systems and of muscular distortions.

"Throughout the years, many of the nation's leading child specialists have concurred with these findings."

(Raymond S. Moore and Dorothy N. Moore. *Better Late Than Early*. p. 69)

Enhancing Development of Contact

Creative hands-on activities help children learn to reach, grasp and release. Remember that learning happens from the inside out: the work of the arms and hands requires good sensation, accurate kinesthetic matching, and hours of practice. Here are some suggestions:

1. Use dry brushing to enhance tactile sensation of the hands. See the instructions in Chapter Five.

2. Use deep pressures to enhance proprioceptive sensation of the hands and arms. See the instructions in Chapter Five.

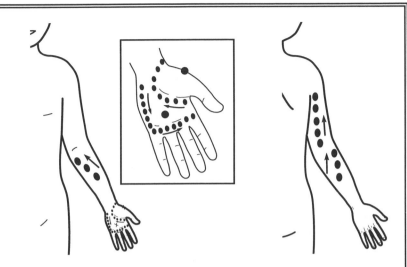

3. Watch how the hands work together. When your child is belly crawling, for example, make sure he uses the whole hand, not just the palms of the hands or the fingertips.

4. Encourage whole arm activities that enhance differentiation of the shoulders, arms, wrists, hands, fingers, and thumbs. Finger painting, drawing in flour or powder, and sandbox play also encourage children to watch their hands as they work. Emphasize large movements that use the whole arm: large circular motions (clockwise and counter clockwise), straight lines (forward and back, side to side, diagonal), and squiggly patterns.

5. Reinforce hand-eye coordination with activities that have the hands and eyes working together at arms length, not close-up. This includes painting at an easel, cutting out cookies, playing with soap suds, and finger plays. Hand-eye coordination also can be enhanced by putting a sticker on the back of the hand.

6. Provide activities to build the muscles of the fingers and hands, such as squishing clay, mud, or dough. Give small foods (raisins, cheese cubes, cereal circles, etc.) that can be best picked up using the "pincer" grasp.

7. Choose toys to enhance manipulation and contact, not toys that require precise dexterity. Good choices include stackable plastic rings, puppets, large blocks, books with thick pages, and vehicles with moving parts (such as firetrucks with ladders that go up and down, dump trucks that dump, bulldozers that scoop).

8. Don't encourage toddlers to use pencils, crayons, and scissors. Toddlers simply don't have the ability to handle them appropriately and will use inefficient ways of holding these small items. Bad habits are hard to break. School-age children who are unable to hold a pencil correctly are likely to have used pencils and crayons before their hands had the sensation and differentiation necessary for holding them properly.

Speech: Self-Expression and Interaction

Although other animals are capable of communicating, only humans use a symbolic language that is complex, stylized, and individualized. Speech gives us the ability to communicate about events and objects in other time periods and other places.

Children usually begin talking when they achieve upright posture, and as the cerebral cortex expands in its audio, visual, and spatial capabilities. Developing language requires postural stability, oral function, regulation of breathing, listening and hearing, speaking, and cognitive maturation. Speech development also reflects numerous emotional and social factors, including relationships with siblings, home and family setting, and childcare.

Recognizing speech as a motor generalization, we see different levels of speech (just as there are different levels of locomotion and contact) which develop sequentially over a period of time. Each level builds on the previous levels, gradually and efficiently leading a child to clear and effective speech.

Speech pathologist Edward Mysak identified four stages of pre-verbal vocalization as stepping stones in the developmental sequence of attaining language:

Crying is baby's first vocal communication with parents. This is his way of expressing hunger, pain, fear, discomfort, or frustration. Crying is a tool of communication throughout our lives.

Cooing includes gurgling, chuckling, snorting, and grunting. These reflexive sounds are baby's early expressions of pleasant feelings, and begin to be heard during baby's first four months. Some forms of cooing continue as part of our adult vocabulary.

Babble-lalling is the first stage of vocal play, and begins when babies are four to eight months old. Now there is more lip action, and some single-syllable sounds (ba, ka, gu, etc.). By about six months, baby can make most vowel sounds. Sitting changes the position of the Eustachian tube to allow more lip and teeth sounds.

Echoing begins when babies are eight to twelve months, as babies imitate the sounds made by others and the sounds they make themselves. By their first birthday, babies have a good repertoire of consonants (developed because the tongue develops back to front). Speech sounds change as baby spends more time sitting; sitting changes the position of the ribs and thorax, and so enables deeper breathing and better articulation. Sounds also change as babies get their first teeth and begin eating with spoons and cups. CN 7.3

These early sounds (crying, cooing, babbling, and lalling) are a child's first expressions of *lingua:* the sounds of speech which surround the child from the very beginning of life. Long before children can understand the meaning of these sounds, they become acquainted with the sounds of their parents, the home, the culture, and they begin to imitate these sounds in primitive ways. From the lingua, children develop language as their unique symbolic communication.

Language is a powerful tool for self-expression, and plays a life-long role in shaping our personality and attitudes. The words we say, even the words we think, reflect our subconscious, our beliefs, our expectations, and our future. Consider the child who says, "I'll never be able to ride a bike." Expressing his discouragement gives his negative feelings greater strength and power; when a child begins seeing himself as a failure, his enthusiasm for learning the skill wanes. How much better if the child instead says, "It's going to be fun to be able to ride a bike!" This message, even when coached, will build the child's positive feelings about his abilities and help him anticipate his expected achievement.

Or consider the parent who begins cleaning the garage by saying, "This won't be easy." Her child will begin envisioning a long day with one disgusting chore after another. The job would begin on a more positive note if Mom says, "I'll bet there are some real treasures hiding here among all this stuff," or "Let's bring the radio out here while we work," or "How about working for a couple of hours and then taking a milkshake break."

It is the parents' responsibility to teach and model language as they want their children to speak it. Positive, creative, empowering language is a tool for positive, creative, empowered lives. Here are some guidelines:

- *Be positive, truthful, and specific.* "I expect you to put away the toys before your bath" tells a child exactly what is expected and when. "I'm angry about the mess in the kitchen" explains your reaction much more accurately and lovingly than saying, "You make me so angry!"

- *Recognize that words direct action and choose words to reflect positive expectations.* Avoid self-defeating phrases and expressions of negative outcomes such as, "I'll never finish this report," "These shoes are killing me," "Don't be such a dummy!"

- *Use the correct pronoun.* Instead of "We're putting on socks" when you are dressing your son, it's more accurate to

say, "I'm putting socks on your feet."   Own your feelings.
Don't say, "This ice cream makes you cold" if what you
really mean is "This ice cream makes me cold."

- *Use language to speak your highest choices about your life.* "I am healthy." "I choose to be home tonight." "I enjoy being with you."
- *Avoid negative words.* "Don't spill your milk" inspires thoughts of spilled milk. Instead, use words that help your children see their own competence: "Carry your milk carefully."
- *Be committed to listening.* Listen with your heart, your mind, and your ears. CN7.4

Enhancing Development of Speech

Parents enhance development of speech by appreciating the sequenced human timeline for developing speech and recognizing the importance of using positive language with children.   Language development is enhanced when parents encourage and imitate the sounds babies make and respond enthusiastically as baby's repertoire of sounds expands. Children should never be punished for crying. Minimizing background noises allows children to focus their ears on spoken sounds.

For children with language disorders, there are no effective home-remedies to enhance speech development. It is most important that parents know when and how speech develops so they will recognize the need for intervention; problems will be minimized by getting help immediately. Therapists who are trained in early oral motor development (a speech therapist, occupational therapist, or physical therapist) can design appropriate intervention that is specific and personal.   Such therapy is "invasive," as the therapist may be touching the mouth, teeth, and tongue in ways that may be unpleasant and stressful. CN7.5

Delays in language development are often preceded by problems "in the background." These may include:

- Problems with sucking or eating: excessive drooling, inability to suck, poor tongue function, inability of lips to close properly. These are indications that the mouth and/or tongue has too much or too little sensation.
- Poor jaw function: the mouth hangs open or shuts tightly even when the child is relaxed.
- Poor breath control or uneven breathing.
- Never putting hands and feet in the mouth.
- No imitative sounds.
- Playing silently: the child doesn't make playtime noises (animal sounds, motor sounds, rumbling, screeching, etc.).
- Poor postural stability.
- Inadequate hearing and/or listening.
- Preoccupation with non-verbal learning that may indicate the child is avoiding speech development.

Self-parenting

Beth's second birthday began when she crawled in bed with Mommy and Daddy. Later Beth "helped" Mommy in the kitchen, played balloon tag with Dad, and accompanied him on a last-minute trip to the grocery store just before guests arrived.

Beth's parents had invited some friends and relatives over for cake and some simple games. As Adam watched his young daughter enjoy the festivities, he was mesmerized by her interactions with people and things in her environment: her delight at the candles on the cake, her playfulness with Grandpa, her curious approach to a music box, her grasp of a handful of sand, her simple descriptions of "big cake," "fuzzy bear," and "noisy mess!"

It seemed just days ago that she had been born yet Adam couldn't imagine life without her. How busy and wonderful the days had become with a two-year old in the house!

Although he loved his work, Adam was now always eager to get home for his daily playtime with Beth. A few months ago, Adam and Beth were completely contented with laptime at the end of the day. Now, they had an endless list of favorite "together-time" activities that included playing ball on the living room floor, reading stories together, "swimming" in the bathtub, and eating ice cream. Last Saturday, they spent most of the afternoon at the neighborhood park, swinging, sliding, and climbing through tunnels. And although she clearly loved both her parents, now there were times when Beth's fears could only be calmed by Adam's presence.

Adam was humbled by his relationship with his daughter. He knew he could never be as all-seeing and all-knowing as Beth believed he was. Yet through her eyes, he saw himself as honest, fun, and strong. Beth helped him remember that a loving embrace is the best way to ease stress and anxiety at the end of a long day, that lying on the floor feels good all over, and that every word has meaning and power. Just recently, in fact, Adam had noticed that his speech had become more specific and positive - an indirect result, perhaps, of teaching his daughter the importance of words. Even when the sink backed up, Adam heard himself say, "I can fix this!" instead of grumbling about the mess, the probable expense, and plumbing in general.

Sometimes Adam felt his two-year old daughter was actually the parent of his own inner child. As he watched and encouraged Beth through each developmental task, some part of Adam was simultaneously re-learning to walk, talk, and move more efficiently. Through her eyes, he was learning to love the child within himself. For his daughter, and with his daughter, Adam was re-discovering the joy of meaningful contact with the world and the joy of being human!

THE PERCEPTUAL-MOTOR STAGE
18 months - 4 years of age

CHAPTER EIGHT:
Systematic Exploration

Since their third birthday, the Larson twins – Nathan and Natalie –have learned to play like never before.

Nathan is the noisy one. He chugs and rumbles as he runs his cars along the lines on the floor. He roars and groans as he climbs on the furniture. He squeals as his tower of blocks falls over. Nathan is always busy – and always noisy.

Natalie keeps busy, too, but her favorite games are quieter and take more concentration. She loves the sandbox, where she pours, packs, dumps, and shovels sand. Sometimes she builds a city in the sand; sometimes she makes a variety of sandcakes and cookies. Natalie usually talks to herself as she plays; at naptime, she often "reads" her favorite books to her dolls and stuffed animals.

Both Nathan and Natalie love to help Mommy and Daddy. They can carry food to the table, put towels on the shelf, and poke seeds in the prepared soil of the family garden.

Their parents try not to compare the children's development. Until puberty, Nathan will follow a developmental timeline that is slower than his sister's. Nathan is less mature emotionally, has been slower to learn to talk, and isn't quite toilet trained. Natalie can run faster than Nathan, and is more interested in dressing herself. Nathan and Natalie seem to be happy to be who they are – and happy to discover something new about the world and about themselves everyday.

Matching Perceptions with Actions

Nathan and Natalie are learning by doing. Because their bodies move easily and automatically, they can pay attention to what's happening around them, using their bodies as their reference point for movement, position, space, and time. Their sensory systems provide information for perceiving the world. And as they match their perceptions with their body movements, they are expanding their matrix of possibility, energy, and safety to relate to the world in a most intimate way.

Matching perceptions to motor activity is the theme of this developmental stage, which spans the time from when children are eighteen months old until their fourth birthday. Named by Newell Kephart as *the perceptual-motor stage,* this is when children learn to accurately perceive the world so they can interact purposefully and meaningfully.

"When the child has developed a body of motor information he begins to match the perceptual information which he receives to this earlier motor information. In the early stages of such matching, motor activities play the lead role."

(Kephart. *The Slow Learner In The Classroom.* p. 233)

Remember that these developmental stages overlap: development doesn't happen steadily in all ages, and each individuals follows a unique developmental timeline. It takes years to learn to use our bodies and to relate to the world. Each new skill and each new perception must be checked against other skills and perceptions – reinforced through practice and experience – and integrated into our ever-growing understanding of ourselves and our surroundings.

When Nathan was first learning to walk, his movements were his only way of perceiving the world. Walking toward a chair that he wanted to explore, he stopped only when he bumped into the chair. In time, he learned to use his eyes to measure distance. Soon he learned to match visual perceptions with the position and movement of his body. With practice, he was able to stop at a precise distance from the chair.

As Nathan becomes more skilled at matching perceptions and movements, he will be able to use a greater variety of perceptions to direct his body even more accurately and purposefully in a greater variety of movements. When asked to "line up for lunch," for example, he will automatically assess perceptual data for positioning his body accurately in relation to other children. He will rely on visual and auditory information about the other children, as well as internal cues (including proprioception and vestibular sensation) about his body position and movement. And he will use his body as the reference point for measuring distance, direction, and position.

Children can't develop accurate and useful perceptual-motor matches if the perceptual data or the motor activity is unreliable:

- Kinesthesia must provide perfect matching of tactile sensations, movement/stability, and body position.

- Auditory and visual information must be accurate.

- Motor generalizations must be well-established so the body can move smoothly and automatically.

- The autonomic nervous system must maintain the body's well-being even under stressful circumstances.

   Marjean's skin is super-sensitive. Because her skin is constantly itching and burning, Marjean doesn't get other sensory information from her skin. In fact, her skin makes her so uncomfortable that she doesn't pay much attention to other perceptual information from her body.

   At age three, Marjean doesn't understand her body's internal messages about body position. She's always fidgety, so she's never quite sure of where she is – and visual and auditory information is often confusing. Her motor skills have also suffered, leaving Marjean poorly equipped for matching perceptions with motor activity.

Marjean's super-sensitive skin is just one example of a problem "in the background" which interferes with perceptual-motor development:

- Children may have visual impairments or hearing problems that affect their perceptions of the world.

- Some children have poor postural stability, so don't have reliable information about the position of their bodies.

- Other children can't walk smoothly, or are unable to use their hands efficiently. Because they must concentrate even to perform simple tasks, they don't notice what's happening around them.

- Many children face emotional stress that overwhelms their autonomic nervous system, putting them in a constant state of anxiety.

Systematic Exploration Uses
Perceptions, Actions, Repetition

Accurate perceptual-motor matching enables children to move freely into the larger world. If this matching process proves to be reliable, children realize it's much quicker to explore a chair with eyes and ears than by touching, grasping, and walking around it. Perceptions, they discover, are the most efficient and reliable way of getting information. Of course, they can always get a "second opinion" with hands-on, walk-around exploration.

At the beginning of the perceptual-motor stage (at about 18 months of age) children have the motor control and the perceptual-motor matching necessary for systematic exploration of their surroundings. Systematic exploration is sequenced but repetitious: each discovery is checked, integrated, practiced, and reinforced.

Marty was given a four-inch red plastic ball when he was just a baby. By the time he was three months old, he was happily exploring how a ball moves when it is touched. He often (but not always) could move the ball with a swing of his arms – and so he practiced his arm-swings thousands of times.

When Marty was five months old, he could bring the ball to his mouth, where he explored it with his sensitive tongue and lips. By his first birthday, he had learned to push, kick, and chase his red ball across the floor. He now had other balls too, and through hours of active play learned that some balls can be held with one hand, some bounce higher or roll faster than others. When he was eighteen months old, he received a set of blocks, and quickly compared his understanding of balls to his new toys: Could they bounce? Did they roll? How do they taste?

Systematic exploration often begins with simple random movements, such as a vague swing of the arm. With practice and repetition, the movement becomes automatic. Marty recognized a pattern of perceptual information that corresponds with the movement, including *tactile sensation* as his hand brushes against a blanket and *proprioceptive sensation* of muscle action. As he learned to control the movement, he began to explore new ways of using that movement – such as pushing the ball. With repetition, each new movement was reinforced by his perceptions, fueling a steady expansion of his understanding of his body, his abilities, and the world.

The developmental timeline ensures that each skill level provides a firm foundation for the next, never overloading the child's ability to organize and assimilate new information and skills. Every learning becomes quickly integrated to pave the way for the next learning, the next stage of development.

> *"The biological plan is a drive for knowledge as ability, not knowledge as information."*
> (Pearce. Magical Child. p. 113)

Body Awareness as Our Reference Point

Children understand space and time through relationships, as they learn to compare one thing with another. Physical activity and systematic exploration teach them that the world has no "absolutes" for understanding space and time. There is no absolute "big" – yet one thing is bigger than another. There is no universal "before" – yet children know that breakfast comes before lunch.

Children soon realize that their physical reality is the most reliable reference point. A healthy body awareness is their only "absolute" for understanding direction, position, and movement in space and time.

Body awareness involves three elements: body schema, body image, and body concept.

Body schema is the internal "roadmap" for operating the body. This roadmap begins to develop with prenatal movement patterns. As we grow, sensation, kinesthesia, motor generalizations, and perceptual-motor matching provide even more control of our bodies. Through activity, a child develops a body schema that includes his innate understanding of his center of gravity, how his body works, and the position of his body in space. He knows his body parts and is always aware of the position of those body parts. He knows how much space his body takes up, and how much space is needed for his body parts.

Body image is how the body appears to us. Intertwining emotions with sensation and movement patterns, this is our physical and emotional understanding of who we are. Body image incorporates body schema with an understanding of how others perceive us. How do I feel about my body? How do other people respond to me? Do people say I'm cute? fat? scrawny? plump? CN8.1

Body concept is our conscious understanding of who we are and how our bodies work. Body concept is more cognitive than body image and body schema: this is our thought-process for understanding, planning, and evaluating the functions of our bodies. A healthy, positive body concept requires on-going opportunities and encouragement for expanding our abilities. Negative experiences and discouraging messages can damage a growing body concept and intimidate efforts.

If Sandra is shamed for soiling her pants, she may understand her body functions as shameful.

If Brady believes daddy's teasing words about being clumsy, he may resist physical activity and may not coordinate his movements.

If Cassie is told that she is quick and graceful, she will have more fun at dance class – and be more enthusiastic and confident about learning and practicing each new step.

"Body awareness is intimately connected with the child's whole physical and emotional adjustment. Although all the child's experiences are reflected in his feelings about his body, movement education can be a highly effective way of influencing these feelings."
(Frostig. *Learning Problems In The Classroom.* p. 162)

Laterality and Directionality Develop From the Inside Out

With the body as our reference point, our understanding of direction begins internally. The symmetry of the body gives us two separate sides: two eyes, two ears, two hands, two feet, and so on. As babies, we move the two sides of the body together: we reach with both hands, kick both legs simultaneously – and so develop motor abilities on both sides of the body.

Our working knowledge of the two sides of our bodies begins with laterality: our internal awareness of the lateral (side to side) dimension of space. Babies begin developing laterality first by using the two sides of the body together, such as by propping themselves up with both arms so they can raise their heads. Soon they learn to use the sides of the body in opposition to do two different things: one side is holding (propping up the body) while the other side is moving (reaching and raking).

Body movement and position are important aspects of laterality. Laterality expands as babies learn to differentiate the parts of the body, and as they establish posture, balance, and stability against gravity. Laterality then gives children the internal awareness of the body's midline as the vertical line of reference for the two sides of the body, and the reference for judging distance, movement, and orientation in space.

The direct result of laterality is the emergence of left- or right-preference. *Preference* means just that: after using both sides together and in opposition, children begin to prefer one hand, foot, eye, and ear over the other. Preference becomes permanently established as *dominance* by age six or seven – but children must first experiment with using both sides of the body, then each side separately. Babies and toddlers often shift back and forth from bilateral to preference, and even shift from preferring one side to preferring the other.

When children begin feeding themselves, parents can encourage them to establish a preference by placing their eating utensils on the right side of the body (or the left side, if there is a strong genetic left-handedness in the family). Preference of the arms, legs, eyes, and ears should also be encouraged in dressing, playtime, and other everyday activities: putting the right stocking on first, holding the telephone to the right ear, and so forth. Parents should lead with one side of the body consistently without worrying about whether their child is becoming left- or right-handed. With healthy motor development and a stable environment, children will develop laterality, preference, and dominance appropriately.

> *"Many children with learning disorders will be found to have very limited motor responses. Such limitations are particularly apparent in areas of relationship to gravity, laterality, and overall coordination."*
> (Kephart. *Learning Disability: An Educational Adventure.* p. 83)

Combined with an accurate body awareness, our internal sense of laterality becomes the basis for perceiving direction in space, or *directionality.* Directionality is the external projection of laterality, using the body as the reference point for understanding above, beside, below, near, far, and other terms about where things are: "The cat is near my hand." "The hat is on my head." Once we can relate objects to the body, directionality enables us to relate the position of one object to another: "The cat is by the sofa." "The balloon is above the table."

As development of laterality and directionality become more complex, children become able to name right and left -- usually by about eight years of age. The highest level of this skill is automatic left-right directionality needed for reading. Laterality and directionality are the foundations for recognizing the difference between d and b, d and q, b and p, was and saw. This will be discussed more in Chapter Nine.

Perceptual-Motor Concepts Translate Motor Actions to Mental Actions

The key to perceptual-motor development is the ability to translate motor action into mental action: to connect what I'm doing with what I'm thinking. Matching movement with perception gives children information about relationships between themselves and the objects in their world, and expands their ability to perceive and interact with the environment.

As adults, our ability to accurately perceive our environment is so automatic that we give little thought to how it develops. Let's look at five of the key concepts of translating motor action into mental action.

- Constructive form
- Form constancy
- Object figure-ground
- Order and direction in space
- Perceptual-motor match

Constructive form means that objects are made of many parts. A take-apart toy animal, for example, might have legs, tail, ears, and nose that snap on and off. Taking the toy apart helps children learn what an animal is: this is how children learn constructive form. Putting things together is cognitive skill which involves perceptual-motor abilities and comes much later. It's a parent's job to provide toys that come apart easily into manageable pieces – and to be willing to put the

toy back together again and again so the child can repeatedly take it apart.

Form constancy means that objects continue to exist even when they are out of sight. Jean Piaget observed that until babies are six to eight months old, they believe that objects don't exist unless they can be seen. They won't look for the ball once it is out of sight; when the ball reappears, they greet it as a completely new object. Even mommy and daddy may be treated like strangers after a few days' absence. Only gradually can children accept the constant existence of an object or a person.

Parents can use a variety of perceptual-motor games to reinforce form constancy: peek-a-boo, simple versions of hide-and-seek with people and objects, and finger plays such as "Where is Thumbkin."

Object figure-ground means distinguishing an object as separate from others in a group, such as when baby points at sister among a group of children, grasps a favorite cup off the shelf, eats the banana out of the fruit salad. To visually identify an object in a group, children must be able to move their eyes systematically from object to object. Object identification is confirmed by sounds, taste, smell, and other sensory channels.

Parents help their children recognize object figure-ground relationships at storytime ("Point to the elephant ... Where is the bunny?"), when shopping ("We'll buy the red socks"), when waiting ("Tell me when you see Mommy's car"), and when offering a selection of toys or foods from which to choose.

Order and direction in space is recognized as children learn to perceive the position of objects in relation to themselves. The blanket is pulled close under baby's chin. The ball rolls from daddy to baby and back again. Blocks are lined up in a row that begins directly in front of the child. These perceptions are confirmed by actions: tactile information matches visual perceptions; auditory clues are confirmed by the eyes; body movement follows visual direction.

Children's recognition of the position of objects in space soon evolves to the next dimension,

as children learn to perceive order and direction in time. With their present position as the base point, they begin to recognize first and last, now and later, before and after. Daily routines will reinforce this understanding of order in time: for example, bedtime routine might include brushing teeth, then putting on pajamas, reading a story, prayers, and finally good night kisses. Altering this routine even slightly may upset children's understanding of order and direction in space and time.

Parents help children experience order and direction in their world by respecting children's need for routine and stability. Daily routines are especially important at wake-up time, mealtime, when dressing, and at bedtime. Playtime also offers numerous opportunities to experience and discuss order and direction: by positioning objects in front of, over, and next to others; rolling a ball back and forth; doing things first, next, and last.

The perceptual-motor match is a child's first effective "processing" of information. By matching perceptual information with motor data, children connect their perceptions of the world with their interior reality. When a child sees a ball, for example, she immediately knows how it will feel against her hand. Her hand moves accurately and automatically to pick the ball up and roll it across the floor. Even the sound of the ball matches her  expectations, and is "in sync" with her visual, tactile, and motor perceptions.

Children develop confidence in perceptions that correspond reliably and accurately with one another – and that prove to be reliable for directing the body. As they grow, children will rely less on hands-on exploration, and instead use visual, auditory, and other perceptual information. Reliable and automatic perceptual information allow them to do one thing while thinking about another. They also then can make mental connections between physical realities and possibilities. In other words, they start to pretend, creating their own world of make-believe.

> "As their eyes begin to lead, the hand follows along to confirm the result.
> If trouble or confusion occurs, the child returns to the use of the hand for
> verification of the information. Thus the transition from a motor to a visual
> match or motor to auditory match occurs."
> (Chaney and Miles. *Remediating Learning Problems.* p. 103)

Television disrupts the perceptual-motor match. The dazzling auditory and visual images of television offer nothing for children's other perceptual channels. Televised images can't be confirmed with hands-on exploration, so kids can't match tactile with television's auditory and visual messages. Even the auditory and visual images are limited by the screen and the editors. Watching television hour after hour, children may develop a perceptual world that is completely separate from their motor experience. In effect, they live in two unconnected worlds: an audio-visual world rich with knowledge, and a motor world of poor physical skills. Not only has television robbed them of time they should be spending in active play, it also has taught them that their eyes and ears aren't in sync with their tactile, proprioceptive, vestibular, and other sensory channels. This is why some kids may be able to talk about their bodies and give detailed descriptions of physical skills that they are completely unable to perform. What they need is the opportunity and encouragement to learn from the inside out – using all channels of perception to explore and experience the world!

Social Growth and Body Care

By age three, Nathan and Natalie are learning to take care of themselves. With pull-on clothing (elastic waistbands, wide necklines, few buttons, etc.) they can dress themselves with just a little help. They rarely wear diapers any more (though Nathan more often than Natalie), and usually use the toilet by themselves. And they are enthusiastic participants in the basic routines of self-care, such as brushing teeth after meals and before bed, putting on a coat when going outside in the cold, and washing hands before and after meals.

Each night before dinner, they stand at the bathroom sink with Daddy to wash hands together. They laugh as they rub bubbles over one another's hands. As they dry their hands (each person using their own bright colored towel), they often sing or chant a nursery rhyme together, then hang their towels side by side on the hooks near the sink.

*With Daddy's patient coaching and side-by-side instruction,
they are learning to do for themselves what their most trusted
caregivers have done for them: to take care of their bodies. And
so their lessons in self-care are intertwined with lessons in
getting along with others – and feeling good about themselves.*

During the perceptual-motor stage, children's interactions with
the world expand to include relationships with an increasing
number of people. At the same time, children become more
aware of their bodily functions and physical needs, and assert
their independence in taking care of their bodies.

Children's social skills also develop from the inside out. Their
skills for relating to other people are rooted in the mother-child
bonds that developed prenatally, when all the child's needs
(physical, emotional, and spiritual) must be fully and automatically met by the mother. Over time, baby's matrix gradually
expands to include father, then siblings and grandparents, then
other people. If baby's needs are fully met by her first caregivers,
she develops confidence in herself and the world. Her ability to
take care of herself and to interact with others will reflect the care
and interactions she has experienced since conception.

This matrix expands even more when children learn to care
for their bodies, and they move from total dependence on others
to inter-dependence and independence. That's why it's so
important that lessons in self-care be grounded in secure
relationships with primary caregivers (the parents). As we teach
children to use the toilet, bathe, comb their hair, and dress
themselves, we are giving them the skills for moving into the
larger world by themselves, and for relating to the world in
positive ways.

Self-care lessons must correlate with the child's physical,
emotional, and intellectual development. Each self-care task
requires specific physical abilities and a particular sequence. To
wash your hands, for example, you first turn the faucet handles in
a specific direction and rinse your hands under the running water.
Then you rub soap between your hands, place the soap in soap
dish, scrub your hands with the bubbly soap lather, rinse your
hands, turn off the water, grasp the towel, dry your hands, and
hang the towel properly on the towel rod.

For this sequence, a tight grasp may be necessary to turn the
faucet handles, and children must know which direction the
handles must be turned. Quick responses may be needed to

handle the slippery soap. The hands must work together and
separately as they rinse, work the soap into a lather, and use the
towel. In addition, there may be lights to be turned on and off,
and a step-stool to place in front of the sink. And what do you do
if there's no soap? If the water is too hot or too cold? If the
towel gets wet? And how do you wash your face?

Self-care skills are more complex than most parents realize.
That's why children learn best from good modeling and positive
coaching. Here are some tips:

- *The way we care for ourselves reflects how we care about
  ourselves.* Be loving. Remember that you are teaching your
  child to take care of himself because you care about him:
  your goal is to give him the skills and confidence for greater
  independence and freedom – not to free yourself of the
  "hassles" of taking care of him. Respect his needs, his
  timeline, his abilities.

- *Body care is complex.* Children need specific instructions,
  step-by-step lessons, and good role models to learn the
  sequence of body care tasks. Be patient. Children won't
  learn these skills the first time they are taught. Coach and
  remind children gently and repeatedly.

- *Children learn when they are ready.* Parents who try to
  toilet-train their children too soon will find that they have
  trained themselves, not their children: they may be able to
  "read" their child's body language well enough to rush their
  child to the toilet long before the child has internal control
  of his bladder and a desire to use the toilet. Every aspect of
  body care and personal hygiene requires specific physical,
  mental, and emotional abilities. Expecting too much too
  soon is apt to frustrate parents and children. What's more,
  without the skills to do things right, children may
  compensate in ways that are inefficient and hard to correct,
  and may impair future learning.

- *Use positive language as you teach body care skills.*
  Demonstrating, modeling, and coaching children in these
  skills communicates attitudes about the body, self-esteem,
  and relationships. Yet because body care skills are complex
  – and because many parents aren't comfortable talking about
  their bodies – children often hear confusing messages that
  interfere with their abilities to take care of themselves and
  damage healthy body awareness.

• *Use correct names for body parts.* Children need to know that a penis isn't a "wienie," the vagina isn't "that place down there." They need to hear that their bodies are good, strong, and need care. They can't afford to hear messages of shame ("Why can't you stay dry like a big boy?"), disgust ("Don't touch yourself there!"), or guilt ("Won't you ever learn?" "You ought to know by now!").

"Who does not know that to teach a child to feed himself, to wash and dress himself, is a much more tedious and difficult work, calling for infinitely greater patience than feeding, washing and dressing the child one's self?"

(Montessori. *The Montessori Method.* p. 97-98)

Social Growth and Play

As children become more social, their playmates and peers begin to define their matrix -- that is, the energy, possibility, and safety which shape their lives. Playing with other children becomes a laboratory for relationships.

For infants, rolling a ball across the floor, and playing peek-a-boo and other games provide a fun structure for interactions with the world and primary caregivers. Small children first play "parallel" to others: playing side-by-side, each is absorbed in her own activities. Play gradually becomes more cooperative, and children learn to take turns, share, give, and receive. Fantasy or "just pretend" is a strong theme to children's play between the ages of two and five, intertwining imitation and imagination. Children will pretend to sleep, to fix a meal, to read a book, to care for a doll, to drive a truck, to be an animal. Through their fantasies, children experience the world in new ways and must expand their social interactions accordingly.

At age three, Nathan and Natalie often enjoy parallel play: she may pretend she is a mouse while he operates a steam shovel. Their play becomes more cooperative if Natalie brings a dump truck to haul away the sand Nathan is scooping with his shovel. But conflict may develop if their fantasies conflict, if Nathan scoops up the mountain Natalie has been building, or if Natalie's truck sets off on a high-speed chase across Nathan's roadway.

In fact, quarreling and competitive behavior are indications that children are becoming more socially aware: they recognize the validity of their playmates, and are asserting themselves in their social interactions. If they don't have confidence in themselves, they won't be able to interact with other people in appropriate ways. How can children be attentive to other people's needs if they are not sure that their own physical, mental, emotional, and spiritual needs will be met?

Second-Line Trauma

During this time of tremendous physical growth, a child is most vulnerable to traumas that upset his emotional balance and personality. As explained in Chapter Three, these are known as *second-line traumas,* for they impact development of the second level of the brain, which is responsible for emotions and personality.

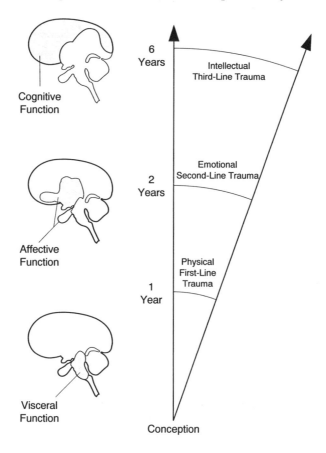

Brain researcher Paul MacLean describes the brain as having three independent but interrelated parts:

The first level is *the visceral brain,* which regulates the function of the internal organs: breathing, digestion, circulation, and other survival functions. This is the brain's first operational center, and receives the impact of the earliest traumas. First-line traumas are discussed in Chapter Three.

The second level is *the feeling brain,* or the limbic system. Excitement, pleasure, anger, shame, and frustration are experienced – or suppressed – at this level. Our physical body becomes the outlet for expressing emotional feelings through tears and smiles – or suppressing feelings and storing emotions as muscle tension. Through these emotional-physical experiences we develop personality characteristics such as independence/ dependence, ambition/ lethargy, and decisiveness/indecisiveness.

The third level is *the neocortex, or the thinking brain.* This system empowers -- or handicaps - our language, memory, reasoning, planning, logic, and problem-solving skills. Third-line traumas are discussed in Chapter Nine.

"The earlier a child masters something, the more deeply it becomes imprinted and the more certain he is of success for the rest of his life. That is why, conversely, negative messages and experiences are so difficult to unlearn."
(Miller. *The Untouched Key.* pp. 10-11)

The three levels of the brain work together to maintain the equilibrium of the whole brain. When that equilibrium is shaken by pain and trauma, the three independent systems respond as well as possible at that moment in time. But because the three levels of the brain develop sequentially, the impact of the childhood pain and trauma will damage the most vulnerable area of the brain: the level presently under development.

Damage from first-line traumas (experienced prenatally, during birth, or during the first year of life) affects survival systems. Asthma, skin rashes, colic, and food allergies can often be traced to first-line trauma.

Second-line traumas are experienced during early childhood, as the brain is developing its sensitive limbic system. Second-line traumas are also caused by an "overflow" of pain from first-line traumas: the physical distress to the survival systems "overflows" into the emotional development of the brain's second level. Second-line traumas will, in turn, create a shaky foundation for third-level development – and increase the risk of learning disabilities and other cognitive dysfunctions. The second level of the brain develops as children are learning and practicing the motor generalizations, movement patterns, motor planning, and sensory/perceptual abilities for relating to the world. At the same time – and through physical activity – emotions and personality are forming *from the inside out.* Children's physical reality at the deepest level is the seed-bed for understanding and expressing happiness, enthusiasm, rage, excitement, and all other emotions. Thus emotions and muscles become interconnected: the emotional impact of physical experiences is stored in the muscle tone and the body wall. As adults, persistent muscle tension can often be traced back to emotional stress from an experience of early childhood, when memory of a second-line trauma was stored in the muscle wall. Decades later, that same pain resurfaces in response to specific emotional or physical experiences. CN8.2

A first-line trauma is usually lurking in the background of second-line traumas: interruptions to bonding and other unmet survival needs of infancy, physical abuse to the mother, an unwanted pregnancy, a difficult birth, or some other trauma that disturbed development at its earliest stages.

During this time frame (usually between ages two-and-half

"Criminal traits have been traced all the way back to infant behavior patterns, such as hyperactivity and unusual fussiness ... which make it harder for a mother to bond with her baby."
(Magid and McKelvey. High Risk: Children Without A Conscience. p. 35)

---

and four), many children remember and talk about their birth experience. Their newly developed verbal abilities become a natural outlet for the physical memories of what most likely was the most dramatic experience they've had: their birth. When parents are open and encouraging to these discussions, they may enable children to release first-level trauma through verbalization. Prenatal and birth experiences may also be expressed through children's physical activity, such as climbing through tunnels (the birth canal), swimming in the bathtub (the womb), and building forts (the womb). CN8.3

Early childhood should be a time for developing positive and healthy ways of relating to an ever-expanding world. These developmental needs are sabotaged by second-line traumas. If children are overwhelmed by stress, traumatized by abuse, neglected, or abandoned, their emotional and physical needs are not being met. The hunger for fulfillment won't go away with time and maturity: unmet needs continue to disrupt development, crippling emotional health and setting an unstable foundation for cognitive growth and stability.

Not all children who are neglected, abused, abandoned, or otherwise traumatized become dysfunctional. The difference is the opportunity to express one's feelings about the negative experience, and to build emotional stability beyond the trauma. Nor is the impact of second-line traumas always obvious. Because first- and second-line traumas occur before we have a good command of language, the pain is stored non-verbally. Resolving these traumas must also be done non-verbally: we won't recover just by talking about it. What's needed is specific, caring, and professional help – and a personal commitment to resolving the wounds of childhood. Swiss psychotherapist Alice Miller notes that a single caring person can empower a child to rise above trauma: "a sympathetic and helpful witness who confirmed the child's perceptions, thus making it possible for him to recognize that he had been wronged." (Alice Miller. *The Untouched Key.* p. 50)

Self-parenting

Donna knew she was doing a good job parenting her three-year old twins, Natalie and Nathan. But some unsettling force seemed to be working within her, as though trying to keep her from loving her children too much. She remembered her own childhood as a happy time. She never doubted that her parents loved her: although they rarely expressed their affection with hugs and kisses, they showed their love by providing her with a stable family life, a clean home, and plenty of food, clothing, toys, and plenty of "extras."

Donna was in kindergarten when she learned that she had been adopted two weeks after she was born. She had been born to a distraught teenager who lived in a church-related institution during her pregnancy. Although she had never felt shame about being adopted, she sometimes felt haunted by her unknown earliest experiences.

When Donna was pregnant with Nathan and Natalie, she was

amazed at the swirl of thoughts and emotions that she experienced. Her instinctive response to her growing belly had been embarrassment and shame. Soon she got caught up in her husband's enthusiasm about the babies and pushed any negative thoughts out of her mind.

Each stage of pregnancy, birth, and parenting brought new thoughts and feelings – and new questions about her own first weeks of life. For the first time, she allowed herself to wonder if her birth mother had caressed her before she was born... if the caregivers in the institution had cuddled her before she was adopted... how her adoptive parents had greeted her. Sometimes she longed to be held, cuddled, and loved.

Now that the twins were older, Donna was often overwhelmed by the intensity of their feelings. They could bounce from hilarity to fury in the blink of an eye; could pound their feet in frustration, squeal with delight, and jump with enthusiasm. Donna couldn't remember ever having such exuberance about her feelings — even as a child. It was such a quiet household, she remembered: feelings weren't to be expressed.

Admitting that she may be jealous of her children's freedom to express themselves – and sure that she wanted to do her best as their mother – Donna registered for a workshop designed to help parents overcome the traumas of their own childhood. Through that course, she soon realized how little she knew about her emotions.

Memories began to surface: a birthday party where she had been shamed for crying, her loneliness at dinnertime when she was expected to keep quiet, her fears after a car accident when her mother was too busy to listen to her. Donna soon recognized that food had become her ally: through compulsive overeating she had tried to fill the emptiness she felt deep within her, and to nurture herself in ways no one ever had.

As time passed, Donna's intrigue with her early memories continued. A therapy center offered a course on the effects of the birth experience, where Donna physically and emotionally relived her own birth – and the abandonment she felt when she had been taken from her mother just moments later. That abandonment continued as emotional abandonment by her adoptive parents. Donna recognized that same abandonment as the "unsettling force" at work to undercut her closeness with her young children. She knew she may never know the full impact of the childhood traumas, but promised to continue the physical and emotional work of restoring wholeness in her life – knowing that it's never too late.

THE PERCEPTUAL STAGE OF DEVELOPMENT
3 1/2 years - 7 years

CHAPTER NINE:
Ready for Action

As she skipped down the block towards Hawthorne Elementary School on her first day of first grade, Candace was excited. Her brand-new bookbag was heavy with its load of pencils, crayons, notepads, and her own scissors -- all new, of course. Her lunch money was in her pocket, and knowing she would be buying her own lunch at school made Candace feel very grown-up.

The teacher greeted each student at the door and helped them find their nametags and their desks. A few minutes later, everyone was busily playing in one of the classroom's activity centers.

After school, Candace was eager to tell Mommy all about her day. She told about the story they read and the game they played at recess, the balloons they decorated and the cake they had for lunch. She told about funny John who wiggled around a lot, and about the "big, fat boy who acted like a baby." Candace had helped a "real quiet girl" cut out her nametag and a boy to pick up his crayons ("he dropped the whole box!").

"School is fun!" Candace said at dinner that night. "It was easy!"

The first day of first grade was easy for Candace because she was ready. Although she was a little anxious about the new experience, she had confidence in herself and her abilities. Going to school all day was an exciting new challenge.

Candace's confidence was rooted in her physical abilities. Every movement she made confirmed that her body worked the way it should, and that she could rely on her body to do what she wanted it to do. The past six years had been a time of experimentation and practice for Candace: she had learned to use a variety of perceptions efficiently and appropriately. By age six, she had confidence that her body would tell her about the world and allow her to function and interact in the world.

Perceiving the World

This budding reliance on perception marks the beginning of *the perceptual stage of development* (from age three-and-a-half to age seven). This stage is the bridge between the perceptual-motor stage, when motor activity is used to confirm sensory perceptions, and cognitive development, when children's thought processes are no longer dependent on sensory or motor information.

Perception is the process for making meaning out of sensation, and is the mental process linking sensation and thought. Percepts come through numerous sensory channels, including the skin, eyes, ears, nose, movement, posture, and balance. A toy, for example, is perceived for its size (larger than a banana, smaller than my bed); color (red, but not as red as my coat); weight (heavier than my toy tractor); and function (wheels that turn, doors that open and close, a horn that honks). These characteristics (or percepts) provide important information for recognizing the toy as a truck and knowing how to interact or play with this object.

Perception is immediate, complete, and unanalytical. Through perception, sensory information is automatically processed to create a complete and unquestioned picture. Although it's rarely examined as a complex skill, perception requires a reliable foundation of sensation, kinesthetic matching, physical stability, and motor planning. For that reason, it's no surprise that the perceptual stage begins when children are just able to walk easily. Once they can move comfortably in the upright position they begin to fully explore the expansive and exciting world around them. Because their bodies work automatically, their awareness moves beyond their inner reality. Sight, smell, sound, and other sensory impressions provide new information about the "outside world."

"All perception and sensation take place on a background of muscular activity. And although we are unaware of it, this activity is most strictly shaped by gravity."
(M. Feldenkrais. *Body and Mature Behavior*. p. 79)

Perception has been important in the two previous developmental stages. First, in the motor-perceptual stage, baby receives information about the world (i.e. percepts) through movement. During the perceptual-motor stage (beginning at 18 months of age), perceptions are confirmed with hands-on exploration and activity. Children move into the perceptual stage as they learn to process sensory information more efficiently, without needing to confirm perceptions with movement. The brain automatically and instantly integrates information from the eyes, ears, skin, and other sensory channels. Each perception is compared and related to other perceptions; looking and listening become the child's primary channels for understanding the world.

Perception involves four steps:

- The initial registration or orientation to what is happening. Sam notices that the cat is sitting on the table. The cat "catches his attention"; his attention span is long enough to perceive the cat.

- An emotional involvement with the object. Sam's curiosity about the cat compels him to look, listen, and pay attention. Watching the cat becomes important to Sam. The emotional involvement reflects survival relevance (hunger, fear, fatigue) and/or emotional relevance (curiosity, anger, pleasure).

- Association with past experience. If Sam enjoys cuddling his cat, his perception of the cat will be quite different than if the cat has scratched or frightened him in the past.

- Some motor response, either verbal or movement, verifying that the perception has taken place.

Completing Motor Generalizations:
Receipt and Propulsion

The automatic processing of the perceptual stage is important for developing *receipt and propulsion,* the last of the five motor generalizations. Receipt and propulsion are at the highest level of all the motor generalizations, and the most interactive.

Receipt and propulsion involve more than just learning to catch and throw. In receipt, we respond to (or receive) objects moving towards us and must orient ourselves in relationship to something moving through space. In propulsion, we make something move away from ourselves; we propel objects by batting, throwing, pushing, and pulling. Receipt and propulsion require that the eyes, hands, and feet are coordinated; that the two hands work together; that children can move efficiently in space and time. Children quickly and easily learn receipt and propulsion when the other motor generalizations are well-established:

Posture and maintenance of balance give head-to-toe stability necessary for automatically moving our bodies into the most efficient position for interacting with the moving object. In other words, the body is the stable reference point children need for relating to an unstable (moving) object.

"We cannot perceive unless we are aware of the attitude and orientation of the body."
(M. Feldenkrais. *Body and Mature Behavior.* p. 79)

Locomotion allows children to move easily from one place to another. Running, walking, and stopping are automatic, coordinated, and efficient movements that place the body in the right place at exactly the right moment.

Contact enables hands to reach, grasp, and release the object. The hands are in position: fingers, wrist, and hand will work together to do exactly what they are expected to do.

Speech allows children to respond and interact verbally during motor activity and is especially important for the highly interactive motor generalization of receipt and propulsion. Children must be able to talk about what's happening ("Here it comes!"), follow directions and give instructions ("Move that way!), and communicate difficulties ("I dropped it!").

If children have established all other motor generalizations by the time they are school-age, the skills of receipt and propulsion will come easily. But when the early motor generalizations are not smooth and automatic, children don't have the background for efficient and appropriate response to moving objects. They will have trouble learning to catch, throw, bat, and kick. They duck and cover their faces when the ball comes towards them (protective survival response to stress). They learn to avoid any interaction with moving objects and become sideline observers, not active players.

Some children just need more time to learn receipt and propulsion; their physical development may be slower than other children their age. Some need a more relaxed opportunity to practice these skills (remember that kids learn best when they are encouraged, not pushed, to learn something new). Some children need more active intervention in establishing the earlier motor generalizations (check the index for suggestions on enhancing posture and maintenance of balance, locomotion, contact, and speech).

Besides providing a firm foundation of previous motor generalizations, parents can enhance receipt and propulsion by: CN9.1

- Rolling objects back and forth across the floor with baby.
- Batting beach balls and balloons back and forth with toddlers in a slow-moving game of catch.
- Playing fun games and exercises such as those described in *T.S.K.H.(Tickle Snug Kiss Hug)*, David Gallihue's *Motor Development and Movement Experiences for Young Children,* and recorded movement-music programs by Hap Palmer.

Readiness:
When Kids Are Ready for the Challenges of School

The classroom is abuzz with activity as the students work on their Halloween mobiles; black cats, ghosts, scarecrows, and pumpkins are to be assembled and hung by string from a wooden dowel.

Candace unconsciously bites her tongue as she concentrates on gluing the bat's wings. Her excitement grows as she finishes each piece of her mobile. Behind Candace, Tom works quietly but awkwardly at the project. No matter how hard he tries, he can't make his crayons color within the lines. Tom is the biggest child in the class but in many ways seems the youngest. He doesn't speak clearly, often forgets to zip his pants after using the bathroom, and can barely write his name. He's already known as "a pleasant boy but a little slow."

Andrea is the smallest child in the class. She, too, seems younger than most of the other children and usually works and plays alone. The classroom is too noisy for her; she sometimes jumps at the sudden sound of a book dropping or another child's laughter. Maybe that's why she so often has trouble completing her work. Now, when most of her classmates are nearly done with their mobiles, Andrea's is still a jumble of pieces. Her scarecrow is missing his hat, she forgot to color the pumpkin's face before attaching it to the string, and she can't find the ghost she cut out a few minutes ago.

John's desk is next to Candace's, but he is rarely there. He dashes from one desk to another, to "borrow" someone's glue, offer advice, tell a story, or just make a nuisance of himself.

Although Keith has been quietly sitting at his desk, he hasn't made much progress on his mobile. His crayons break every time he uses them and he keeps dropping pieces of paper on the floor. He's never been able to make his scissors cut right so nothing looks at all the way it should. He knows what he is supposed to be doing and he knows he won't be able to do it. So he just slumps down in his chair and idly plays with a crayon.

Even simple craft projects are difficult for Tom, Andrea, John, and Keith. These children, and thousands like them in classrooms everywhere, don't have the skills necessary for schoolwork. Because they have difficulty with basic activities, they are learning the skills of compensation that allow them to avoid what they are unable to do.

When children are fully ready to come to school and learn, their bodies, minds, emotions, and spirits are adequately developed for the demands of the classroom. They are challenged by new experiences, and have the confidence, skills, and maturity to handle tasks appropriate for their age. If children aren't developmentally ready for school, they can't succeed in school. It's no wonder that school classrooms are filled with children with "behavior problems" and "learning disabilities"!

A child's chronological age is, unfortunately, the most commonly used standard for admittance to school and public school districts usually establish "cut-off birth dates." Yet, it is no secret that boys mature more slowly than girls and that each child's developmental timeline is unique.

Tom, for example, does not have the maturity for first grade work. Clumsiness, babyish speech, and a short attention span are signs that his body, mind, and emotions are not developed as well as his classmates. Because he is big for his age, people expect him to be capable. In truth, Tom has poor body awareness and inadequate muscle tone. Unless he is given more time to develop, the expectations of what he should be able to achieve will soon overwhelm him: he may become known as a social misfit, an academic failure, a clumsy fat kid.

Because Andrea is so small, her immaturity is more obvious. Her body size and physical abilities are a full year behind her classmates. To her mother, Andrea's emotional balance has never seemed normal; even as an infant, she was "jumpy" and easily startled. Her premature birth was a first-line trauma which has overwhelmed her survival system; she desperately needs integrated therapy to help her learn trust and confidence "from the inside out."

A simple way to evaluate Tom and Andrea's level of maturity (their developmental age) is to look at their teeth. Studies have confirmed that children whose teething is behind their chronological age are more likely to have difficulty in school. Children with advanced teething tend to be advanced in behavioral maturity. Although there are exceptions, parents and teachers have reason to question a child's readiness when his/her teething schedule is significantly different than this norm. CN9.2

Because readiness involves more than developmental maturity, assessment of perception and motor skills is the best tool for predicting how a child will perform in the classroom. Such assessment also will help parents, teachers, and therapists position children for success in school by uncovering problems in the background of present academic difficulties.

John is allergic to glue, paste, and other basic school supplies. He also has a highly sensitive sense of smell. Every breath John takes disturbs his survival system. Because he has never developed fine motor skills or even midline stability, John doesn't know how to sit still. He continues to disrupt the class and he learns and accomplishes little himself.

Keith's posture is the key to understanding why he has so much trouble with simple activities: he stands in the typical fatigue posture, with knees locked back, tummy out, shoulders slumped, head forward. His body has poor stability and poor kinesthesia. Keith's mind is so busy running his body that he can't concentrate on learning.

"No child sets out in life to be a failure, a retardee, a drop-out, or a juvenile delinquent. He learns to be one... by being literally forced to become one because of his inability to adjust himself to the learning stimuli presented to him in school."
(Louise Bates Ames. *Is Your Child In The Wrong Grade?* p. 9)

Screening for Integrated Motor Skills

As an occupational therapist specializing in children's development, Margot Heiniger developed the *Integrated Motor Activities Screening* in 1980 as an outgrowth of a project on early prevention of school failure. Field-tested and evaluated by scores of teachers and therapists, the *IMAS* provides highly accurate insights into readiness for school and is an effective tool for identifying children who are likely to have learning disabilities. The *IMAS* examines eight characteristics of readiness: CN9.3

Eye control

Eye, hand, and foot preference

Body awareness

Posture, muscle tone, and movement patterns

Appropriate behavior

Auditory-visual-motor discrimination and sequencing

Eye-hand coordination

Gross motor control

- *Eye control:* Children's eyes should be able to follow the movement of objects horizontally and vertically without moving their heads. This is important for following a line of text when reading, adding columns of numbers, copying material, and performing numerous physical tasks.

- *Eye, hand, and foot preference:* By their fourth birthday, most children consistently prefer either the right or the left eye, hand, and foot. Children are more likely to develop mixed preferences if they haven't adequately differentiated the parts of their bodies or haven't developed internal laterality. This is more common among children who, as infants, spent too little time belly crawling, or who were propped in a vertical position (such as in a baby walkers or jumpseat) before their bodies were stable. Lack of preference, therefore, may indicate lack of laterality, differentiation, and/or stability.

- *Body awareness:* Children should be able to locate and name their nose, ears, chin, shoulders, and other parts of their bodies. Although there is little correlation between body awareness and school success, children must know the location of their body parts in order to use them automatically. A child who holds onto other children, runs a hand along the wall while walking, or frequently bumps into others may be demonstrating a lack of body awareness.

- *Posture, muscle tone, and movement patterns:* When a child's body is properly aligned, the "segments" of the body make a perfect vertical column; an imaginary straight line could be drawn through the child's ankle, knee, hip, shoulder, and head. If one segment is out of line, it is because other segments must compensate for distortions in the child's kinesthesia, muscle tone, and movement.

- *Appropriate behavior:* School-age children can be expected to be sometimes distractable, restless, and talkative. Their attention span is shorter when they are under stress, such as on the first day of school, when surrounded by strangers, in an unfamiliar setting, during a test, or when they are tired. Over an extended period of time, these same behaviors can interfere with a child's performance at school. Typical misbehaviors include distractibility, restlessness, and talkativeness. CC9.4

  - Distractibility is a problem when children frequently must be redirected to a task. Some children are easily distracted by sounds; others are distracted by visual stimuli such as decorations on the bulletin board, moving objects, even the sound and flicker of fluorescent lights.

  - Restlessness is often a sign of poor muscle tone: children must change positions every few seconds just to rest their muscles. Other children wiggle to release tension, or to avoid a difficult task. Restless kids can't sit still.

They constantly squirm in their chairs, run around the classroom, fidget, and distract their classmates.

- Talkative kids may be using language to direct attention away from their inadequacies. By giggling, laughing, and talking, kids can get the attention they crave while avoiding tasks they are unable to do.

• *Auditory-visual-motor discrimination and sequencing:* To succeed in school, children need to be able to pay attention to sounds, discriminate between various sounds and sights (words as compared with background noise, for example), remember auditory and visual information, and coordinate muscle activities in a specific time sequence. These skills are essential for such basic tasks as listening and paying attention in a school environment, following verbal directions, learning rhymes and songs, repeating story sequences, and learning names and addresses.

• *Eye-hand coordination:* Coordinating the eyes, hands, and fingers becomes increasingly important as children learn to dress themselves, play with toys, and write. Eye-hand coordination is necessary for using a pencil with appropriate grasp and pressure, making written symbols of a consistent size, copying information from the chalkboard, and organizing written material on a page. The *Integrated Motor Activities Screening (IMAS)* evaluates three indicators of eye-hand coordination which affect hand function and use of tools:

- Being able to make a noise by snapping the fingers indicates fine motor control.

- Making bunny ears (a "V") with proper positioning of the fingers and thumb indicates proper strength in the fingers and hand, and good tactile sensation. Children should be able to make the bunny "wave" the ears by bending the hand up and down at the wrist: this indicates good muscle tone and differentiation of the wrist.

- Using crayons and/or pencils properly is an indication of eye-hand coordination, fine motor skills, motor development, visual acuity, laterality, and attentiveness.

• *Gross motor control:* Good physical skills (including laterality, body image, and neuromuscular control) enable children to devote maximum energy to visual and auditory information in the classroom. Chronic fatigue posture, restlessness, right-left confusion, number or letter reversals, clumsiness, excessive leaning on elbows, and low endurance are signs that children are without adequate automatic control of their bodies. The *Integrated Motor Activities Screening (IMAS)* observes a child's gross motor skills through four specific activities:

- Balancing on each foot requires muscle strength and control, as well as kinesthetic feedback, and shows that children can coordinate the two sides of the body to maintain balance.

- Being able to hop on one foot continuously for ten seconds indicates that children have good balance, endurance, and muscle strength in their legs.

- Skipping continuously in a straight line involves a complex hierarchy of skills that has been integrated into a flowing movement. Being able to skip is an excellent indicator of a child's ability to sequence, time, and coordinate his movement and is an indication of balance, flexibility, and endurance.

- Tossing and catching indicate a child's ability to judge movement through space, as well as the child's balance, timing, coordination of both sides of the body and eye-hand coordination.

"The slow learner has had a long history of failure. From this experience he has learned one thing: the best way to reduce the probability of failure is to never do anything new."
(Newell Kephart. *The Slow Learner In The Classroom.* p. 64)

A Classroom View of Readiness

A few years before Candace enrolled as a first grader, Hawthorne Elementary School's resource room had begun using the Integrated Motor Activities Screening (IMAS) *for evaluating the readiness of the school's first grade students. Using the test each fall, the school gained valuable insights on students' readiness, and teachers were better able to identify students whose academic progress would be greatly improved by intervention programs. Because the* IMAS *is given one-on-one, away from the classroom in an isolated setting, the evaluator has an opportunity to objectively evaluate each child without distractions.*

Based on the results of the IMAS, *the resource room teacher recognized that some students would benefit from minor adjustments in diet, sleep habits, even classroom seating arrangements. For other students, she recommended programs involving regular therapy, specific physical activity routines, and emotional support. Many parents received invitations to attend a series of parenting classes led by one of the school's resource room teachers, the school counselor, and a therapist.*

The Integrated Motor Activities Screening (IMAS) *showed Candace and her classmates to be a fairly "average" group of first graders, with a wide range of abilities, maturity, and concerns.*

Tom – 5 yrs. 10 mos.

"Tom"

At school and home: Tom is the biggest in his class. He is clumsy and awkward, and still talks in the high-pitched, simple language of a child much younger. Tom uses both left and right hands, whichever is closest to the pencil or eating utensil. When writing or coloring, he moves his body and/or the paper frequently. At home Tom goes downstairs one foot at a time and still needs training wheels for his bicycle.

The IMAS shows: Tom functions a full year below his age level (scoring 4 yrs. 10 mos.). Because of his size, he is expected to perform better than his peers which accentuates his feelings of inferiority. He stands in a typical fatigue posture, indicating poor sensation and muscle tone. Tom has poor laterality. He is unable to balance on one foot, hop in place, or skip, and has equally poor balance on left and right. His gross motor skills are extremely weak.

Recommendations: Tom should be placed in a developmental kindergarten. This program should emphasize body development, basic motor skills, and manipulation skills to better prepare him for first grade academics. His left-right preference will become more clearly established as Tom develops integration of the two sides of his body, kinesthesia, and sequencing.

Because both of his parents work, a developmental after-school program is recommended for Tom, where he can receive regular physical activity and therapy under supervision. His parents should be advised to encourage his development of basic motor skills and de-emphasize fine motor skills. They also should be taught how to enhance Tom's kinesthesia and muscle tone using dry brushing, deep pressures, and patterns for movement and non-movement. Most of all, Tom needs time to mature, plus appropriate activity and encouragement to master the control of his body.

The resource room teacher will plan to meet at least twice each year with Tom's therapists and parents to assess his progress and monitor other problems that may appear.

Keith – 6 yrs. 9 mos.

"Keith"

At school and home: Keith is a daydreamer. He plays quietly, often staring at the television or out a window. He is slow to complete his work. He often drops things.

The IMAS shows: Keith has poor eye-hand coordination, poor gross motor skills, poor posture, and poor muscle tone. Because his body doesn't work automatically, he uses his mind to run his body. His brain's "higher circuits," therefore, are not available for cognitive functioning. Without the *IMAS* screening and appropriate intervention, Keith could quietly "slip through" the cracks in the system without achieving his potential, academically or physically.

Recommendations: Keith will benefit tremendously from a home program for enhancing his kinesthesia through dry brushing, deep pressures, and patterns of movement/non-movement. Instead of competitive sports, Keith should be enrolled in developmental gymnastics, martial arts, swimming, or tumbling to ensure the much-needed development of his body.

Andrea - 5 yrs. 11 mos.

"Andrea"

At school and home: Andrea is the smallest child in class. She was identified a year ago as having attention deficit disorder (ADD) without hyperactivity. Andrea was born prematurely. The school counselor and principal have been informed that Andrea was physically abused by her father when she was an infant. Her parents have since divorced and her mother is now a single parent. Grandparents often care for Andrea while her mother is working.

In class, Andrea is quiet, withdrawn, and easily distracted. She stares at other children, and plays nervously with her crayons and books.

The IMAS shows: Andrea had difficulty with portions of the exam simply because she is so easily startled. She was able to repeat only the most simple clap-tap sequences of the auditory-visual-motor segment because she jumped whenever the examiner made a sound. She resisted the eye exams, obviously scared by these "invasive" activities. She relaxed considerably as she named her body parts (indicating body awareness), and she readily demonstrated dominance of her right eye, hand, and foot. Her confidence with these components of the exam indicate that she has benefited from some one-on-one time with an adult.

Recommendations: Andrea's difficulty in the classroom seems to be more directly related to emotional trauma than to physical problems. Because of the non-invasive nature of the latter portions of the IMAS, Andrea was able to relax enough to participate and do relatively well on fine motor components.

Yet Andrea was tense throughout the exam, just as she is at school. The examiner recognized that the resting state of Andrea's autonomic nervous system is dangerously close to her stress threshold; Andrea is almost constantly at the edge of a "flight" response of her survival system, which is the reason she is so easily distracted and startled, and why she so often withdraws from the world around her. The examiner correctly surmised that Andrea was the victim of first-line and second-line traumas which continue to interfere with her ability to concentrate, learn, play, and relate.

Andrea's teacher and her mother were advised to reduce the stress in Andrea's environment and to stimulate her peacekeeping system with dim lights, quiet voices, soft music, encouragement, and some changes in her diet and sleep schedule. Andrea's mother and grandparents were invited to parenting classes at the school.

A physical therapist was eager to begin stabilizing the sensitivity of Andrea's skin using dry brushing but knew Andrea might be threatened by this procedure. First, Andrea's grandparents agreed to give Andrea a positive experience of nurturing touch each day, usually by holding her in their laps while reading a story. A month or so later, they began gently massaging Andrea's skin. It was more than two months after Andrea's *IMAS* evaluation when the therapist first tried dry brushing. The brief session convinced the therapist that Andrea was operating a little further from her stress threshold but that her skin was still super-sensitive and would benefit greatly from the regular therapeutic stimulation of dry brushing and, later, deep pressures.

John - 6 yrs. 7 mos.

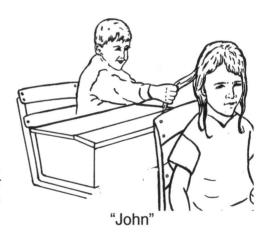

"John"

At school and home: John never sits still. His constant activity often makes him a nuisance. During the spring of his kindergarten year, he was labeled as having attention deficit disorder (ADD) with hyperactivity. He has been on Ritalin for six months and his dosage of the medication has been increased several times.

The IMAS shows: John has mixed dominance, with preference of his right hand, left eye, and no preferred foot. His restlessness is a sign of poor midline stability: he shifts his body as soon as his muscles become fatigued, every five to ten seconds. It is no surprise that he hasn't developed left-right preference because he hasn't integrated the two sides of his body. Nor has he established the kinesthetic figure-ground necessary for motor functioning and stability. Ritalin hasn't helped John overcome these problems, which stem from his poor background of sensation and a lack of kinesthesia. He will continue a cycle of dysfunction, discomfort, and failure unless intervention is directed at that level.

Recommendations: John will benefit tremendously from a program of developmental therapy at home and in a clinical setting. His parents should be taught to do dry brushing and deep pressures regularly with John; he should re-learn basic patterns of movement/non-movement under the direct supervision of a therapist.

Stability of his entire body should come as John learns to keep his body still and as he develops kinesthesia. Soon he will spontaneously try activities he hasn't attempted before, such as cartwheels and jumping on trampolines. As kinesthesia develops, so will his confidence in his body; his enthusiasm for organized activities will continue to grow as his capabilities expand. As his behavior becomes less annoying, John's other social skills will improve and he should begin making more friends.

In the meantime, his daily sessions of dry brushing and deep pressures will cement his relationship with his parents and provide new direction for family interactions. His parents will benefit from the school's parenting classes and may be advised to obtain additional counseling in behavior modification and other healthy parenting techniques.

Candace - 6 yrs. 5 mos.

At school and home:
Candace is highly motivated and enjoys new experiences. She began school at age four and has taken lessons in swimming, gymnastics, and ballet. She is secure and self-confident and does well at school. She has many friends but also enjoys playing alone. Her artwork is regularly displayed on the family

"Candace"

refrigerator and often is enclosed in letters to grandparents.

The IMAS shows: Candace rated well on all portions of the test. Her body works automatically without conscious control. Her body awareness and coordination should enable her to do well in any organized game or playground activity.

Recommendations: Candace is ready for school and should do well in all areas. Even so, her progress might be interrupted at any time by a family crisis, injury, illness, or other major event. Her performance is sure to be affected by her teachers, peers, and after-school activities.

Like all children, Candace should be regularly evaluated so that her parents and teachers can assess all aspects of her development. Her parents will be her most important advocates and Candace's achievement will be boosted by their involvement in parent-teacher organizations at school, classroom activities, and extracurricular programs.

Is Ritalin the Answer for Hyperactive Kids?

Attention deficit disorder (ADD), hyperactivity, and attention deficit hyperactivity disorder (ADHD) are familiar terms to many parents of school-age children. Estimates vary greatly but some experts say as many as one-fifth of all school-age children are hyperactive; others put the count at one in a hundred. CN9.5

The disagreements don't end there. As therapists, we've talked with parents at odds with principals, teachers debating with school psychologists, and therapists disagreeing with physicians about hyperactivity and attention deficit disorder.

One problem is the diagnosis itself. What exactly is hyperactivity, or ADD or ADHD? Although attention deficit disorder may occur with or without hyperactivity, the term "ADD" is commonly used for both. Hyperactivity is probably the most popular term and the least definitive. The clinical definition includes mental inattention, impulsivity, and hyperactivity. To be diagnosed with ADHD, problem behaviors must have been noticed before the child was seven years old and have persisted for at least six months. Specialists use a list of fourteen characteristic symptoms of which ADHD children must exhibit eight. That list includes excessive fidgeting, driven or frantic behavior unlike that of peers, distractibility, talking excessively, and losing things. These characteristics aren't easily evaluated, especially by strangers (the school psychologist, for example, or even the family physician). What's more, these same symptoms are often seen among children with other problems and also may be indicative of stress, hypersensitive skin, and allergies.

Hyperactivity and attention deficit disorder would be easier to diagnose and treat if scientists could identify a distinguishing characteristic. Researchers have studied various explanations for why kids are restless, impulsive, or distractable. No biochemical or biological difference (or cause) has been found.

What researchers **do** know is that behavior can be changed using certain drugs. The most popular is Ritalin, a stimulant available by prescription which has "shown to have dramatically positive effects upon most hyperactive children," according to a 1989 article in *Parents* magazine.

Ritalin (methylphenidate) was first approved for use with children in 1961. Like morphine and barbiturates, Ritalin is classified among those drugs with the greatest potential for abuse; the Drug Enforcement Administration (DEA) regulates its manufacture.

On Ritalin, children with ADD or ADHD are more able to pay attention, stay on task, and sit still but the effects are temporary; only with repeated dosages and sustained-release tablets will the benefits last all day. At best, Ritalin is prescribed as part of an intervention strategy that involves the child's family, school, physicians, counselors, and therapists. Unfortunately, Ritalin is often used alone, with no on-going program to help the child in other ways.

There is evidence showing that Ritalin has no behavioral effect for up to forty percent of all hyperactive children. Among those who are helped by Ritalin, a placebo (sugar pill) often works just as well; the benefit of Ritalin is apparently due to its expected benefits, not chemical changes it induces. There's also the "magic bullet" effect: parents and children may see Ritalin as the only effective way to modify behavior. Kids say their behavior is beyond their control; parents abandon efforts to discipline the kids; Ritalin dosages are increased.

The problem is that Ritalin doesn't affect the basic problems. Ritalin may make children easier to manage but it doesn't make them smarter or happier. Ritalin may help the kids get through today but it doesn't make them better prepared for tomorrow. By making kids more manageable, Ritalin may make teachers and parents happier but it doesn't make school and home more effective. Ritalin may be the easiest solution for children with attention deficit disorder and/or hyperactivity but it isn't the best.

Behavioral problems and inattentiveness are symptoms of other problems and the answer isn't to be found in medication. Instead of a prescription for Ritalin, these children need a comprehensive, individualized program that evaluates behavior and motor skills; corrects problems with sensation, muscle tone, kinesthesia, and body awareness; boosts confidence and self-image; and teaches skills in behavior management. Parents must understand the problem is in the background; their commitment to a program that addresses this can change behavior and physical problems.

In recent years, Shirley Randolph has achieved remarkable results with over 50 children, between ages 5 and 15, diagnosed ADD and ADHD. Her program includes daily sessions at home (five days a week) of dry brushing, deep pressures, and resting in a supported flexion position. In addition, the children have weekly sessions with Randolph where they receive intensive muscle stimulation, differentiation, and belly crawling in a controlled environment.

About half of these children were on Ritalin when they started the program. All were taken off Ritalin from three to six months later with no need to be put back on Ritalin or other behavior-modifying medication.

The duration of Randolph's program has varied from 34 weeks to 48 weeks. For each child, the result was that behavior problems were eliminated, grades came up, and coordination was dramatically improved. Many children were able to ride bicycles, jump rope, and/or participate in team sports for the first time. Social skills improved significantly; many children enjoyed a remarkable boost in popularity and earned awards for achievement, behavior, and attitude.

Of the first fifty children in the program, seven dropped out or did not achieve as expected. In each case, the parent had not made a firm commitment to the program; they refused to do the activities, were inconsistent in the five-day-a-week implementation, and/or failed to bring the child to therapy regularly.

In many of the fifty cases, the behavior worsened for a period of time while the child released years of frustration, inadequacy, and failure. While being held in the therapists' arms at the end of a session, many of the children spontaneously apologized for their outbursts: "I'm sorry! I didn't really mean those awful things I said to you!" CN9.6

Correcting behavioral problems is not easy. Effective intervention requires a long-term, holistic approach that reaches to the problems in the background and provides an environment of love, support, and encouragement. To be successful, most families require a strong positive support system and assurance that consistent persistence will pay off. The rewards are immeasurable. There is nothing that builds success like being successful with your body and feeling good from the inside out! A case study documenting this effective program is found in the Appendix section.

Third-line Trauma

As personality and intellect expand during childhood, the brain becomes vulnerable to a new level of traumas. The third level of brain development is the expansion of the neocortex, which equips children for reasoning, word patterns, theoretical thinking, problem-solving, and illusions. Because this level of brain development occurs in early childhood, traumas experienced after age three are most likely to impact intellectual functioning. The cognitive memory of childhood abuse, neglect, injury, or other trauma can impact speech, academic progress, personality, and other mental functions.

Most third-line traumas are built upon earlier traumas. As skills of speech and reasoning are developed, children become able to intellectualize or rationalize problems, even to talk their way through distress. Their words may offer insights to the hidden pain of long-ago trauma: phrases such as "I'm stuck," "I'm lost," "No one's there," and "I'm doing this all myself" may be verbal clues to prenatal distress, birth trauma, or other painful experiences.

> *"Each level discharges excess Primal energy in order of its development. Early on, when the system is not fully developed, the discharge is almost totally visceral (first level); as physical and muscle coordination and emotional expression develop, the energy can flow into body wall or muscle release (second level) where we can become tense physically so that the muscles are tensed up; and finally, when the neocortex (third level) is fully developed, ideas can absorb and discharge the energy."*
>
> (Arthur Janov. *Imprints*. p. 227)

Because we learned from the inside out, resolving inner pain often happens best by reaching through the outer, most recent layer of learning -- our intellectual awareness. Through our intellect, we can accept an awareness of our imperfections; recognize the need for information; begin probing our conscious understandings and memories; appreciate the interconnectedness of body, mind, emotions, and spirit; develop and embrace the strategy that will bring the greatest peace, happiness, and fulfillment in our lives.

And that's only the beginning; we know that the conscious mind is only one aspect of who we are. Inner pain may have lodged in our emotions (second-line trauma) and physical functioning (first-line trauma). To reach that pain, we must delve far into the past, far beyond conscious memory, to uncover layers of unhealthy background that has prevented us from optimal functioning, and to correct the subsequent compensation that has enabled us to function as well as we do.

How much better the world would be if all children were nurtured from the beginning; if each child were loved from the moment of conception; if all children received all they needed of food and clothing, housing and health care, guidance and freedom, love and security; if every child had every opportunity to grow and develop according to the perfectly sequenced human timeline. That's our deepest wish and the reason for this book.

> *"Healthy self-esteem is the internal experience of one's own preciousness and value as a person. It comes from inside a person and moves outward to relationships."*
>
> (Pia Mellody. *Facing Codependence*. p. 7)

Where Do We Go From Here?

For childhood to be a magical time for growth and discovery and for optimum growth to occur along the human timeline, we must rethink our cultural priorities. Too many children today are growing up without the environment and the nurturing they need to reach their fullest potential.

What emotional trauma is suffered because birth is rushed or delayed, difficult or drugged? How many babies are deprived of the security of mother's loving arms? What happens to children who don't have opportunities to move their bodies freely? How do kids cope when they live with constant stress, uncertainty, and fear? What happens to the human matrix when children can't be children?

Enhancing the human matrix may be the key to the survival of the human race. For it is the human matrix that interconnects *each* of us with *all* of us. It is the human matrix that weaves the genetic code of humankind with the experience of this place and time. It is the human matrix that directs human development from the inside out and that's why all of humankind suffers – from the inside out – when the human matrix is damaged by neglect, abuse, stress, or dysfunction. That is why we must change the way we care for today's children.

- We need to embrace a broader, more holistic view of parenting and care-giving: to care for the bodies, minds, emotions, and spirits of all children.

- We need to learn to be parents: to teach teens and young adults the skills of parenting, the important sequence of human development, and the fragile nature of the human matrix.

- We need to be families that cherish the privilege of loving and nurturing children, who take the responsibilities of parenting seriously yet lovingly, always placing our children's highest good as our highest priority.

- We need schools whose primary concern is to help children learn, and where curriculum is designed for the needs of children of all capabilities and interests.

- We need therapists who work together, going beyond traditional boundaries to contribute professional and personal perspectives for a holistic, comprehensive approach to prevention and treatment of disabilities.

• We need to be a society that loves its children and is committed to the well-being of our youngest and most vulnerable generation.

It is for these reasons that this book is being presented – for all children, for all of humankind.

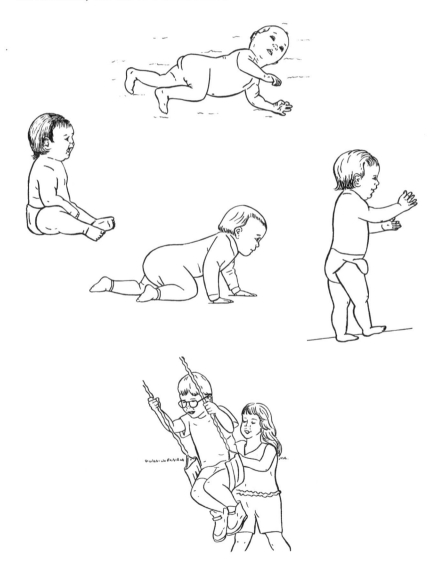

APPENDIX

APPENDIX A
Chapter Notes

The following pages refer to items noted CNx.x in the text. In the Chapter Notes, we offer our comments about primary reference sources for *Kids Learn From the Inside Out,* and assist readers in pursuing additional information on specific topics.

Chapter One Notes: Learning From the Inside Out

CN1.1, page 3

Heiniger and Randolph's first book, *Neurophysiological Concepts in Human Behavior: The Tree of Learning* (1981), was written to offer medical professionals a holistic understanding of the function of the nervous system. The book presents a strategy for evaluating problems and techniques for early intervention. The same concepts are the foundation for *Kids Learn From The Inside Out,* supplemented by new material and the authors' experience, and written for a general audience.

CN1.2, page 5

First developed by Newell Kephart, this understanding of human development was expanded by Kephart's co-workers Clara M. Chaney and Nancy R. Miles. Their developmental sequence of human learning is best explained in *The Slow Learner in the Classroom* (1960, 1971).

Kephart's stages of development include innate automatic (referred to in his first work as "motor"), motor-perceptual, perceptual-motor, perceptual (or perceptual-perceptual), perceptual-conceptual, and conceptual (or conceptual-conceptual). Because we focus on development only up to age seven, we have not included the latter two stages in this book. The value of Kephart's work has not diminished with time and we heartily encourage readers (especially developmental therapists) to study his writings. We especially recommend the second edition of Kephart's *Slow Learner in the Classroom* (1971).

Kephart's *Purdue Perceptual-Motor Survey* uses problem solving tasks as a setting for assessing children's motor-perceptual and perceptual-motor development and examining how children use their bodies. This survey is not a pass-fail exam but an excellent tool for task analysis.

Remediating Learning Problems: A Developmental Curriculum (Clara M. Chaney and Nancy R. Miles, 1974) is a systematic guide for using motor activities to enhance learning. Their work is referred to more extensively in the later chapters of this book.

Margot Heiniger trained directly with Kephart, Chaney, and Miles; she and Shirley Randolph have incorporated their principles and techniques extensively in their work as therapists.

CN1.3, page 8

Born in 1870, Maria Montessori left a legacy of educational methods and theories that still influence the world's children today. After graduating from medical school in 1896, she cultivated her special interest in the education of children through her studies of anthropology, philosophy, and psychology. Her first work as an educator was as director of a school for retarded children, where she incorporated the work of Jean-Marc-Gaspard Itard and Edouard Seguin with the "ineducable." In doing so, Montessori quickly earned recognition as an innovative and effective educator.

Montessori was convinced that her theories could be "applied to normal children" and would "set free their personality in a marvelous and surprising way," as she explained in *The Montessori Method*. In 1907, she opened her first "Casa dei Bambini" (Children's House) using the "Montessori Methods" that have retained their popularity and effectiveness for nearly a century. Basic to her methods was her understanding of the sequential development of sensory systems.

Elizabeth G. Hainstock's *The Essential Montessori* (1978) is a concise guide to Montessori's life, work, and writings. The book includes a useful overview of the Montessori movement today, and a list of informational sources.

CN1.4, page 8

Joseph Chilton Pearce's *The Magical Child* (1977) is an urgent and informative guide to "help you rediscover nature's plan for our children." The book outlines the biological plan for the growth of intelligence, and how that plan is damaged in modern societies. Pearce writes as a parent, a teacher, and a human concerned about the reintegration of self and child. His work is greatly influenced by Jean Piaget's developmental stages, biologist Herman Epstein's explanation of brain growth spurts, and Jerome Bruner's recognition that "intent precedes the ability to do."

CN1.5, page 10

Ashley Montagu has written more than 40 books, including *Growing Young* (1981), *Touching* (1971), *Prenatal Influences* (1962), and *Life Before Birth* (1961). A distinguished anthropologist, his books are well-researched, provocative, and timely. He has written on an amazing variety of subjects related to human behavior, including superiority of women, aggression, and prenatal development.

In *Growing Young,* Montagu offers a delightful list of 26 characteristics of childhood ("neotenous drives of the child"), beginning with a child's need for love and including curiosity, sense of wonder, playfulness, openmindedness, resiliency, optimism, compassionate intelligence, dance, and song (p. 131). Montagu uses his background in anthropology as he compares human development to that of other species and he argues that the key to staying young is to embody the 26 childhood traits.

CN1.6, page 12

This information comes from the *World Almanac* and *Book of Facts* 1992; *Newsweek* (Nov. 18, 1991); *Statistical Abstract of the United States* (1991); *Newsweek* (June 18, 1992); and *Statistical Record of Women Worldwide* (1991).

CN1.7, page 14

David Elkind's books and articles trace the problems of education and child-raising practices. In *The Hurried Child* (1981), Elkind examines children and stress: how society pressures children to "hurry and grow up," how children cope (and don't cope) with those pressures, and how these problems must be solved. Elkind is a professor of child study and a resident scholar at Tufts University.

Chapter Two Notes: Development and Stress

CN2.1, page 20

Konrad Stettbacher is a Swiss psychotherapist known for his work on early trauma (primal wounding) as a primary cause of suffering. His 1991 book, *Making Sense Of Suffering* (with foreword and afterword by Alice Miller), outlines a holistic, four-step self-help primal therapy to "resolve primally induced anxiety, pain, and confusion by uncovering their origins." (p. 39) The book begins by defining and describing psychic illness and primal trauma as injuries to a person's ability to live consciously and function fully. He also examines the traumas of birth: "How you were born is how you will live." (p. 89)

CN2.2, page 21

John-Roger and Peter McWilliams' popular and easy-to-read book, *You Can't Afford the Luxury of a Negative Thought* (1990), analyzes negative thinking as "one of the primary diseases of our time." With vivid descriptions and numerous quotes, the authors explain the powerful effects of thoughts and emotions (negative and positive) on our bodies and our lives. Their problem-solving model is a pyramid of thoughts, feelings, and actions: the structure and power of this pyramid (and our ability to access situations and solve problems) requires positive thoughts and feelings, plus physical action.

CN2.3, page 23

Heiniger and Randolph's 1981 book, *Neurophysiological Concepts in Human Behavior,* offers a more complete and technical explanation of stress responses. The book's first concept (and first chapter) includes a review of Hans Selye's description of the psychophysiology of stress and explains how stress reactions affect and are affected by the autonomic nervous system, endocrine system, immune system, brain function, and nutrition.

"The body's adaptive processes to external or internal stressors may be altered by manipulation of the ergotropic-trophotropic elements," the authors explain (p. 3). Stress reactions are sympathetic or ergotropic; the parasympathetic system (relaxation) is the trophotropic.

CN2.4, page 25

Julio B. deQuiros, M.D., Ph.D. and Dr. Orlando L. Schrager, M.D., are Argentine physicians and developmental specialists with an extraordinary knowledge of children's development and learning disabilities. Their book, *Neuropsychological Fundamentals In Learning Disabilities* (1979), is written for educators, therapists, and doctors. Although difficult to understand, the book provides a valuable analysis of human learning development, neurological and neuropsychological assessment, therapy, and remediation for learning disabilities. Heiniger and Randolph were fortunate to have heard a lecture by deQuiros and Schrager; Heiniger worked with Schrager in 1983.

CN2.5, page 29

Pia Mellody is well-known for her outstanding work with codependency, dependency, and addiction – and helping people reclaim their innate child-like characteristics. Therapists and codependents may be familiar with her lectures and tape series, "Permission to be Precious."

In her book, *Facing Codependence* (1989), Mellody describes how codependence operates in everyday life and relationships; she offers a practical model for healing codependent persons. "Painful childhood experiences (are) a common snake pit in addictive and other kinds of dysfunctional families," she writes (p. xix). She defines child abuse in broad terms ("any experience in childhood [birth to age seventeen] that is less than nurturing" p. xx), and uses the term "abuse" interchangeably with "dysfunctional." Pia Mellody is a consultant at The Meadows, an Arizona treatment center for people with addictions. Her 1992 book is *Facing Love Addiction: Letting Go Of Toxic Love.*

CN2.6, page 35

Heiniger's *Integrated Motor Activities Screening* (1990) is a quick, comprehensive instrument for identifying preschool and kindergarten children who are at-risk for learning disabilities. The *IMAS* is based on the premise that basic motor functions are the foundation and the building blocks for developing the complex perceptual-motor skills required for academic learning. By indicating a child's specific areas of weakness, *IMAS* directs educators in implementing the most appropriate intervention strategies. The *IMAS* is discussed in more detail in Chapter Nine and Appendix F.

Chapter Three Notes: Life Before Birth

CN3.1, page 40

In *Nurturing the Unborn Child* (1991), Thomas Verny and Pamela Weintraub offer a nine-month program to assist parents in soothing, stimulating, and communicating with their unborn baby. The book also helps parents re-examine their own memories of childhood and resolve old conflicts in preparation for a positive parenting experience.

CN3.2, page 41

Thomas Verny's book, *The Secret Life of the Unborn Child* (1981), is a magnificent introduction to the possibilities of an extensive prenatal experience. The book is based on solid research in this newest field of psychology, and includes case histories that are startling in their clarity and complexity.

CN3.3, page 41

With full color photos, drawings, and vivid descriptions, Lennard Nilsson's beautiful book, *A Child is Born* (1965/1981), illuminates the mystery of human development from conception to birth. Nilsson is a pioneer in scientific medical photography, and his book is an excellent resource for parents. For more detail, parents can refer to a basic embryology textbook (such as Moore's *Before We Are Born* or Rugh and Shettles' *From Conception to Birth*). See the Bibliography for more information.

CN3.4, page 54

Czech psychoanalyst Stanislav Grof is well-known for his amazing work in exploring the dimensions of consciousness and for offering new perspectives in psychotherapy and inner exploration. Grof has been in the United States since 1967 and is former Chief of Psychiatric Research at the Maryland Psychiatric Research Center, and Assistant Professor of Psychiatry at Johns Hopkins University School of Medicine. His books include *Beyond the Brain: Birth, Death and Transcendence in Psychotherapy* (1985), *The Adventure of Self-Discovery* (1988), and *The Holotropic Mind* (1992).

Grof identified four distinct levels or realms of the human psyche: the sensory, the individual unconscious, the level of birth and death, and the transpersonal domaine. To access the deeper levels of consciousness, he developed a technique known as Holotropic BreathworkTM, which combines breathing, music, and other media.

Through this technique, persons can reach memories of their birth, express emotions which may have been suppressed for years, and begin to heal the impact of an original trauma.

CN3.5, page 54

Environmental psychologist Leni Schwartz's 1991 book, *Bonding Before Birth*, is a compassionate and insightful perspective on prenatal life. The book is an excellent guide for expectant parents and offers guidelines for starting support groups, performing breathing and relaxation exercises, and selecting a birth center. Throughout the book, Schwartz emphasizes and explains how our birth experience influences physical and psychological health and affects how we live our lives.

Schwartz has studied extensively with psychoanalyst Stanislav Grof and he helped pioneer the holistic approaches to childbirth that are now widely accepted.

CN3.6, page 57

In *Prenatal Influences* (1962) and *Life Before Birth* (1977), Ashley Montagu outlines a sound and practical program for prenatal care. From the moment of conception until birth, the human being is more susceptible to his environment than ever again. In his usual thorough and convincing style, Montagu explains how the embryo or fetus is affected by mother's nutrition and emotional state; he depicts the impact of drugs and the causes and effects of prematurity and offers other information that every prospective parent should know prior to conception.

CN3.7, page 57

Klaus and Kennell's 1976 book, *Maternal-Infant Bonding*, is considered a classic work on bonding. This book identifies principles governing mother's attachment to the infant and explains crucial components to the process of attachment. The authors (both neonatologists) suggest improvements in hospital care policies, including care for parents if the baby is premature, full term, malformed, or if the newborn dies.

CN3.8, page 58

Jerrold Lee Shapiro's 1988 book, *When Men are Pregnant*, is an excellent resource on the issues men face during pregnancy. Shapiro explores in depth the doubts, fears, and psychological pressures of fathers-to-be, and laments that medical establishments often fail to support men's participation in pregnancy and birth.

CN3.9, page 60

French obstetrician Frederick Leboyer's *Birth Without Violence* (1982) includes a stark description of the trauma, anxiety, and pain experienced at birth and explains simple techniques for making birth a more gentle and loving experience for baby. His poetic style is matched by dozens of black and white photos, for a most memorable and informative book.

CN3.10, page 70

Statistics on cesarean deliveries are from the *Statistical Abstract of the United States* (1991); *The Los Angeles Times* (January 26, 1989); and Gannett News Service/*The Idaho Statesman* (May 12, 1992).

CN3.11, page 72

Arthur Janov's 1983 book, *Imprints: The Lifelong Effects of the Birth Experience* documents and explains how our individual experience of the birthing process can profoundly color the rest of our lives. "It will no doubt be surprising to see that what happened to a tiny baby during the first hours of life decades ago can have lifelong ramifications... And it will be equally surprising to see how the reexperience of that event liberates the human system as nothing else can." (p. 19)

Janov explains how birth imprints can determine whether we become aggressive or passive, compulsive workers, heavy smokers, alcoholics or asthmatics. This book documents the dangers and delicateness of the intrauterine environment. Janov explains what steps are needed to protect the unborn, and advises adults in overcoming their traumas by "reliving" their birth experience.

CN3.12, page 74

Dr. Frederick Levenson, author of *The Causes and Prevention of Cancer* (1985), is a graduate of New York University, the Center for Modern Psychoanalytic Studies, and the California Graduate Institute. In this book, Levenson presents an important and exciting explanation of how cancer is caused by external and internal irritation and explains how cancer development can be prevented and treated successfully.

Levenson understands prenatal fusion as essential for the fetus's ability to handle irritants and stress. "The mother's defenses, both physically and emotionally, serve to absorb the fetus's defenses," he explains (page 29-30). He refers to this as "emotional entropy between mother and child." If this emotional entropy is not established prenatally, the results may be extreme and can be best understood as three stages:

Marasmus, the disease of "wasting away," is the most severe reaction to lack of emotional support as the baby's well-being is severely disrupted. This extreme failure to thrive occurs because there is a total lack of fusion and bonding.

The second most severe is childhood autism or schizophrenia. These children behave as if there is no outside world; they are incapable of responding to other people, cannot protect themselves from environmental dangers, and usually do not develop communication skills. Emotionally neglected infants often show specific symptoms of withdrawal known as anaclitic depression: immobility, avoiding strangers, weight loss, insomnia. (Rene Spitz, M.D. is credited for identifying these symptoms in 1947.)

The third stage, according to Levenson, is cancer, which develops as a defense against marasmus or death. Explains Levenson, "In schizophrenia, the attempt to dissipate hyperirritation is through the mind. In cancer, the hyperirritation that does not get adequately dissipated during infancy is stored in body cells." (p. 46) Mind and body can be conditioned to be self-contained and to view life as a fundamentally irritating experience. Irritation is thus channeled through genetic translocation or shifting of the genes along the chromosomes and will become fully evident when additional irritants are introduced later in life.

Levenson is convinced that medical research is misdirected in its pursuit of the causes of cancer. "The complex biological aspects of cancer have not been integrated with the psychological aspects," he writes (p. 17). "Yet this integration can provide the answer" to how and why irritants lead to cancer in some people and not others. "The answer to all these questions lies in how cancer is caused rather than in what causes cancer." His book is written for professionals and the general public, and offers astounding insights on human development, stress, and disease.

CN3.13, page 74

In her 1993 book, *The Primal Wound: Understanding the Adopted Child,* adoptive mother and therapist Nancy Verrier, M.A., presents a revolutionary perspective on adoption. Verrier clarifies how the separation of adoption affects the birthmother and the adopted child. The book gives validation to the feelings of adoptive children and explains their behavior. The insights into abandonment and loss will help heal adoptees, their adopted families, the birth mother and others who have felt abandoned.

CN3.14, page 75

Psychologist David Chamberlain is known for his ground-breaking work in understanding the beginnings of human consciousness, and for his convincing documentation of how prenatal and birth experiences profoundly affect us throughout our lives. His books include *Consciousness at Birth: A Review of the Empirical Evidence* (1983) and *Babies Remember Birth* (1988). He became president of the Pre- and Perinatal Psychology Association of North America in 1991.

In his 1988 book, *Babies Remember Birth,* Chamberlain presents scientific and medical evidence of the wide variety of emotions experienced prenatally, and shows the amazing cognitive and reasoning abilities of newborn infants. The book includes numerous true accounts of adults who, under hypnosis, recall the details of their own birth. Chamberlain systematically disproves seven myths about newborns (such as babies don't feel, have very poor brains, have no sense of self, and don't need their mothers). The book includes an excellent list of resources and readings.

Chapter Four Notes: The Fourth Trimester

CN4.1, page 78

Margaret Ribble's slim volume, *The Rights of Infants* (1943, 1965) is a classic work on the emotional needs of infants. "It is unquestionably true that adverse emotional experiences between child and parents in the first two years of life can evoke serious problems in the child's personality development," the author explains in the preface to the 1965 edition.

Ribble (a medical doctor, psychiatrist, and psychoanalyst) systematically discusses the infant's basic needs: the right to a mother, the effects of "oxygen hunger," the importance of sucking, patterns of early behavior, early sleep habits, the role of fathers, and other pertinent topics. Ribble explains clearly and simply the biological reasons for infants' behavior from birth through the first critical months of life. The book includes case studies tracing the nurturing needs of adults back to developmental issues of infancy.

Another excellent book on newborn infants is *The Amazing Newborn* (1985), a delightful and thorough (yet easy to understand) portrayal of the amazing talents and abilities of newborn infants. Developed by husband-wife team Marshall and Phyllis Klaus (pediatrician/neonatologist and psychotherapist/educator), the book includes a fascinating overview of pertinent research and is illustrated with more than 125 black and white photos of infants less than ten days old.

CN4.2, page 80

Magid and McKelvey were noted in Chapter One for their studies relating childhood trauma to developmental disorders and personality. This information is presented in *High Risk: Children Without a Conscience* (1987), where the authors describe the formation of attachment during the infant's first year and explain how factors can break or interrupt the bonding cycle. Relying on research and expert testimony, the authors explain how unattachment leads to a deep-seated rage which festers to produce a variety of dysfunctions: "It's now clear that one of the primary causes of rapidly increasing crime, particularly by children, is unattachment... The distinguishing characteristic of the diseases of nonattachment is the incapacity of the person to form human bonds." (p. 63)

The authors continue to explain that these children without a conscience "personify an attachment process that has gone very wrong."

Their profile of character-disturbed children includes fourteen characteristics:

1. Lack of ability to give and receive affection
2. Self-destructive behavior
3. Cruelty to others
4. Phoniness
5. Severe problems with stealing, hoarding and gorging on food
6. Speech pathology
7. Marked control problems
8. Lack of long-term friends
9. Abnormalities in eye contact
10. Parents appear angry and hostile
11. Preoccupation with fire, blood, or gore
12. Superficial attractiveness and friendliness with strangers
13. Various types of learning disorders
14. Pathological "crazy" lying

Besides linking criminality to bonding and attachment, the authors show a spectrum of deviant behavior related to poor childhood attachment. They also discuss "state of the art treatments for unattachment," offer guidelines for choosing childcare, and address foster families, adoption, teenage pregnancy, and children of divorce.

CN4.3, page 80

Mary Salter Ainsworth's research is documented in numerous publications including Robert Karen's article, "Becoming Attached: What Children Need." (*The Atlantic,* February 1990).

CN4.4, page 81

These six states of infant consciousness are the result of the work of Boston's child psychiatrist Dr. Peter Wolff (1959) and Dutch researcher Dr. Heinz Prechtl (1964). Working independently, their observations and documentation led these two researchers to the same conclusions. Klaus and Klaus describe and depict (with text and photos) these states of consciousness in *The Amazing Newborn.*

CN4.5, page 82

Brazelton's Neonatal Behavioral Assessment Scale is well known as a reliable tool for evaluating behavior and determining basic personality of newborn infants. This is an excellent tool for helping parents get acquainted with their newborn's behavior and states of awareness. For health care professionals, the scale is uniquely designed to identify abnormal behaviors which may eventually affect development and functioning.

CN4.6, page 83

Salk is well-known for his writings on childcare and parenting. For more information on this study, see Salk's article, "The Effects of the Normal Heartbeat Sound on the Behavior of the Newborn Infant: Implications for Mental Health" (*World Mental Health,* Volume 12 (1960).

CN4.7, page 84

An excellent resource on the importance of bonding is Jean Liedloff's book, *The Continuum Concept* (1977) which explains the importance of time-in-arms as the foundation for security and happiness; for developing kinesthesia; for emotional, mental, and spiritual wholeness.

Liedloff's understanding of human nature was radically changed as she studied the Yequana Indians, a primitive tribe living deep in the Venezuelan jungle. Liedloff contrasts this ancient culture with modern child-rearing practices which, says Liedloff, are taking the human species far from the natural continuum and to the very brink of human extinction.

CN4.8, page 84

For an insightful description of the functional abilities of the skin, see the 1978 edition of Ashley Montagu's book, *Touching,* which presents the skin as a tactile organ, and discusses how the tactile experiences of infancy affect behavior and personality. Montagu explains how the sensation of touch is a necessary stimulus for physical survival of the individual, and places its importance beside human needs for oxygen, water, food, rest, and activity. We consider this book an absolute "must read" for parents, therapists, and health care providers.

CN4.9, page 92

LaLeche League International is an excellent source of information and encouragement on breastfeeding. Contact them at 9616 Minneapolis Avenue, Franklin Park, Illinois 60131 (telephone 708/455-7730).

CN4.10, page 92

The four factors in bonding come from Joseph Pearce's book, *Magical Child* (p. 63).

CN4.11, page 98

Economist Sylvia Ann Hewlett's 1991 book, *When the Bough Breaks,* documents the extent of child neglect in the United States through statistics, case studies, and examination of public and private policy. Extensively footnoted, the book includes shocking facts:

- 20 percent of all children are growing up in poverty, a 21 percent increase since 1970.

- 330,000 children are homeless.

- The rate of suicide among adolescents has tripled since 1960.

- In 1987, less than 5 percent of the U.S. federal budget was devoted to programs that benefit children, one-fifth the amount spent that year on persons over age 65.

Hewlett outlines an "action plan" of ten key policy initiatives: establishing a National Task Force on Children, mandating job-protected parenting leave, guaranteeing free access to prenatal and maternity care, improving access to quality child care, increasing government support of education, subsidizing family housing, shifting tax policy to support families with children, and other much-needed changes.

Chapter Five Notes: The AHA! of Kinesthesia

CN5.1, page 104

Clara Chaney first became acquainted with Newell Kephart when she came to him for help with her own children's learning disabilities. She became the key person in his parent training program at Purdue University, and continued to work and write with him for decades. Chaney was especially interested in the lower levels of Kephart's stages, and was primarily responsible for expanding those stages downward from motor-perceptual to innate automatic.

In 1965, Chaney and Kephart co-authored *Motoric Aids to Perceptual Training,* which offers many activities to enhance gross motor differentiation. In 1974, Chaney and Nancy Miles co-authored *Remediating Learning Problems: A Developmental Curriculum,* explaining the background of children's problems with movement control. In this book they discuss kinesthesia, developing movement and non-movement, differentiation of extremities, and establishing kinesthetic figure-ground.

Heiniger and Randolph have trained with Kephart, Chaney, and Miles, and continue their relationship with Clara Chaney.

CN5.2, page 112

These strategies for enhancing kinesthesia developed out of our work with physical therapist Ed Snapp, former director of the polio ward at Jefferson Davis Hospital (Houston) and a graduate of the University of Texas Medical Center. Snapp's Chronologically Controlled Developmental Education began as a program for children in public schools, especially those in kindergarten through second grade.

Snapp's unique approaches are based on the sensations and movement patterns of the three prenatal trimesters. He continues to refine and expand his theories and techniques as he works with persons with a variety of physical disabilities and learning disorders, including polio and post-polio syndrome.

Heiniger and Randolph began working with Snapp in 1980, as he was developing his Chronologically Controlled Developmental Therapy for use by occupational and physical therapists, and have adapted his techniques for deep pressure stimulation and his specific application of the belly crawl. His work has also enhanced their awareness of the significance of the environment as an aid to treatment.

CN5.3, page 123

Heiniger and Randolph met Dr. Alfred Tomatis and his wife Lena in Paris at the Third International Congress of Tomatis Method, 1988, where they were guests at a four-hour private lecture; they have since attended other training sessions related to the Tomatis Method in the United States.

Tomatis's work has revolutionized the understanding of the ear and its importance for learning, communication, language, music, creativity, and self-esteem. His breakthrough method is now used in over 180 facilities in 15 countries. Most of his extensive writings are available only in French. English-readers will find his work well presented in *The Conscious Ear* (1991) and *Education and Dyslexia* (1978).

Chapter Six Notes: Moving Up in the World

CN6.1, page 128

In *Children Adapt,* occupational therapists Grady, Gilfoyle, and Moore present children's development as a spiraling continuum taking children from prone to vertical. Each step includes a primitive or reflex phase, a transitional phase, and a mature phase. Written primarily for therapists, the book's first section offers a clear and concise explanation of the development of the nervous system. Using text, photographs, and graphs, the book does a tremendous job of analyzing the step-by-step progress of each skill.

The authors are best known for their emphasis of early sensory-motor-sensory integration. Many years ago the emphasis was on motor, then sensory-motor, and finally to sensory-motor-sensory: every motor activity returns its own specific set of sensory information to the nervous system.

CN6.2, page 135

Clara Chaney and Nancy Miles present excellent activities for enhancing the prone progression in their 1974 book, *Remediating Learning Problems: A Developmental Curriculum.* In chapter five, they discuss "moving to learn," beginning with relaxation. Chapter Seven offers activities that incorporate balance and locomotion.

CN6.3, page 138

In *The Slow Learner in the Classroom* (second edition), Kephart presents detailed progression of four motor generalizations. Development of motor generalizations happens in three stages: as an individual piece of information, then elaboration as the experience is repeated, then integration.

Kephart makes a strong case for the importance of free play, which provides children with opportunities to experiment without having to come up with "right" or "wrong" answers. Adults tend to organize children's play with rules, parameters, materials, and adult expectations. Instead, adults should provide many possible variations and assist children through any rigidities, resistances, and frustrations.

The first edition of *The Slow Learner in the Classroom* does not include motor generalizations or space and time, yet contains Kephart's Perceptual Survey Rating Scale (which became the *Purdue Perceptual-Motor Survey*) and training activities.

CN6.4, page 142

Jean Ayres' approach to posture and maintenance of balance offers helpful insights on disorders in postural and bilateral integration. These disorders result in poorly integrated postural reflexes, immature equilibrium reactions, poor ocular control, and lack of integration of the two sides of the body. Ayres' concepts are presented in *Sensory Integration and Learning Disorders* (1972). The book is written primarily for professionals, but may also be helpful to parents.

CN6.5, page 142

Kephart's understanding of space and time was influenced by his work in industrial psychology and his association with Ernest J. McCormick, a leader in the field of industrial psychology and professor of psychology at Purdue.

Chapter Seven Notes: Making Contact

CN7.1, page 155

In a 1976 article in *Journal of Learning Disorders* ("Diagnosis of vestibular disorders in the learning disorders." 9[1]:39-47), Julio deQuiros documents how vestibular disorders and postural disturbances can produce learning disabilities associated with motor skills, the acquisition of language, and the development of normal competencies in reading and writing. Vestibular disorders can be diagnosed medically just hours after birth; just as some children are born with visual or auditory defects, newborn infants may also have deficiencies in proprioception or vestibular function. DeQuiros recommends evaluating vestibular proprioceptive mechanisms using a caloric test and a turning test. Early detection gives parents and medical professionals the greatest opportunity for obtaining needed intervention.

DeQuiros's studies are explained more fully in Heiniger and Randolph's earlier book, *Neurophysiological Concepts in Human Behavior,* pages 69-71.

CN7.2, page 160

Raymond and Dorothy Moore are known as the pioneers of the home-school movement. Their 1975 book, *Better Late Than Early: A New Approach to Your Child's Education,* offers persuasive evidence that formal education is inappropriate for children before they are eight. The first half of the book presents the need for later entry into school. The latter half of the book examines specific reactions, needs, playthings, activities, and opportunities for five age groupings (birth to 18 months, ages 1 through 3, 2½ through 5, 4 through 7, and ages 6 through 8 or 9).

CN7.3, page 162

As early as 1954, speech pathologist Edward D. Mysak was instrumental in overcoming what he recognizes in brain-impaired children as "contradictions in management." He reasoned that children with limited movement should not be strapped and constrained in fixed positions and that therapy can enhance the natural evolution of movement, speech, and other human functioning.

Mysak's work with handicapped children led him to insights that are extremely valuable in understanding normal speech development. His work is well-presented in the third edition (1980) of his well-respected book, N*eurospeech Therapy for the Cerebral Palsied: A Neuroevolutional Approach.*

CN7.4, page 164

Mastery of Language is an exceptional program for learning and practicing positive language which supports one's highest choices. The program was developed by Robert and Helena Stevens, a husband-wife team. Their simple but highly effective tools include simple statements of empowerment: "I can, I am, I will, I choose, I have, I love, I create, I enjoy, I empower." The program teaches the technique of mind-mapping for gaining insight into emotions and traumas as well as for positive organization of one's daily life. For more information, contact Robert and Helena Stevens: 323 Ridgeview Drive, Asheville, North Carolina 28803. Telephone (704) 299-3388.

CN7.5, page 164

Excellent material on speech development is offered in Chaney and Miles' 1974 book, *Remediating Learning Problems.* Body movement and speech are discussed in the first chapter, with suggestions for oral motor activities in preparation for speech. The book also discusses preparation for language arts (including sounds, vocabulary, and preparation for writing) and includes activities for listening, sound-making, and communication.

Chapter Eight Notes: Systematic Exploration

CN8.1, page 171

Marianne Frostig is well-respected for her practical, effective, and comprehensive guides to movement education. These are designed primarily for classroom teachers of kindergarten through primary grades and can be adapted to be effective with upper grades. It is unfortunate that so many educators use only her worksheets while ignoring her excellent theoretical and practical guides on the necessary background for using paper and pencil to complete the worksheets. Frostig's material is unparalleled for its theoretical background to physical education and its concern for the emotional needs of children.

Says Frostig, "Movement education can help children gain self-awareness and prepare them to withstand the pressures and anxieties of their lives as adults.... Movement education provides the most direct means of enhancing body image." (*Movement Education: Theory and Practice, p. 19*)

CN8.2, page 183

Among those now working on the concept of the inner child, John Bradshaw may be most recognized because of his popular tapes, workshops, and books. Bradshaw explains that, as adults, our "wounded child" has unresolved grief as a result of childhood abandonment, abuse, and neglect of childhood dependency needs. To heal this grief, Bradshaw has people "go back" to claim the inner child developmentally, from infant to toddler, preschooler, school-age child, and adolescent.

Bradshaw uses the three brain levels (explained in Chapter One of *Kids Learn*). Damage to the visceral brain occurs prenatally and during the first postnatal year; the limbic brain is damaged during the first six months as emotional bonding is occurring; the neocortex is still developing in our early years, and a true thinking brain develops at around age six or seven. Since the visceral brain is poor at forgetting, the permanence of early traumas will dominate the future. "Whatever a child survives in the first year of life, a time of intense vulnerability, will be registered with survival benefits in mind," Bradshaw says in *Homecoming* (p. 72).

Bradshaw's systematic style makes *Homecoming* an excellent self-help book. Each stage is presented with key components, a questionnaire, discussion, and tools for reclaiming the inner child.

CN8.3, page 183

Prenatal-perinatal psychologist William Emerson uses these and other activities to simulate birth as part of his intensive therapy for healing birth traumas. For more information, contact Emerson at 4940 Bodega Avenue, Petaluma, California 94952.

Chapter Nine Notes: Ready For Action

CN9.1, page 191

Many excellent books and recordings are available for helping children with the motor generalization of receipt and propulsion and for enhancing basic motor functions. Our favorites include:

Yoga: Beginning Techniques for Youth and Exeptional Children (by Mary Martin, Kimbo recordings).

Yoga for Children by Eve Disken. (For children ages 5 - 12, with excellent illustrations of each activity.)

Motor Development and Movement Experiences for Young Children, 3 - 7 by David L. Gallahue. (Fun, basic activities that are easily taught and require few props. Activities are presented to help adults select activities to meet specific needs.)

CN9.2, page 193

Child psychologist Louise Bates Ames confronted modern understandings of school readiness in her 1966 book, I*s Your Child in the Wrong Grade?* Ames was co-founder of the Gesell Institute of Child Development and a prolific writer on child development and parenting. Her concerns and recommendations are still valuable 25 years later. Too many children are starting school too soon, and parents today should demand effective methods of assessing children's readiness for school.

CN9.3, page 194

For more information on Margot Heiniger's *Integrated Motor Activities Screening,* see "Using the Integrated Motor Activities Screening" (Appendix F).

CN9.4, page 195

To assist in analyzing a child's difficulties, Chaney and Miles (in *Remediating Learning Problems*) developed a chart tracing general behavioral problems and difficulties with language, math, physical education, reading, and writing. This excellent tool integrates Kephart's stages of motor development for practical and effective use.

CN9.5, page 203

Sources for this section include *Consumer Guide/Prescription Drugs* (September 1989), p. 191; *Science News* (June 18, 1988 and May 27, 1989); *The Atlantic Monthly* (November 1989); and *Parents Magazine* (February 1989); and the authors' training and experience.

CN9.6, page 205

Heiniger and Randolph's first book, *Neurophysiological Concepts in Human Behavior* (1981), includes an extensive discussion on the causes of undesirable behavior, halos of behavior, levels of breakdown of behavior, restructuring the environment, and specific management. (p. 196) Movement control procedures are presented using specific body part movements similar to the belly crawling movements. This mode of behavior management should only be done with the direction and supervision of a therapist knowledgeable in the procedure.

APPENDIX B
Glossary

The glossary includes definitions of technical terms used in this book as well as our definitions of everyday terms which may seem ambiguous or hard to understand. Chapter references note where the term is first explained.

abduction: (Chapter 3) See *body movements.*

adduction: (Chapter 3) See *body movements.*

asymmetric tonic neck reflex: (Chapter 4) The fencing reflex: one arm is flexed and one arm extended. The head turns to the side and the arm on that side extends while the other arm flexes. May or may not affect the legs.

attachment: (Chapter 4) See *bonding.*

autonomic nervous system: (Chapter 2) The system responsible for internal control of the body's involuntary functions such as circulation, respiration, metabolism, digestion, etc.

body image: (Chapter 5) Our sense of who we are, using the body as our reference point. Also known as body scheme. Body image is the starting point for every human function and movement. **Schema** refers to movement patterns. Don't confuse body scheme and schema.

body movements: (Chapter 3)

    flexion: Movement of body parts which make the angle at the joint smaller and more bent.

    extension: Movement of body parts which straighten the joints.

    adduction: Movement of body parts towards the midline of the body. For fingers and toes, adduction is movement towards an established line.

    abduction: Movement of body parts away from the midline of the body. For fingers and toes, abduction is movement away from an established line.

    internal rotation: Movement of body parts at shoulders and hips, rolling inward toward midline of the body.

    external rotation: Movement of body parts at shoulders and hips, rolling outward from midline of the body.

bonding: (Chapter 3) The parent-child connection established prenatally and during the first months of life, essential for healthy physical, psychological, and spiritual development. **Fusion** is a state of prenatal bonding when the emotions of mother and baby are completely interconnected. **Attachment** describes the stage of bonding when the infant is physically and emotionally secure in his/her relationship with primary caregivers. **Emotional entropy** is the process during prenatal fusion when fetal defenses are absorbed by mother's physical and emotional defenses.

cephalocaudal: (Chapter 4) The normal direction of development proceeding from head to toe.

colostrum: (Chapter 4) The "early milk" produced by the human breast. A protein-rich fluid containing antibodies for fighting infection and preparing the digestive tract for functioning.

compensation: (Preface) Adjustments to normal functioning made by an individual when normal functioning is unavailable.

consciousness: (Chapter 3) The level of awareness on which an individual normally operates.

cruising: (Chapter 6) A stage of development before independent walking when babies use tables, chairs, and other furnishings for stability.

detachment: (Chapter 4) A defense mechanism used to minimize the pain of separation.

differentiation: (Chapter 4) The process of "sorting out" body parts from each other in a specific pattern (head from trunk, arms from body, legs from body, and then each piece of the limbs from each other).

directionality: (Chapter 8) External projection of laterality, first to the body and then to objects in space.

dyspraxia: (Chapter 5) Impaired ability to plan motor movements resulting in clumsiness.

ectoderm: (Chapter 3) The top cell layer of the embryonic disk: building blocks for skin, hair, eyes, tooth enamel, and the nervous system.

embryo: (Chapter 3) The unborn human from conception through eight weeks of development.

endoderm: (Chapter 3) The bottom layer of the embryonic disk: building blocks for the lining of the gastrointestinal tract, respiratory tract, and other organs.

extension: (Chapter 3) See *body movements.*

external rotation: (Chapter 3) See *body movements.*

fetus: (Chapter 3) The unborn human from eight weeks after conception until birth. The developmental timeframe from eight weeks until birth is called the fetal period.

figure-ground: (Chapter 5) An intensity-frequency relationship. What is most intense and at the highest frequency is the figure (foreground or primary focus); everything else is background. **Kinesthetic figure-ground** is separating the moving tone of extremities (head, arms, legs) as the figure from the holding tone of the trunk as the ground, all on an automatic internal basis. **Auditory figure-ground** is separating the important sounds (such as mother's voice or teacher's voice) from environmental sounds (such as the television, air conditioner, or fluorescent lights). **Visual figure-ground** is separating the important part of a picture from the background or separating the letters from the lines on the page.

fine motor skills: (Chapter 9) Ability to use the body's small muscle groups for detailed tasks such as buttoning, snapping, zipping, coloring, cutting, and writing.

flexion: (Chapter 3) See *body movements.*

fusion: See *bonding.*

gross motor skills: (Chapter 9) Ability to use the body's large muscle groups such as belly crawling, creeping, walking, running, jumping, hopping, skipping, throwing, and catching.

homeostasis: (Chapter 2) Optimal balance of the body's internal functions.

innate automatic reflexes: (Chapter 3) The body's "pre-wired" circuits for survival and adaptation outside the womb, formed prenatally and during the first months after birth.

integration: (Chapter 2) Automatic functioning of a body system which requires coordination of the system with itself and with other body systems

internal rotation: (Chapter 3) See *body movements.*

kinesthesia: (Chapter 5) The matching of tactile, proprioceptive, and vestibular sensations into one single sensation. Frequently referred to as the sixth sense.

laterality: (Chapter 8) An internal awareness of the difference between the two sides of the body and how they work together and in opposition. Laterality is the internal awareness of the lateral dimension of space.

locomotion: (Chapter 7) Moving from one point to another by belly crawling, creeping, walking, etc.

maternal sensitive period: (Chapter 4) The period immediately after birth (the first hour or so) when the newborn baby is especially alert and responsive to interaction. This is a turning point for parent-child bonding as the baby receives the gentle welcome necessary to make the transition between the intrauterine environment and the world outside the womb.

mesoderm: (Chapter 3) The middle layer of the embryonic disk: building blocks for the skeleton, muscles, connective tissue (cartilage, ligaments, etc.), and circulatory system.

midline: (Chapter 3) An imaginary line dividing the body into equal parts: two sides, top and bottom, front and back. The midline has a critical relationship to the function of eyes, hands, and feet.

Moro reflex: (Chapter 4) The primitive reflex response to fear of falling with the body going into complete extension (arms stretched out, head back, back arched), then flexion (pulling inward toward the center of the body).

motor generalizations: (Chapter 6) Generalized areas of movement that are landmarks of a child's growth and development: posture and maintenance of balance, locomotion, contact, speech, and receipt and propulsion.

muscle tone: (Chapter 2) The basic readiness or foundation of a muscle to work. **Hypotonicity** (low muscle tone) is when the muscle is not ready to work and results in weakness and too much range of motion. **Hypertonicity** (high muscle tone) is when the muscle is overly prepared for work and results in limited range of motion.

ovum: (Chapter 3) The egg.

oxytocin: (Chapter 4) The hormone responsible for release of the richest milk from the milk glands.

parasympathetic system: (Chapter 2) The portion of the autonomic nervous system responsible for maintaining homeostasis or well-being of the body's involuntary systems (digestion, circulation, respiration, metabolism).

peacekeeping system: (Chapter 2) Our term for the parasympathetic system of the autonomic nervous system.

posture: (Chapter 6) A stable body position against the force of gravity.

praxia: (Chapter 5) Efficient motor planning. Praxia involves healthy sensation, motor response, and sensory feedback.

primal wounding: (Chapter 3) A profound first level trauma caused when postnatal separation interrupts bonding.

prone progression: (Chapter 6) The sequence of skills that takes us from the horizontal (prone) position to vertical (upright). The progression includes rolling over, propping on arms, up on all-fours, sitting, and standing.

proprioception: (Chapter 5) The inner sense of muscles, tendons, joints and pressure, as supplied by proprioceptors, to give us constant, accurate, and automatic knowledge of the movement and position of our bodies as a whole and of the individual parts (arms, legs, fingers, toes, etc.)

quickening: (Chapter 3) Fetal movements that can be easily felt by the mother.

rooting: (Chapter 3) The reflex for turning the head towards a light touch at the corner of the mouth. With the rooting reflex, newborn babies turn their heads towards the nipple to suck.

self-parenting: (Chapter 1) A process of identifying and resolving early childhood experiences that were less than nurturing or not optimal physically and/or emotionally.

stress: (Chapter 2) The tension and pressure of everyday living. Positive stress gives a zest for life and results in rewarding achievements. Negative stress undermines well-being and interferes with human potential.

stress continuum: (Chapter 2) An imaginary line with minimal stress and optimal functioning at the right end, intense stress and survival functioning at the left end.

stress threshold: (Chapter 2) The point on the stress continuum where an individual's sympathetic (survival) system will be activated, resulting in a total fight-or-flight reaction.

survival system: (Chapter 2) Our term for the sympathetic system; the "crisis management" part of the autonomic nervous system.

sympathetic system: (Chapter 2) The portion of the autonomic nervous system responsible for survival by fight-or-flight reactions.

tactile sensation: (Chapter 5) Sensory information supplied through the skin; the sense of touch.

task analysis: (Chapter 9) The step-by-step assessment of a physical task which enables a therapist to identify and confront a problem and see what's in the background.

teratogen: (Chapter 3) Any drug, virus, irradiation, or other non-genetic factor which can cause malformation of the embryo or fetus.

trauma: (Chapter 2) Unresolved stress which creates a significant disruption to development. The earlier the trauma occurs, the more disruptive.

vestibular system: (Chapter 3) The system which coordinates the relation between the orientation of the head (its motion and position) with the force of gravity. The vestibular system integrates sensory-motor impressions into a coherent picture with the image and orientation of the body in space.

viscera: the internal organs of the body, including the stomach, intestines, heart, lungs, liver, and kidneys.

APPENDIX C
Case Studies

Nurturing children along their developmental timeline is at the core of the work of physical therapist Shirley Randolph and occupational therapist Margot Heiniger. For more than 30 years, they have used the principles of human development to improve children's physical coordination, muscle strength, and behavior. At the same time, their continuing training and studies led them to the innovative, effective, and holistic therapy strategies outlined in this book.

Here are the stories of how their work has impacted three individuals: a child labeled as having Attention Deficit Disorder with hyperactivity, an infant diagnosed with cerebral palsy, and an adult coming to terms with learning disabilities and early traumas.

Tyler: Attention Deficit Disorder and Hyperactivity

Tyler was diagnosed as having Attention Deficit Disorder with hyperactivity at age five, the beginning of his kindergarten year, and was immediately put on Ritalin. He was restless and hyperactive and simply could not sit still.

Eighteen months later, Tyler was evaluated by Randolph and Heiniger. He had not grown or gained any weight in the 18 months he had been on Ritalin. He stood in the typical extreme fatigue posture: flat feet, hyper-extended knees, upper trunk and shoulders projected backward excessively, and slightly exaggerated lumbar curve. His deep pressure sensation was extremely poor: the entire skin felt loose and lifeless and excess stimulation was needed to produce redness. Muscle tone was extremely low with very poor coordination. His parents agreed to weekly therapy and made a commitment to a home program. Here is a dated report of Tyler's progress during the next fifteen months.

March 16: Tyler began a program of brushing and deep pressures on his back. From then on, therapy sessions always began with dry brushing and deep pressures. Tyler's parents were instructed to do dry brushing and deep pressures at home, twice daily, five times a week. Within two weeks, his parents noticed that the skin on his back looked and felt different than on his arms where brushing was not being done.

March 30: Tyler began receiving pressures on his hands and feet. He loved it! The pressures had an immediate calming effect and Tyler occasionally fell asleep during the procedure. Tyler was given a large inner tube, cut open and hung from the ceiling as a hammock, where he could rest in a flexed position. Tyler was told to rest in the inner tube for at least 30 minutes daily. His appetite soon increased dramatically.

April 20: The muscle mass in his trunk and shoulders had doubled in size. In therapy, Tyler began the individual movement patterns of the belly crawl, a greatly frustrating experience!

April 27: Tyler had gained four pounds in seven weeks. His belly crawling movements were becoming more organized.

May 11: Other family members had commented on how calm Tyler is and noted changes in his behavior.

May 25: Tyler began doing arm patterns with the individual belly crawl movements.

June 8: Tyler's family was taught to help Tyler do belly crawl patterns at home. Tyler showed strong resistive, manipulative behavior with intense verbal outbursts directed at the therapist.*

July 6: Tyler celebrated the recent holiday weekend with his extended family on a camping trip. Tyler did very well with other children and adapted well to the different schedules and activities. Tyler was taken off Ritalin.

July 20: Tyler refused to do belly crawl patterns, and had a major tantrum during therapy. After his blow-up, he and the therapist had a good talk. Tyler said he didn't know why he acted that way sometimes.

July 27: Tyler started moving in the belly crawl pattern. He could do "supermans" for only four seconds.**

August 3: Tyler often slept in his inner tube. Tyler could now do a smooth belly crawl for 100 feet.

September 14: Therapists were told that Tyler had "three terrible days" at school; his parents were considering starting Tyler on Ritalin again. The therapist was called to a child study team conference at school. The teacher was willing to work with the therapists and parents

---

*Tyler's behavioral outburst is common among children with learning disabilities, hyperactivity, and difficulties with movement control and sensory/perceptual processing. In their 1980 book, *Neurophysiological Concepts in Human Behavior,* (pp. 192-208), Heiniger and Randolph discuss the reasons for these behavior problems – and offer effective strategies for behavior control through movement control.

**Supermans, done lying on the tummy, are a super exercise for total back extension, which includes shoulder-girdle stability and contributes to hand-eye coordination and hand function. Supermans are done in three arm positions: hands at the buttocks, hands at the shoulder, and hands extended forward with arms reaching overhead.

to keep Tyler off Ritalin and to help him through movement and behavior control strategies.

September 21: Tyler broke three fingers, so could use only the heel of his left hand when doing the belly crawl.

September 28: Tyler began the homolateral belly crawl pattern in place.

October 5: Tyler turned cartwheels for the first time ever! He was still very active, now because he enjoyed using his body and not, as before, because of fatigue-induced restlessness. When playing, Tyler had perfect posture but his posture collapsed when he stood still. Tyler began the homolateral pattern of the belly crawl for movement.

November 2: Tyler tried the cross-pattern/moving belly crawl but it is too difficult, so his therapist continued homolateral pattern.

November 30: Tyler was excited about being able to jump rope for the first time.

January 5: Tyler's therapy was reduced to every other week. He was now a muscular, active, well-coordinated boy!

February 1: Tyler broke his arm, so could only do crawling patterns in place.

March 8: Arm cast was removed and arm was extremely sensitive so couldn't be used for crawling for two more weeks.

March 22: Tyler did basic and cross-pattern crawling without hurting the arm; homolateral was still too painful. Deep pressures were now done only once a week on Tyler's bottom, thighs, and feet; back, hands, and arms continued to receive pressures five days a week.

April 19: Tyler's arm no longer hurt when hanging or supporting his weight so he was given full clearance for all activities.

May 3: Tyler's time in the inner tube was reduced to 15 minutes daily.

May 17: Tyler's therapy was reduced to an "on call" basis.

Summary

Tyler had a total of 42 treatments. His success was largely due to the commitment of his parents and their conscientious use of the home program.

Two years later, Tyler continues to do very well in school. His grades are exceptional and he receives many awards for extra activities and superior behavior. He is known for his compassion, is well-liked by teachers and peers, and says he has "lots of friends." He plays soccer, baseball, golf, and basketball and is an excellent fisherman.

It will be important to continue monitoring Tyler as he grows, especially during times of stress: when he changes schools, during adolescence and other growth spurts, and in times of family transition or crisis (such as divorce, death, moves, or birth of a sibling).

Jonathan: Early Intervention In Cerebral Palsy

When Jonathan was two months old, his mother noted that he had poor head control. He had a difficulty breast-feeding and his arms and legs seemed stiff. His pediatrician referred him to a pediatric neurologist who examined Jonathan and diagnosed him as having cerebral palsy.

Jonathan was four months old when he was referred to Shirley Randolph for physical therapy. Her examination showed that Jonathan's tongue was hypersensitive: when his tongue was touched, he gagged and thrust his tongue. His lips didn't purse to close on the nipple. When lying on his tummy he could lift his head and support himself on his extended arms but his head was always tilted to the left. He had excessive muscle tone of the arms and legs.

For Jonathan, Randolph developed a physical therapy program with a strong home component. His mother was taught to stimulate his mouth, lips, tongue, and cheeks to improve sensation and muscle tone. A flexion chair was made to position Jonathan's body in total flexion in order to reduce the excessive extension that had been dominating his body. In addition, Jonathan had weekly sessions with the physical therapist, where he received stimulation to specific muscle groups and was taught movement patterns to advance him through the prone progression.

After six months of therapy, the pediatrician noted the progress Jonathan had made. Jonathan was sitting, babbling, and socially responsive. By 13 months, Jonathan was walking independently. He could carry an object while walking, patty-cake while walking, and move from standing to squatting and back again without holding on.

Jonathan's progress continued for the next two years. At age three, he began preschool, which offered him social interaction within a structured environment. By then, he had no signs of cerebral palsy.

When Jonathan was four years and five months, Margot Heiniger used the *IMAS* to screen him for pre-kindergarten readiness. She observed that Jonathan showed typical cerebral palsy spasticity patterns when under stress. The *IMAS* also revealed that Jonathan had not established left- or right-preference and was having significant difficulty with his eyes. He was left-eyed, right-handed, and inconsistent about foot preference. He consistently showed reversals when using a pencil or crayon with his right hand, which some may have interpreted as evidence that he was left-handed. Further examination convinced Heiniger that Jonathan was genetically right-handed but that his lack of preference was inhibiting function. When asked to look through a cardboard tube, Jonathan held the tube to his right eye while using only his left eye for seeing. Other activities indicated that Jonathan's right eye was nonfunctional, even though it was his preferred eye.

Jonathan was unable to follow vertical and horizontal movement, especially across the midline of his body. His behavior was impulsive and he was easily distracted. He was tense when trying to balance his body and had difficulty with hopping and skipping. Overall, Jonathan was below average in all areas, even when compared to the norm for children five months younger.

Jonathan's program was immediately altered to prepare him for kindergarten. He needed low-level ocular activities (eye exercises done while lying on his back: fixating at an object with both eyes working together, then separately, with extra work on the right eye). His new program also included enhancing kinesthesia and motor skills with dry brushing, deep pressures, and movement patterns. Family and caregivers were encouraged to offer the security of a daily schedule, hearty encouragement, and regular opportunities for Jonathan to demonstrate his competence.

After a full year of therapy (daily sessions at home plus weekly sessions with Shirley Randolph), Jonathan was re-tested with the *IMAS*. The right eye and right hand were now dominant; foot preference was still mixed. He no longer did reversals while writing and his impulsivity and attention span had improved dramatically. Jonathan still was unable to visually track a moving object across the midline of his body. He had difficulty hopping and skipping, and had little endurance. Under stress, he no longer showed the cerebral palsy spasticity patterns. Jonathan still needed work in two areas:

1. With ocular pursuits, to strengthen the eye's ability to track horizontally and vertically.

2. With lower extremities, to establish preference and enable him to hop, skip, and play for extended periods of time.

The *IMAS* should be used annually as a basis for evaluating Jonathan's progress, at least through the fourth grade, with revisions in his therapy program as appropriate. Evaluation will also be needed in conjunction with Jonathan's growth spurts (usually at about grades three and six), and at any time when increased stress may affect his function and development.

Summary

There is no way to know the extent of Jonathan's difficulties if he had not received intensive, individualized intervention. It is clear that his function and potential were improved far beyond initial expectations of the pediatric neurologist who first diagnosed him as having cerebral palsy.

Margot: Learning Disabilities And Early Trauma

Margot Heiniger's own story is an example of the importance of looking into the background when seeking to resolve present-day problems. After years as an occupational therapist, Margot began her own self-parenting efforts to overcome learning disabilities and other difficulties. Her personal work shed new light on her professional work and allowed her to gain first-hand experience with Ed Snapp, the Tomatis Method, William Emerson and Michael Irving, and Barbara Findeisen.

Margot was first examined for learning disabilities when she was seven years old. More than 40 years later, an educational therapist was astonished to find Margot's reading abilities at about a third grade level, astonished because she knew Margot as a successful therapist, teacher, and author and as a woman who had completed high school, college, and graduate school.

At age 52, Margot began a program of intensive educational therapy. A year later she was reading at the twelfth grade level. She continues to work on her reading skills, concentrating on fluency, comprehension, and written language skills. She now recognizes her learning disability as a third-line trauma built upon second- and first-line traumas. Educational therapy would not have been successful if she had not also been working to uncover and re-learn what was in the background of her problems with reading.

Margot's childhood was a rocky path of abandonment, neglect, and fear. Adopted when she was three months old, she had spent her first weeks of life in institutions. Her adoptive parents provided well for her physical needs but were unavailable emotionally. Margot and her older brother (also adopted) were expected to stay out of the way; Margot was reprimanded for "acting like a tomboy." Her best times were at her grandmother's country home where she was cuddled and cared for with love and acceptance and allowed the freedom to play, swim, and explore.

When Margot was seven, her mother disappeared mysteriously for a period of time. Margot's questions about her were dismissed. Years later she learned that her mother had gone away to give birth; the child lived only three days. Soon thereafter, Margot's mother was diagnosed with breast cancer. Home care nurses were hired and Margot was allowed little contact with her mother.

By then, Margot knew that she was "different" from the other kids because she could not read. Instead of seeing words on a page, Margot saw letters that seemed to dance, split, and glow. She refused to read except when using what her parents called "funny staring behaviors." Only by staring at the page would the letters hold still long enough for her to read them. For Margot, it was the only way she could read, but to her parents, it was an indication that something was terribly wrong with their daughter. They scheduled a complete psychological and neurological examination but told Margot nothing about the procedure beforehand. Margot still remembers having wires on her head and clamps on her body and her incredible fear that she was about to be electrocuted. The tests revealed that Margot was not mentally retarded and that she had a congenital heart defect, yet another cause for her to be afraid.

Margot was ten when both her grandmother and mother died. During the last stages of her mother's illness, Margot was virtually ignored and soon thereafter she was enrolled in a boarding school where she spent the next seven years. She gained her high school diploma with hundreds of extra hours studying and the help of a few dedicated teachers. She was guided towards occupational therapy where she could combine her artistic skills with her interest in people. At graduation, Margot was on the school honor roll and received awards for art and athletics, and earned the school's highest award for exceptional overall achievement.

Because of her difficulties with reading and writing, college and graduate school were extremely frustrating. Her work in special education was highly rewarding, yet required significant extra effort from Margot. Over the years, she maintained a special interest in children with physical and academic difficulties and was always intrigued by the connection between physical, emotional, and academic well-being.

In 1980, Margot was evaluated by Ed Snapp and she began his 18-month intensive individualized program for enhancing kinesthesia and learning movement patterns. (See Appendix A, CN5.2, for more information on Ed Snapp's work.) It was then that she first recognized the enormous effort she had made in compensating for her disabilities and she began to acknowledge her own achievements. Through the program, she gained significant improvements in kinesthesia and movement patterns.

In 1986, Margot was evaluated at the Tomatis Center in Toronto and soon began the Tomatis Intensive Program which produced significant changes in her posture, movement patterns, and breathing. (Read more about the Tomatis Method of Auditory Stimulation in Chapter Five.)

At age 48, Margot began an intensive search into her personal history. Under the supervision of a psychologist, she had a regression that revealed the impact of the immense traumas she experienced as a youth and child and her subsequent decision to "create a wall" around herself as protection from further pain. It was then that she realized the power of her subconscious and made a commitment to delve deeper. A few days later, she had a second regression, this time going back to her birth experience. During the regression, she went through a series of movements while feeling people pull and turn her infant body. She turned to resist their pulling, then felt confused as her mother was drugged.

Margot's interest in birth memories continued. Four years after her first birth regression, she began working with prenatal-perinatal psychologist Dr. William Emerson* and psychotherapist Michael Irving to continue to recover her birth memories. Through art therapy and subsequent regressions, she learned of numerous physical traumas during her prenatal and birth experiences. Because of her birth regressions and intensive work in psychotherapy, Margot believes she was born by cesarean section after four days of labor and that her mother died in childbirth (contrary to what she was told when she contacted the adoption agency as an adult). Her feelings of abandonment deepened during her adoptive mother's absence, illness, and death, as well as through the repeated rejection by other caregivers and her own difficulties in school.

Through additional work she has resolved much of her birth trauma and is now working on prenatal trauma. With therapist Barbara Findeisen,* Margot has continued to explore and heal first-line and second-line traumas. She also works on issues resulting from decades of psychological repression including eating disorders, unresolved grief, learning disabilities, and self-esteem.

---

*Contact Emerson or Findeisen for information about their programs. See the bibliography for addresses.

Throughout her efforts at self-parenting and healing, Margot has maintained a passion for helping others uncover and overcome early traumas. As an occupational therapist, Margot's work intertwines neurophysiological concepts with her recognition of the life-changing impact of early traumas.

APPENDIX D
Working with Developmental Therapists

Therapy is both science and art; to be effective, a therapist must apply proven scientific principles in a manner that is individualized, creative, and ever-changing. Not only is each child unique but each child brings to each session a unique set of needs, physical sensations, perceptions, emotions, and thought patterns.

Parents are a child's number-one advocate in an adult world. It is the parent's job to determine when a child needs additional help, to attain that help, to monitor the child's progress, and to support the therapy in every way possible.

The Many Branches of Developmental Therapy

Not all developmental therapists work with children. For children, developmental therapy includes several branches:

Occupational therapy uses specialized equipment, toys, games, and activities to help children develop the skills essential for school. These skills include balance, right- or left-handedness, fine motor skills, and eye-hand coordination.

Physical therapy uses hands-on techniques for basic physical intervention with motor skills, sensation, and physical function.

Speech therapy uses a variety of physical and instructional techniques to enhance the mechanics of speech: mouth, tongue, teeth, and jaw.

Language therapy enhances the child's use of language and usually is accompanied by speech therapy.

Instructional therapy is remediation in basic academic skills (such as reading, writing, and math) and "learning how to learn." These programs should include individualized testing and educational evaluation to determine the child's learning styles and to monitor academic achievement as well as to detect problems "in the background" which interfere with learning (such as problems with sensation, kinesthesia, or posture).

Finding the Right Therapist

Look for a therapist whose strategies are interdisciplinary, holistic, neurologically appropriate, comprehensive, and systematic:

Interdisciplinary - a team approach involving parents, therapist(s), school (teacher and counselor, psychologist, principal, specialists), physician, and others.

Holistic - caring for the child's physical, mental, emotional, and spiritual well-being.

Neurologically appropriate - using sequenced learnings that nurture the child's progress according to the human developmental timeline.

Comprehensive - recognizing that the problem is in the background and implementing strategies to address today's symptoms as well as the underlying problem.

Systematic - using a program that makes sense to you. The plan should be sequenced and cumulative (so that each level reinforces and builds on what was done previously) and repetitive (so yesterday's lesson is reviewed today and tomorrow).

For lists of therapists who may be able to help your child, talk with your school principal, psychologist, special education department, and/or physician. Referrals also may be available through support groups for parents of children with special needs; these groups may be listed in the newspaper or a community guide, or through hospitals, churches, and civic groups. Other parents are often the best referral source. Talk with parents at school functions, children's sports events, and other gatherings.

Your first contact with the therapist should be by telephone. Begin by asking a few questions. If you are satisfied with the therapist's responses, schedule a session with the therapist for yourself before your child's first appointment. Use this opportunity to talk about your observations and concerns, to review the therapist's philosophies and techniques, and to tour the setting. Examine the therapist's qualifications: ask about training, experience, certification. Ask for references: names and telephone numbers of the therapist's clients/patients.

Ask about your role in therapy: What will be the best way for you to tell the therapist about your on-going observations and concerns? How often will you receive progress reports? Can you watch the therapist work? How can you reinforce therapy at home, at school, and elsewhere? How will other caregivers (physicians, childcare providers, therapists) be involved? Is there a support group for clients, parents, and/or families?

Consider logistics of location, scheduling, fees, insurance coverage, the therapist's personality and your general impressions of the therapy setting. Is the environment clean, friendly, and professional? Will you and your child feel comfortable there?

Participating in Your Child's Therapy

Accompany your child to the first therapy session. Remember that first impressions are important: as you introduce your child to the therapist, model the courtesy, respect, and confidence you expect your child to use. Your words and attitude should say to your child and the therapist:

> I trust you.
>
> I respect you.
>
> I expect you to respect me.
>
> I will follow the therapist's directions.

As therapy proceeds, continue to treat your child's therapist with courtesy, respect, and confidence. Expect competence. Expect to be informed about your child's progress. Expect opportunities to provide the therapist with your observations and concerns. Expect the therapist to be human: she won't have all the answers and won't perform miracles for your child. Respect the therapist's clinical judgement. Be patient.

Remember that you always have the option of changing the care plan. Of course, if you believe your child's therapist is inept, unprofessional, or incompetent, you must immediately make other arrangements. This type of therapist is the exception, and we encourage parents not to let one bad experience lead them to believe that all therapists are incompetent or that all therapy is ineffective. The risks are minimized when you do your homework in selecting a therapist and maintain a healthy relationship with your therapist and with your child. Remember, too, that developmental therapy is a three-way relationship between therapist, parent, and child.

APPENDIX E
Choosing Childcare

Many children spend a large portion of their growing years in day-care facilities where their development and attitudes are shaped not by their parents, but by paid caregivers. In the United States, one fourth of all children under age five are enrolled in organized care facilities (2.22 million children as related in *Statistical Record of Women Worldwide,* Linda Schmittroth, editor, 1991.).

The demand for quality childcare has resulted in a wide range of options. By any standards, many childcare options are far from ideal. To provide children with the best environment for learning from the inside out, parents must carefully select a childcare setting that is in harmony with a child's developmental timeline and personal needs.

Certainly parents need basic information about a childcare center's licenses, schedule, fees, parental participation, meal service, health care, emergency procedures, and so forth. Numerous parenting resources include guidelines to help parents evaluate childcare and preschool arrangements. In addition, parents need guidelines for assessing how each childcare setting nurtures the holistic development of children and helps children follow the developmental sequence for kinesthesia, movement patterns, motor generalizations, and other learnings from the inside out. These insights are woven through each chapter of this book. Here are some additional tips for selecting care for growing children:

Infants: Birth to 8 months

Babies most need the comfort and security of home and family. Childcare settings must provide appropriate stimulation and maximum security. Important characteristics include:

1. *Low staff ratios.* Babies are held and carried, not left in cribs or playpens.

   Human contact (time-in-arms) is critical for infants to bond to the primary caregiver and to develop trust and is the best way to provide the necessary tactile, proprioceptive, and vestibular stimulation necessary for developing kinesthesia. Infants can and should be carried about while caregivers perform routine tasks, even while infants are sleeping. Fabric snuggli carriers and slings may be used.

2. *Few mobiles, drawings, and pictures.*

    Visual stimuli distract babies from the internal focus that is so
    important during the early months of life.

3. *Tummy time on a slick surface.*

    Parents may need to be innovative in providing opportunities
    for babies to lie on their tummies. Ideally, infants are placed on
    an enclosed slick surface area several times each day. An
    alternative is to place a piece of smooth, no-pattern vinyl
    flooring in the crib. Parents may wish to obtain a two-by-four
    foot piece of vinyl flooring to ensure that their babies always
    have a clean, appropriate place to play and sleep.

    Parents must remember that babies' free movement is restricted
    by carpeting, cushioned mats, and cluttered floors. During
    tummy time, clothing should cover arms, legs, and feet so skin
    doesn't stick to the slick surface.

4. *No infant seats, jump seats, walkers.*

    These appliances restrict babies' movement. In addition,
    propping babies upright puts their bodies erect prematurely. Of
    course, infant seats are required for transportation in the car.

Pre-toddlers (8 months to 14 months)

During this time, children's development is on two tracks: becoming
erect and walking, and manipulation of objects. The motor-perceptual
stage emphasis here is upon mastering the body's movement patterns
and orientation in space and time so the body can move automatically
and instantaneously. Important qualities of a childcare setting for pre-
toddlers include:

1. *Low staff ratios for continued bonding, trust, and safety.*

    As babies become more active, their exploration and
    experimentation requires that caregivers be available to give
    constant positive reinforcement of achievements and immediate
    attention when problems arise.

2. *Large open areas with safe, stable objects for babies to move
    in, over, around, and through.*

    A variety of activities is necessary to meet the needs of babies
    who are only creeping as well as those who are pulling
    themselves up and cruising. Children should be free to move
    from activity to activity.

3. *Safe, appropriate objects for hands-on manipulation.*

As babies are developing the motor generalization for contact (reach, grasp, and release), they need a variety of objects to take apart using their gross (large muscle) manipulation skills.

Toddlers (14 months to 2 years)

Toddlers should still be primarily concerned with body activity and perfecting their basic movement skills. Children should have good muscle tone, and should have established the motor generalizations of posture and maintenance of balance, locomotion, contact, and speech. Important characteristics of quality childcare for toddlers include:

1. *Staff ratios slightly higher than with younger ages.*

Staff should meet children's on-going needs for attachment, security, safety, and positive reinforcement.

2. *Large spaces inside and outside for big muscle activity.*

3. *Variety of toys for manipulation.*

Preschoolers (ages 2 through 4)

Children's bodies, minds, and spirits need a healthy, safe environment supervised by caring, competent adults. Many preschoolers are enrolled in social and academic programs which over-emphasize children's cognitive growth. Preschoolers are much better served by childcare programs emphasizing physical activity and social interaction. Important characteristics of childcare and preschool programs for these children include:

1. *Staff ratios slightly higher than for toddlers, but still low enough to meet the needs for attachment, security, safety, and positive reinforcement.*

2. *Large spaces inside and out.*

Children now need apparatus for climbing, sliding, and swinging, as well as tricycles and Big Wheels bicycles. A variety of toys should be available for manipulation.

3. *Fine motor activities (such as painting and drawing) should only be done at arms' length.*

Look for easels, blackboards, newsprint pads, large markers, chalk, and fat crayons.

4. *Opportunities for listening, sharing, and music limited to short sessions (10 minutes or less).*

5. *Opportunities for self-help, home-making activities, and multisensory play (sandbox, water tables, finger painting, etc.).*

6. *The majority of the day's schedule as time for "free play"* with ample opportunity to experiment with many opportunities. Children should be provided with a vast number of slightly different interactions with the environment and should be encouraged to try each activity.

APPENDIX F
Using the Integrated Motor Activities Screening (IMAS)

The *Integrated Motor Activities Screening (IMAS)* was developed
to identify pre-kindergarten children who are likely to have learning
difficulties. It is designed for use by teachers and paraprofessionals
who may encounter children with minimal overt clues of learning
problems. The results of this screening can indicate weaknesses in
specific areas so that appropriate intervention can be promptly
implemented.

Background

In 1971, a motor activities screening was developed through the Title
III, ESEA, Early Prevention of School Failure Project. Occupational
therapist Margot Heiniger recognized the potential of a screening based
on a stronger neurophysiological orientation, and developed the *IMAS* to
emphasize integrating auditory and visual input with kinesthetic-tactile
feedback and motor responses. A preliminary version of the *IMAS* was
published in Heiniger and Randolph's 1980 book, Neurophysiological
Concepts in Human Behavior. Performance guidelines were based on
data from 391 children ages four through seven. Following extensive
field testing, *IMAS* was published in 1990. Clinical judgments and
statistical data confirm that the *IMAS* is a powerful tool for identifying
children with potential learning disabilities.

Theory and Rationale

IMAS is based on the premise that basic motor functions are the
foundation and building blocks for developing the complex perceptual-
motor skills required for academic learning. During the early preschool
years, children learn to control neuromuscular movements. This control
initially requires a great deal of time and energy: children must pay
close attention to the internal awareness or kinesthesia associated with
their movements. As this internal awareness develops, more and more
actions become automatic and children can spend less energy on maintaining balance and more to become skillful in other activities. By
kindergarten age, children should have learned the automatic movement
adjustments necessary to maintain balance and posture and should no
longer consciously attend to their movements. A keenly developed
internal awareness frees a child to direct attention to concentrate on the
perceptual information within the immediate learning environment, the
school, and to explore the external environment. The child's body
becomes an excellent reference point for this exploration.

IMAS assesses the degree to which motor activities have been integrated into a child's behavior. It pinpoints the child's methods of problem solving and simultaneously identifies the interfering factors that prevent satisfactory completion of the screening tasks.

General Description of IMAS

The *IMAS* test manual contains all information necessary to administer and interpret the screening and includes a scored sample of the *IMAS* test and a sample screening report for a child. To ensure valid results, it is important to read the test manual before attempting to administer the *IMAS*.

Administration Time

IMAS is a performance test, not a speed test. Only three items are timed. It requires approximately 20 minutes per child to administer and score the test.

Ages

IMAS is targeted for pre-kindergarten children, generally ages $4\frac{1}{2}$ to $5\frac{1}{2}$ years of age. Test items are selected to appeal to children from 4 to $6\frac{1}{2}$ years of age. Suggested performance guidelines are presented for numerous age intervals.

Organization of the screening

IMAS consists of unscored observation items and scored performance items. Observation items are interspersed in the scored portion of the screening to facilitate recording behavioral observations and to enhance the interpretation of a child's performance. The test form is designed so key observations can be noted quickly.

Five general observational sections precede the testing section. The *IMAS* consists of three scored sections: Auditory-Visual-Motor, Eye-Hand Coordination, and Gross Motor.

Administering and Interpreting Screening Items

The *IMAS* is given individually to each child. A quiet area is required, completely separate from any distractions. Required materials include two yarn balls, crayons, a pencil with an eraser, and other common school supplies. A watch with a second-hand is also needed to time some elements of the screening.

The manual contains descriptions of each observed and scored item on the screening. Correct performance and all problem indicators are operationally defined. In addition, common classroom behaviors are described. Classroom implications are explained in some detail; suggestions are offered for remediating specific problems through classroom programs, consultation with specific therapists, and obtaining additional testing.

Obtaining the IMAS

The Integrated Motor Activities Screening (*IMAS*) is available through Margot Heiniger. Contact her at Box 516, Canyon City, Oregon 97820.

APPENDIX G
Bibliography

Ames, Louise Bates. *Is Your Child in the Wrong Grade?* New York: Harper and Row. 1967.

Ayres, A. Jean. *The Development of Sensory Integrative Theory and Practice: A Collection of the Works of A. Jean Ayres.* (compiled by Anne Henderson, et. al.) DuBuque, Iowa: Kendall/Hunt Publishing Company. 1974.

Ayres, A. Jean. *Sensory Integration and Learning Disorders.* Los Angeles: Western Psychological Services. 1972.

Ball, Thomas. Itard, Sequin, and Kephart: *Sensory Education, A Learning Interpretation.* Columbus, Ohio: Merrill.

Bradshaw, John. *Healing the Shame That Binds You.* Deerfield Beach, Florida: Health Communications, Inc. 1988.

Bradshaw, John. *Homecoming: Reclaiming and Championing Your Inner Child.* New York: Bantam. 1990.

Brazelton, T. Berry. *On Becoming a Family: The Growth of Attachment.* Dell Publishing. New York: Delta/Seymour Lawrence. 1981.

The Annie E. Casey Foundation. *Kids Count Data Book: State Profiles of Child Well-Being.* Washington D.C.: Center for the Study of Social Policy. 1992.

Chamberlain, David B. *Consciousness at Birth: A Review of the Empirical Evidence.* San Diego, California: Chamberlain Communications. 1983.

Chamberlain, David B. *Babies Remember Birth.* Los Angeles: Tarcher. 1988.

Chaney, Clara and Miles, Nancy. *Remediating Learning Problems: A Developmental Curriculum.* Columbus, Ohio: Merrill. 1974.

Cratty, Bryant J. *Active Learning: Games to Enhance Academic Abilities.* Englewood Cliffs, New Jersey: Prentice-Hall. Second edition, 1971.

deQuiros, Julio B. "Diagnosis of Vestibular Disorders in the Learning Disabled," *Journal of Learning Disabilities.* Vol. 9, No. 1: January 1976.

de Quiros, Julio. "Significance of Some Therapies on Posture and Learning," *Academic Therap.,* pp 261-270. Vol. 11: Spring 1976.

deQuiros, Julio and Schrager, Orlando L. *Neuropsychological Fundamentals in Learning Disabilities* (Revised edition). Academic Therapy Publications. Novato, California. 1979.

Ebersole, Marylou; Kephart, Newell C.; and Ebersole, James B. *Steps to Achievement for the Slow Learner.* Columbus, Ohio: Merrill. 1968.

Einon, Dorothy. *Parenthood: Pregnancy, Birth and Childcare - The Whole Story.* New York: Athena. 1991.

Elkind, David. *The Hurried Child.* Reading, Massachusetts: Addison-Wesley. 1981.

Elkind, David. "Formal Education and Early Childhood Education: An Essential Difference." *Human Development 90/91.* Larry Fenson and Judith Fenson, editors. Guilford, Connecticut: The Dushkin Publishing Group, Inc. 1990. pp 60-65.

Erikson, Erik. *Childhood and Society.* New York: Norton. Second edition, 1963.

Feldenkrais, M. *Body and Mature Behaviour: A Study of Anxiety, Sex, Gravitation and Learning.* New York: International Universities Press Inc. 1949, 1979.

Fraiberg, Selma. *The Magic Years: Understanding and Handling the Problems of Early Childhood.* New York: Scribner's Sons. 1959.

Frostig, Marianne. *Beginning Pictures and Patterns.* Chicago: Follett. 1972.

Frostig, Marianne. *Movement Education: Theory and Practice.* Chicago: Follett. 1970.

Frostig, Marianne, and Horne, David. *Program for the Development of Visual Perception.* Chicago: Follett. 1973.

Frostig, Marianne, and Maslow, Phyllis. *Learning Problems in the Classroom.* New York: Greene and Stratton. 1973.

Gilfoyle, Elnora M.; Grady, Ann P.; and Moore, Josephine C. *Children Adapt.* Thorofare, New Jersey: Charles B. Slack. 1981.

Grof, Stanislav. *Beyond the Brain: Birth, Death and Transcendence in Psychotherapy.* Albany, New York: State University of New York Press. 1985.

Hainstock, Elizabeth G. *The Essential Montessori.* New York: New American Library. 1978.

Heiniger, Margot C. *Integrated Motor Activities Screening.* Tucson: Therapy Skill Builders. 1990.

Heiniger, Margot C., and Randolph, Shirley L. *Neurophysiological Concepts in Human Behavior: The Tree of Learning.* Boise, Idaho: Tree of Learning Press. 1981.

Hewlett, Sylvia Ann. *When the Bough Breaks: The Cost of Neglecting Our Children.* New York: Basic Books. 1991.

Ingelman-Sundberg, A. (with photography by Nilsson, Lennart). *A Child is Born: The Drama of Life Before Birth.* New York: Dell/Merloyd Lawrence. 1965/1981.

Janov, Arthur. *Imprints: The Lifelong Effects of the Birth Experience.* New York: Coward-McCann. 1983.

Janov, Arthur. *Primal Scream.* New York: G.P.Putnam's Sons. 1970.

Janov, Arthur. *Primal Man: The New Consciousness.* New York: Crowell. 1975.

Jensen, Margaret Duncan; Benson, Ralph C.; Bobak, Irene M. *Maternity Care: The Nurse and the Family.* St. Louis, Missouri: Mosby. Second edition, 1981.

John-Roger and McWilliams, Peter. *You Can't Afford the Luxury of a Negative Thought.* Los Angeles: Prelude Press. 1990.

Karen, Robert. "Becoming Attached," *The Atlantic Monthly.* February 1990. pp 35-50, 63-70.

Kephart, Newell C. *Learning Disability: An Educational Adventure.* West Lafayette, Indiana: Kappa Delta Pi Press. 1968.

Kephart, Newell C. *The Slow Learner in the Classroom.* Columbus, Ohio: Charles E. Merrill. Second edition, 1971.

Klaus, Marshall H., and Kennell, John H. *Maternal-Infant Bonding.* St. Louis: C.V.Mosby Company. 1976.

Klaus, Marshall H., and Klaus, Phyllis H. *The Amazing Newborn: Making the Most of the First Weeks of Life.* Reading, Massachusetts: Addison-Wesley. 1985.

Knickerbocker, Barbara M. *A Holistic Approach to the Treatment of Learning Disorders.* Thorofare, New Jersey: Charles B. Slack. 1980.

Kuczen, Barbara. *Childhood Stress: Don't Let Your Child Be a Victim.* New York: Delacorte. 1982.

LaLeche League International. *The Womanly Art of Breastfeeding.* Franklin Park, Illinois. 1981.

Leboyer, Frederick. *Birth Without Violence.* New York: Knopf. 1982.

Leboyer, Frederick. *Loving Hands.* New York: Knopf. 1976.

Liedloff, Jean. *The Continuum Concept.* New York: Warner Books. 1977.

Magid, Dr. Ken, and McKelvey, Carole A. *High Risk: Children Without a Conscience.* New York: Bantam. 1987.

May, Betty. *T.S.K.H.* * Tickle Snug Kiss Hug: Exercises and Tricks for Parent-Child Fun.* New York: Paulist Press. 1977.

Mellody, Pia (with Andrea Wells Miller and J. Keith Miller). *Facing Codependence: What It Is, Where It Comes From, How It Sabotages Our Lives.* San Francisco: Harper & Row. 1989.

Miller, Alice. *Breaking Down the Wall of Silence.* New York: Penguin. 1991.

Miller, Alice. *The Untouched Key: Tracing Childhood Trauma in Creativity and Destructiveness.* New York: Doubleday. 1990.

Miller, Alice. *For Your Own Good: Hidden Cruelty in Child-Rearing and the Roots of Violence.* New York: Farrar Straus Giroux. 1984.

Montagu, Ashley. *Growing Young.* New York: McGraw Hill Paperbacks. 1983.

Montagu, Ashley. *Life Before Birth.* New York: Signet. 1977.

Montagu, Ashley. *Prenatal Influences.* Springfield, Illinois: Charles C. Thomas. 1962.

Montagu, Ashley. *Touching: Human Significance of Skin.* New York: Harper and Row. 1978.

Montessori, Maria. *Secret of Childhood.* Notre Dame, Indiana: Fides/Claretian. 1966.

Moore, Keith L. *Before We Are Born: Basic Embryology and Birth Defects.* Philadelphia: W.B. Saunders Company. 1977.

Moore, Raymond S., and Moore, Dorothy N. *Better Late Than Early: A New Approach to Your Child's Education.* New York: Reader's Digest Press/Crowell. 1975.

Mysak, Edward D. *Neurospeech Therapy for the Cerebral Palsied: A Neuroevolutional Approach.* New York: Teachers College Press. 1980.

Namikoshi, Toru. *Shiatsu Therapy: Theory and Practice.* Tokyo: Japan Publications. 1974.

Nilsson, Lennart. *A Child is Born: The Drama of Life Before Birth.* New York: Dell. 1965/1981.

O'Quinn, Garland, Jr. *Developmental Gymnastics: Building Physical Skills For Children.* Austin, Texas: University of Texas Press. 1978.

Pearce, Joseph Chilton. *Magical Child.* New York: Bantam. 1977.

Pelletier, Kenneth R. *Mind as Healer, Mind as Slayer: A Holistic Approach To Preventing Stress Disorders.* New York: Delta. 1977.

Pryor, Karen. *Nursing Your Baby.* New York: Pocket. 1973.

Ribble, Margaret A. *The Rights of Infants.* New York: Signet. 1965.

Ridgway, Roy. *The Unborn Child: How to Recognize and Overcome Prenatal Trauma.* Great Britain: Wildwood House. 1987.

Rugh, Roberts, and Shettles, Landrum B., with Einhorn, Richard N. *From Conception to Birth: The Drama of Life's Beginnings.* New York: Harper & Row. 1971.

Salk, Lee. "The Effects of the Normal Heartbeat Sound on the Behavior of the Newborn Infant: Implications for Mental Health," *World Mental Health.* Volume 12, 1960.

Schmittroth, Linda, editor. *Statistical Record of Women Worldwide.* Detroit: Gale Research, Inc. 1991.

Schwartz, Leni. *Bonding Before Birth: A Guide to Becoming a Family.* Boston: Sigo Press. 1991.

Selye, Hans. *The Stress of Life* (rev. ed.). New York: McGraw-Hill. 1976.

Selye, Hans. *Stress Without Distress.* Philadelphia: J.B. Lippincott. 1974.

Shapiro, Jerrold Lee. *When Men Are Pregnant.* San Luis Obispo, California: Impact. 1988.

Simpson, Dorothy M. *Learning to Learn.* Columbus, Ohio: Charles E. Merrill. 1968.

Solter, Aletha Jauch. *The Aware Baby: A New Approach to Parenting.* Goleta, California: Shining Star Press. 1984.

Stettbacher, J. Konrad. *Making Sense of Suffering: The Healing Confrontation with Your Own Past.* New York: Dutton. 1991.

Tomatis, A.A. *Education and Dyslexia*. Fribourg, Switzerland: Association Internationale d'Audio-Psycho-Phonologie. 1978.

Tomatis, A.A. *The Conscious Ear*. New York: Station Hill Press. 1991.

Verny, Thomas, M.D., with Kelly, John. *The Secret Life of the Unborn Child*. New York: Dell. 1981.

Verny, Thomas R. M.D., editor. *Pre- and Peri-Natal Psychology: An Introduction*. New York: Human Sciences Press, Inc. 1987.

Verny, Thomas, and Weintraub, Pamela. *Nurturing the Unborn Child*. New York: Delacorte. 1991.

The World Almanac 1992. New York: Pharos/St. Martins. 1992.

FOR MORE INFORMATION

William Emerson
4940 Bodega Ave.
Petaluma, CA 94952

Barbara Findeisen
Star Foundation
P.O. Box 516
Geyserville, CA 95441
    (707) 857-3359

International Congress on Pre- and Perinatal Psychology
D/S Whyte Association
1600 Prince Street #509
Alexandria, Virginia 22314
    (703) 548-2802

La Leche League International
9616 Minneapolis Avenue
P.O. Box 1209
Franklin Park, IL 60131
    (708) 455-7730

Mastery
Robert and Helena Stevens
RR1, Box 163A
Horse Shoe, NC 28742-9801
    (704) 891-8884
Fax (704) 890-2626

Tomatis Internationale
2, rue de Phailbourg
75017 Paris
     (1) 43-80-92-22

The Tomatis Method
The Listening Center
99 Crowns Lane
Toronto, Ontario M5R 3P4
     (416) 922-1170

The Tomatis Center
2701 E. Camelback Rd., Suite 205
Phoenix, Arizona 85016
     (602) 381-0086

———————————————

Shirley L. Randolph retired from her physical therapy practice in December 1995. She continues to be involved in the Tree of Learning Center in teaching and promoting developmental fitness as presented in this book. She is available to present lectures, workshops, trainings and individual evaluations and interventions. She can be contacted at her home address of 4333 West Plum Street, Boise, ID 83703; (208) 342-4336.

Margot C. Heiniger-White has a B.S. in occupational therapy and a M.A. in special education. She is author of Integrated Motor Activities Screening (IMAS) and coauthor of Neurophysiological Concepts in Human Behavior. She has more than 30 years experience healing and re-patterning children labeled as having developmental/neurological disorders, hyperactivity, and learning disabilities. Active with the STAR Foundation in California, she assists adults through developmental assessments and programming. She assists schools and teachers in implementing developmental programs. For information, email margot@eoni.com or call Legendary Publishing Company at 800/358-1929.

INDEX

Shirley L. Randolph is the owner and director of the Tree of Learning Center in Boise, Idaho, and has an MA degree in physical therapy from the University of Southern California. She has more than 35 years of experience teaching at the university level as well as in seminars. In addition, she has assisted in the healing and repatterning of children labeled as having development/neurological disorders, attention deficit disorder, hyperactivity, and mental retardation.

Margot C. Heiniger has a BS degree in occupational therapy from the University of Kansas and an MA degree in special education (EMH) from Bradley University in Peoria, Illinois. She is the author of the 1990 book, *Integrated Motor Activities Screening (IMAS)*. She has more than 30 years of experience in healing and repatterning children labeled as having development/neurological disorders, hyperactivity, and learning disabilities. She has also led extensive training of teachers in administration of IMAS and individual programming in the classroom. She is presently on staff at Pocket Ranch Institute in California.

In 1981, Shirley and Margot co-authored their professional book, *Neurophysiological Concepts of Human Behavior: The Tree of Learning*. As a team, they have taught throughout the United States and abroad for twenty years.

Dear Reader:

We are interested in knowing how our book has assisted you personally and with your children, and welcome your comments, insights, ideas, and personal reactions to *Kids Learn From the Inside Out: How to Enhance the Human Matrix.*

We look forward to reading every letter we receive but cannot promise to answer each one personally.

If you are interested in networking with others in your area, please indicate that desire and grant us permission for your name to be given to others.

Send your letters to:

Integrated Human Dynamics
4333 West Plum
Boise, Idaho 38703

Phone (208) 342-6463

Thank you. We look forward to hearing from you.

Shirley L. Randolph   Margot C. Heiniger
MA, PT   MA, OTR

Did You Borrow this Book?
Want a Copy of Your Own?
Need a Great Gift for a Friend or Loved One?

Yes, I want to invest $18.95 in my future and have a personal copy of this book. Send me _____ copies of *"Kids Learn From the Inside Out: How to Enhance the Human Matrix."*

Please add $2.50 per book for postage and handling. Idaho residents include 5% state sales tax in the amount of $.95. per book. (Canadian orders must be accompanied by a postal money order in U.S. funds.) Allow 20 days for delivery. Send check payable to:

LEGENDARY PUBLISHING COMPANY
Lorry Roberts, Publisher
P.O. Box 7706
Boise, Idaho 83707-1706

Name _____

Address _____

City _____ **State** _____ **Zip**_____

**Here's my check/money order for $_____.
I have included $2.50 per each book for postage and handling.**

Quantity Orders Invited
For bulk discount prices, please call:
(208)342-7929